S0-ADG-800

EARLY CHILDHOOD EDUCATION SERIES
Leslie R. Williams, Editor
Millie Almy, Senior Advisor

ADVISORY BOARD: Barbara T. Bowman, Harriet K. Cuffaro, Stephanie Feeney, Doris Pronin Fromberg, Celia Genishi, Dominic F. Gullo, Alice Sterling Honig, Elizabeth Jones, Gwen Morgan, David Weikart

(Continued)

CHILDREN'S PLAY AND LEARNING

Perspectives and Policy Implications

Edited by
EDGAR KLUGMAN
SARA SMILANSKY

TEACHERS
COLLEGE
PRESS

Teachers College, Columbia University
New York and London

Published by Teachers College Press, 1234 Amsterdam Avenue, New York, NY 10027

Library of Congress Cataloging-in-Publication Data

Children's play and learning: perspectives and policy implications/
   edited by Edgar Klugman, Sara Smilansky.
      p.   cm.—(Early childhood education series)
Based on presentations given at a binational workshop held in Boston, Mass., Jly, 1988
Includes bibliographical references and index.
ISBN 0-8077-3033-5. —ISBN 0-8077-3032-7 (pbk.: alk paper)
   1. Play—United States—Congresses.   2. Play—Israel—Congresses.   3. Learning—Congresses.   4. Early childhood education—United States—Curricula—Congresses.   5. Early
childhood education—Israel—Curricula—Congresses.   1. Klugman, Edgar.   II. Smilanksy,
Sara.   III. Series.

Printed on acid-free paper

Manufactured in the United States of America

96   95   94   93   92   91   90   8   7   6   5   4   3   2   1

To our grandchildren,
Takara Klugman, Aubrey Robertson, Shira Smilansky,
Alma Smilansky, and Alexander Smilansky,
who represent the children of the world,
and to our soon-to-be-born grandchildren,
who represent the children of the future.

Contents

Foreword

Marjorie Bakken
Academic Dean, Wheelock College

Wheelock College was proud to host the conference, Implication of Children's Sociodramatic Play: Learning and National Policy, co-sponsored with the United States–Israel Binational Science Foundation. The conference on play was an appropriate way to begin the celebration of the College's Centennial. Lucy Wheelock founded the College because she had become inspired by the work of the international educational thinker, Friedrich Froebel. Her international perspective and their joint commitment to the importance of children's play became the foundation stones of Lucy Wheelock's new college in 1898. In 1909, Lucy Wheelock, as a member of the International Kindergarten Union, signed the Liberal Conservative Report.

> Play [is] the self-active representation of the inner life from inner impulse and necessity. The child who is absorbing from his environment materials with which he is building his own world, clarifies and orders his own experience through its constant expression in play. (Froebel, F. [1887]. *The education of man.* NY: Appleton)

The report, in its most bold and comprehensive statement, asserted "Play is history and poetry and prophecy."

The history of childhood and the history of an individual child are linked to play. Those who attended the Play Conference believed that play, indeed, can be prophetic about an individual's life. Our play as children foretells something profound about our destiny as adults. This volume on play reminds us eloquently that play is transforming and can reveal the poetry of a child's inner life and the history of childhood itself.

Foreword

Zeev Rotem
Executive Director
Binational Science Foundation

The Binational Science Foundation (BSF) is a grant-awarding institution that promotes research cooperation between scientists from the United States and Israel. It was established by the two governments in 1972. The BSF funds highly rated research projects in a wide range of sciences. Projects are funded on the strength of their scientific merit, collaborative arrangements, and appropriateness to the guidelines of the BSF.

In 1984 the Foundation began supporting joint United States–Israel workshops on subjects of mutual interest to scientists in both countries in the fields sponsored by the Foundation. These are held either in Israel or the United States. To retain the workshop nature of the meetings in a free, informal, friendly setting, the number of participants is limited to approximately 50 from the United States and Israel and a few experts in the field from elsewhere. We try to keep a reasonable balance between the outstanding representatives of the field and institutional distribution. We have found that such workshops facilitate a quick and broad interchange of knowledge. They foster close relationships between the communities that benefit both the aims and the charter of the BSF.

Such was the 1988 joint United States–Israel workshop on "Implications of Children's Sociodramatic Play: Learning and National Policy," which was sponsored by the BSF and Wheelock College in Boston, Massachusetts, and is reflected in this book.

The coordinators of the workshop, Professor Edgar Klugman from Wheelock College and Professor Sara Smilansky from the Tel Aviv University in Israel, managed to bring together people from different disciplines to discuss their topics. I myself, being a biologist, enjoyed my participation in the meetings and would like to thank Professors Klugman and Smilansky for exposing me to an area with which I was not previously familiar. As an observer, I found that the intention was to focus on future topics and directions. Besides the exchange of information and analysis of research topics, the aim was to try to influence and bring about positive changes in policy. With this in mind, I hope that there will be a follow-up of the work that has been done and that an action plan will be designed and developed, both individually and collectively, to apply the conclusions reached at the workshop and design future aspects of this endeavor.

I would like to take this opportunity once again to thank Wheelock College for their warm hospitality and arrangements made to facilitate the workshop and contribute to its success.

Preface

This volume on children's play and national policy can be viewed within the context of the events of the present day. In both the United States and Israel early childhood education has now become a focal point of interest and concern. Increasingly, women with children under five years of age find themselves in the work force and therefore require preschool care and education for their young. This development greatly expands the need for an increased pool of well-prepared preschool and early childhood personnel, which, in turn, puts pressure on preschool settings as they search for appropriate staff for their classrooms. The current annual staff turnover rate in the United States for the early childhood field is 35.2 percent (Galinsky, 1989). Added to these pressures is the wide popularization of early childhood education in its many forms and the special promises it extends to children of poverty and children with special needs. The widely publicized study by Berrueta-Clement, Schweinhart, Barnett, Epstein, and Weikart (1984) of the Perry Preschool Project has contributed to the emerging realization that early childhood education is important. In both the United States and Israel it is the expectation of many parents and many communities that when children go to school at an earlier age, they can and must be taught the skills and concepts that have traditionally been taught to older children when they first entered school.

It must be remembered that the medium of play is accepted by knowledgeable professionals as the core of the early childhood curriculum. The editors of this book, representing two different cultures (the United States and Israel) and two areas of specialization (early childhood policy and early childhood play) have collaborated in presenting this carefully documented publication focused on many aspects of children's play.

The dream from which this book has emerged developed simultaneously with the dream for a week-long binational workshop on play, which was held in Boston, Massachusetts, in early July, 1988. People from varied professions gathered in an attempt to understand the major reasons for growing pressure on young children (between the ages of two and eight) to learn through formalized academic approaches such as reading, worksheets, writing, and workbooks rather than through play, the young child's natural and efficient learning mode. It was noted with concern that in the recent past, play has gradually ceased to be a major part of the core curriculum in early childhood programs. Indeed, in some programs it is hard to find play at all.

In general, the chapters in this volume are based on the presentations given at the 1988 summer workshop. Every chapter has, however, been revised, deepened, and broadened. Each contributor is a specialist in a professional area of expertise. Through this book the reader gains an overview of the problems and can find opportunities to think about the issues around play from a variety of perspectives.

Among the contributors are educators, psychologists, administrators, philosophers, policymakers, and teacher educators. Some of the authors are Americans and others are Israelis, and this mix exposes the reader to issues relevant to play and to ways of coping with those issues through the perceptual fields of two countries with diverse cultures.

A major focus of the book is dramatic and sociodramatic play as a medium for the development of the cognitive and socioemotional abilities in young children. This is the pretend–make-believe type of play in which most children around the world engage between the ages of two and eight years. In "dramatic play" a child undertakes any make-believe role he or she chooses. The child imitates that person or animal in both action and speech pattern, using toys, nonstructured materials, gestures, and words. When such play activity involves the cooperation of at least two children and the play proceeds on the basis of interaction between the players who are acting out their roles, the dramatic play becomes "sociodramatic play."

This volume deals with important problems relating to the role of dramatic and sociodramatic play in the overall development of young children. It urges the inclusion of play in the curricula of a wide variety of early education programs. Part I cites research evidence indicating the significance of play in the development of young children's cognitive, creative, and socioemotional abilities. Part II analyzes both the historical context and the current perspectives of play. It also addresses the reasons that play, including sociodramatic play, is not included in the required curriculum for all children in early childhood education programs in either the United States or Israel.

Part III raises questions about whether the universities, teachers' colleges, and inservice training programs in the United States and in Israel are preparing teachers to facilitate and assess the development of young children's play. Part IV examines the implications of sociodramatic play for children who have special needs or who come from less-advantaged socioeconomic settings. Part V provides an analysis of the attitudes of administrators and policy makers toward the inclusion of sociodramatic play as part of the core curriculum for early childhood education programs.

In Part VI a review of the research literature relative to play is presented and an agenda for future research is suggested. In conclusion, the Epilogue suggests ways to address problems relative to young children's need to play and recommends ways to enhance play opportunities for children through the design of the psychosocial structure of the institutions that influence early childhood education.

In summary, the goal of this volume is to provide the reader with a broad view of the role of play in early childhood. Each chapter has been written from a different perspective, and each reflects a specific facet of current thinking and research into children's play. Taken together, the chapters offer an unusual "gestalt" that includes both the uses of play and the impinging factors. The editors offer this volume in the hope that it will be useful in enhancing the rediscovery of the power of play in children's lives for the present and for the future. It is hoped that it will assist educators in structuring supports for play both in teacher education and in children's classrooms, as current early childhood programs move into traditional elementary school settings. It is also hoped that ways will be found to incorporate play in a wide variety of nontraditional child care settings and raise levels of awareness and knowledge about the profound impact on current and future development that can result from the myriad of possibilities emerging through children's play.

REFERENCES

Berrueta-Clement, J. R., Schweinhart, L. J., Barnett, W. S., Epstein, A. S., & Weikart, D. P. (1984). Changed lives: the effects of the Perry Preschool Program on youths through age 19. *Monographs of the High/Scope Educational Research Foundation* (No. 8). Ypsilanti, MI: High/Scope.

Galinsky, E. (1989). The staffing crisis. *Young Children, 44*(2), 2–4.

Acknowledgments

Both the binational workshop and this volume have benefited greatly through the collaboration of many dedicated people who together have helped both to move from dream into reality. But we would like to recognize here a few of the many people and organizations who have made important contributions.

We are particularly grateful to the United States–Israel Binational Science Foundation and its Director, Zeev Rotem, whose support cannot be measured. Dr. Rotem's attendance and participation in the workshop were impressive and greatly appreciated by all. We also thank the administration of Wheelock College for its fine support of the workshop, which was given at every level. Our special gratitude goes to Evelyn Hausslein, former Dean of the Wheelock Graduate School, for encouraging and supporting the conference, as well as to President Daniel Cheever and Dean Marjorie Bakken for their ongoing leadership and support of early childhood efforts.

Our immeasurable gratitude goes to Amy Raffety for her invaluable assistance throughout the many phases of the workshop and ensuing preparation of our manuscript. She not only gave her skill and thoughtfulness to our effort but also contributed a quiet, steadfast presence, incredibly hard work, and a generous spirit that helped both efforts in truly impressive ways. We thank Marilyn Day and Andrina Buffong for their many hours of careful typing and Scott Shane, our former graduate assistant, who conscientiously attended to the many conference details, both expected and unanticipated.

The editors at the Teachers College Press, Sarah Biondello, Susan Liddicoat, and Kathleen McClure, have helped enormously in the shaping of each chapter and this volume as a whole.

We are grateful to Shimshon Shoshani, former Director General of the Israeli Ministry of Education, and Rina Michalovitz for their belief and trust in play as a medium that supports young children and for their provision of the needed resources, which allowed selected early childhood supervisors to travel to the United States in order to participate in the workshop.

Finally, we want to acknowledge the ongoing support we have received from both of our spouses, Hertha Klugman and Moshe Smilansky. We are especially grateful to Hertha Klugman for her many helpful suggestions for this volume, her enthusiastic support and her editorial work on a number of the chapters.

Part I
IMPORTANCE OF PLAY IN YOUNG CHILDREN'S LEARNING

The authors present three different perspectives of play, each arriving at the conclusion that the play of young children is not held in as high a priority in either the United States or in Israel as their academic learning and achievement is. The concern of parents and of both societies is for productiveness (a work orientation) rather than for what is commonly perceived as the frivolous waste of time in play. In addition, and of great concern, is the pressure for premature academic achievement, which is succinctly described by Elkind in his statement that "'earlier is better' has become an entrenched conviction." Although this is not always an overt message, nevertheless it is strongly implied by the heavy emphasis by schools and parents on the idea that the earlier a child meets the cognitive and academic expectations of schools, the better it will be. Elkind traces the historical roots in the United States of "the conception of ability as a matter of the individual rather than as that of a group of individuals." He explains this phenomenon in terms of the historical concerns and goals of American society.

In the second chapter, Smilansky reports both on her original research and on her more recent research findings about dramatic and sociodramatic play. She concludes that although classrooms frequently have "the tools" for play, dramatic and sociodramatic play are usually neither addressed nor supported in those educational environments. She emphasizes that educators' professional preparation does not include formal training in the facilitation and appropriate support of play.

Eisner states in Chapter 3 that play in the United States is considered the antithesis of work. He defines and clarifies the varieties of play and describes commonalities between play and art. He states that both "require reflection, both profit from skill, both seek to generate new forms of experience, both lead to invention."

All three authors conclude that play is marginalized in their respective societies. The reader is left to ponder the question of why child's play, in its variety of forms, has not received much more widespread attention to its manifestations, enhancement, and profound implications in the years since the original Smilansky research in 1968.

CHAPTER 1

Academic Pressures—Too Much, Too Soon: The Demise of Play

David Elkind

Over the last two decades in the United States, a new conception of young children has emerged with many different consequences. As far as the well-being of young children goes, most of these consequences have had negative impacts. And perhaps the most negative impact of all has been the demise of play as the major and legitimate occupation of young children. In this chapter I first describe what has happened to early childhood in this time period, then try to explain it in sociohistorical terms, and then describe some of the consequences. A final section focuses on the nature and importance of play in contemporary society and offers an explanation of the forces that mitigate against play activity of young children.

THE NEW CONCEPTION OF EARLY CHILDHOOD

"Earlier is better" has become an entrenched conviction among many contemporary parents and educators. According to this premise, it is never too early to start children on reading or mathematics, swimming, violin lessons, cooking, or karate. Children, we hear, are little sponges who soak up skills and information with effortless ease. Indeed, it would be a glaring error to pass up this "window of opportunity" for giving young children a head start in life.

Nor do parents have to wait until the child is born before they begin sloshing information over this little sponge. There is now a "Prenatal University" where pregnant mothers and expectant fathers learn the curriculum and how to teach it to the fetus. Musical talent is encouraged by playing Mozart while the mother sits comfortably in a chair. The father promotes the child's literary good taste by reading Shakespeare to his as yet unborn child.

Once the infant has made its way into the world, there are a host of academic programs from which parents can choose. Among these is a computer math program for six month olds, reading tutorials for three year olds, and of course, Logo programming for four and five year olds. To ensure that young children are well rounded, preschool children can be enrolled in violin, ballet, tennis, cooking, and a host of other classes. In keeping with the current fitness craze among adults, exercise courses are now available for tots.

Extent of the Earlier Is Better Phenomenon

The earlier is better conviction has made itself felt across the whole spectrum of early childhood education ranging from nursery schools to day care centers. Some 50 percent of parents want the out-of-home program for their preschooler to be "educational." Increasingly, this pressure for early education is confounded with the needs for child care. Currently, for example, a controversy is going on all over the country over full- as opposed to half-day kindergarten. Those who oppose the full day assume that it will be a full day of academics, which they regard as too much. Those who argue for full-day kindergarten see it as providing full-day child care rather than education.

The same is true for the publicly supported prekindergartens being advocated in New York and some other states. Those who oppose the prekindergarten are concerned that it might mean that academics would be taught at that level. Those who want such programs feel they will help fill the need for high-quality child care slots that are not available elsewhere. Schools are safe environments for children; teachers are licensed and sufficiently well paid that they can be expected to stay on the job and be consistent figures for children.

Schools are often caught in the middle. Although they may not wish to push academics down to the kindergarten and prekindergarten levels, they often believe that this is the only way to get funding. School boards will not fund publicly supported child care. But they will fund educational programs touted as giving children a head start and ensuring academic excellence. Put more concretely, school boards are more likely to vote funds for workbooks than they are for blocks and finger paints.

In short, all across our country the conviction that earlier is better—aided and abetted by contemporary family styles and international economic competition—has led to the early formal instruction of infants and young children in everything from academics to sports.

Demise of Early Childhood Play

The major victim of the earlier is better ideology has been the play of infants and young children. In our contemporary climate, play is a bad word.

Given children's sponge-like abilities to learn, the purported rapidity of brain growth, and the time-limited nature of this window of opportunity, play is extremely wasteful of time and energy that might be put to more important and more long-lived activities. In our contemporary world, childhood is a period for work, not for play.

This is far from being a new idea. No less an early childhood innovator than Maria Montessori regarded this stage of life as one that should be devoted to work, or social adaptation, rather than play, which to her seemed self-centered and egocentric. When Montessori observed children using their imagination to create fairy tales, she remarked that the imagination might be better used for envisioning faraway countries or peoples, rather than for imaging make-believe characters. It was from that perspective that Montessori (1967) could make her pronouncement (built on the work of Groos [1914] and his observations that young animals play at activities that adult animals employ for survival) that "play is the child's work" (p. 180).

In her statement Montessori meant to emphasize the Groos observation in the sense that she believed that children's play was a kind of preparation for adult life. Children who played house were in effect rehearsing adult roles. Likewise, children who played doctor or nurse were also practicing for professions they would pursue when they were adults. Montessori was thus arguing for the value of play, albeit as a kind of practice for serious adult roles. Today, however, perhaps because domestic roles have been devalued and many adult occupations have become too technologically sophisticated to be easily dramatized, play is no longer seen as a preparation for life, but rather as indulgence at best and regression at worst. In contemporary parlance the best preparation for the work of adulthood is childhood work.

HISTORICAL BACKGROUND OF THE
EARLY IS BETTER IDEOLOGY

How and why did the "earlier is better" ideology emerge as an underlying principle of childrearing and education? Although the origins of this ideology are complex and intertwined, it is instructive to at least try and understand some of its roots.

The Informal Tradition

The idea that the early years of life are important for later development has a long past. The following examples from literature emphasize the importance of the early years:

> Just as the twig is bent the tree's inclined. (Pope, *Moral Essays*, "Epistle I, To Lord Cobham," line 150)

> The childhood shows the man, as morning shows the day. (Milton, *Paradise Regained*, l.220)

> The Child is father of the Man. (Wordsworth, "My Heart Leaps Up When I Behold," line 7)

> The clew of our destiny, wander where we will, lies at the foot of the cradle. (Richter; cited in Catrecas & Edwards [1952], p. 73)

There are also a number of writers who emphasize the special qualities of childhood as a unique period rather than, as in the examples above, one exclusively concerned with preparing for adulthood.

> The child's grief throbs against its little heart as heavily as the man's sorrow; and the one finds as much delight in his kite or drum, as the other in striking the strings of enterprise or soaring on the wings of fame. (Chapin; cited in Catrecas & Edwards [1952], p. 74)

> The plays of natural lively children are the infancy of art. Children live in a world of imagination and feeling. They invest in the most insignificant objects with any form they please, and see in it whatever they wish to see. (Orhlenschlager; cited in Catrecas & Edwards [1952], p. 76)

The informal attitude toward children, in fact, reflects not one but two different attitudes. One sees childhood as the origin of adult character and personality. This attitude emphasizes the importance of training and education and thus the influence of the environment. This "nature" emphasis is given clearest expression in Pope's metaphor of the twig and the tree.

The other attitude is what might be called the "child nature" argument. In the second group of quotes the unique nature of childhood is emphasized rather than its importance for later development. Certainly Rousseau (1762/1956) is the most explicit in this regard:

> Nature wants children to be children before they are men. If we deliberately depart from this order we shall get premature fruits which are neither ripe nor well flavored and which soon decay. We shall have youthful sages and grown up children. Childhood has ways of seeing, thinking, and feeling peculiar to itself; nothing can be more foolish than to seek to substitute our ways for them. I should as soon expect a child of ten to be five feet in height as to be possessed of judgment. (pp. 38, 39)

Historically, therefore, the nurture views of child nature have viewed childhood as a "preparation for adulthood" and have stressed the importance of early education because of its long-term consequences. In contrast, nature views of children have stressed the unique qualities of childhood and the valuing of these qualities. It has to be said that both views contain childrearing and educational implications. But these are based on two different conceptions of human ability and how this should be addressed. Inasmuch as these two different conceptions are very much in conflict today, it is important to be more explicit about them.

Two Conceptions of Ability

Human abilities can be viewed in at least two different ways. One of these, implicit in the nurture view, is that ability is an individual matter. For example, the "twig" analogy suggests that every individual has the potential to grow up straight or inclined and whether or not that happens depends upon the kind of environmental intervention the twig received while still a twig. Some twigs grow straight, some grow crooked depending upon the environment. Implicit here too are the notions that there are "bad" interventions and "good" interventions and that these designations hold true for young people across the board. That is, what is "good" for one child will necessarily be good for another and what is "bad" for one child will of necessity be bad for another.

The second notion of ability is reflected in the second set of quotations, which look at childhood as a unique period of life. When childhood is looked at in this way, ability becomes a group rather than an individual matter. As Rousseau (1762/1956) says, "children have their own ways of seeing and knowing" (p. 40). From this point of view, ability is an age group rather than an individual affair. While there are "good" and "bad" interventions, they are limited by age group. What is a "good" interaction at one stage—say, on demand feeding of an infant—may be a "bad" interaction at another stage—say, at adolescence when parents should probably not be at teenagers' beck and call for the serving of snacks.

Both of these conceptions of ability presuppose subject-environment interactions but in quite a different way. The individual approach suggests that individuals vary and how that variation will be realized depends upon the goodness or badness of environmental input. This type of interaction is a one-to-one interaction and might be called the "unmarked" path in the sense that it is not clear in what direction things are going and how they will turn out.

In contrast the concept of "group" ability presumes that those abilities will emerge across a wide range of "normally" expected environmental conditions. Children can, for example, grow in a healthy way on a wide variety of different diets. This is not to say that the environment is not important; it clearly is. It is to say only that children can make use of many different environments to achieve their abilities, at least at the early stages of development.

That is why, for example, one can observe the early Piagetian stages in children all over the world.

From this point of view, then, groups vary and the effective progress of any group is insured so long as there is a "normally expectable environment" of physical and intellectual nutrients to make normal growth possible. This path of development is, therefore, clearly marked.

As we shall see, the contemporary emphasis on "earlier is better" clearly reflects the victory of the individual conception of ability over the group conception. It should also be clear from the foregoing discussion that the idea of play as an important activity of early childhood is part of the group conception of ability but not of the individual conception. In short, the victory of the individual over the group conception of ability has also been a victory of "learning" at all ages over "age-relative learning" activities.

VICTORY OF THE INDIVIDUAL CONCEPTION OF MENTAL ABILITY

The ascension of the individual conception of mental ability in contemporary society has been aided and abetted by many changes, as well as by many abiding characteristics of American society. We need to look briefly at both sets of factors to gain some idea of why the individual conception of ability is so firmly rooted in the United States today.

Abiding Characteristics of American Society

Individualism. One characteristic of American society that contributes to the acceptance of the individual conception of ability is our individualistic ideology. Our Bill of Rights speaks eloquently of the rights of the individual over the state. The Fifth Amendment to the Constitution gives the individual the right not to testify if such testimony would be incriminating. Likewise, the First Amendment to the Constitution guarantees the individual the right of free speech and discussion.

These are accepted, hard-won individual freedoms that Americans would not be willing to give up—even if they were willing to do away with some of the interpretations of these amendments that have come down from the Supreme Court. It is not really surprising, then, to find that in our society the conception of ability as a matter of the individual, rather than as that of a group of individuals, finds a ready and welcome home. It is consistent with our well-ingrained thinking about individual rights.

It is also true, however, that there have also been times in our society when we were concerned with group rights. Certainly the Civil War was fought on behalf of groups rather than on behalf of individuals. In our own times, both the civil rights movement and the women's movement were fought to win rights for groups, not just individuals. The group emphasis also appears elsewhere in our society. The introduction of ramps, special parking places, and sloped curbs reflects a consideration of a particular group within our society. So, while we are a highly individualistic society, we have also sought to protect the rights of various groups.

Egalitarianism.   Another characteristic that contributes to the widespread acceptance of the individual approach to ability is our egalitarianism. Except for the time when we were a "crown colony," we have no history of monarchy, of any individual or group who governed by "divine right." Nor do we have any history of rigid social class boundaries such as those found in many other countries. In many countries today, individuals are still born into a social class that effectively marks them and from which they cannot ascend. The "untouchables" in India are a case in point.

To be sure, there are social classes in America, but there is also much more social mobility than in any other country. Only in the United States is it possible for so many people to go from rags to riches on the basis of talent and ability rather than of this or that accident of birth. Television personality Oprah Winfrey is one of the latest examples of an individual rising to fame and fortune from exceedingly humble beginnings.

This egalitarianism, one of the great strengths of our society, does have a dark side. The dark side is the idea that effort and motivation can count for more than ability in the attainment of wealth and fame in our society. We are, as a people, reluctant to admit talent. At the Academy Awards, the awardees go to great lengths to thank everyone who made their success possible. Indeed, it would appear highly egocentric, even narcissistic, for an awardee to say, for example, "Thank you, I am happy to receive this recognition of my talent and hard work." We play down the talent and play up the hard work. Success, we say, is achieved by 99 percent perspiration and 1 percent inspiration.

While such modesty is becoming, it masks a deeper unwillingness to take seriously differences in ability such as those that exist between age groups. Even the current concern with "gifted and talented children" reflects our belief in effort as more important than ability. Many parents believe they can make their child gifted and talented by putting them in the right classes. Some entrepreneurs in our society have established their careers on promises to create geniuses. Indeed parents can now find books on how to raise their child's IQ and how to make them brighter. If intellectual ability is not just motivation, it is also the right teaching.

Given this egalitarian ideology, it is not surprising that the conception of group difference in ability should never have taken firm hold.

The frontier mentality.   Unlike Europe and the Far East, the United States still has a great deal of land. Compared with most societies, where even middle-class people live in relatively small apartments, our spacious homes and apartments are both extraordinary and unique in the world scene. No other nation in the world has as much independent housing as is found in the United States. This openness with respect to space is also reflected in a willingness to move, to live in other cities or in other parts of the country.

While this "go west, young man" mentality can be beneficial, it too has its downside. The willingness to change residence reflects an underlying belief that change is always possible if not inevitable. And that idea of change being possible extends to children and learning. When Piaget came to this country, he was always asked what he came to call the "American" question, "Why do we have to wait for children to be six or seven before they know these things; why can't we teach them these ideas earlier?" (Ripple, 1964)

Part of the frontier mentality is also impatience. If you do not like something, you can leave, go somewhere else, and start over, rather than try making a go of a relationship or job. It is reflected in the concept of "built-in obsolescence"—if we get tired of something, we can throw it out and get something new. We almost rebuilt many of our older cities before realizing, many times too late, the rich historical heritage we were destroying. The various facets of the frontier mentality all work against the acceptance of age group differences. From the viewpoint of this mentality, age differences are challenges to be overcome, not real differences that need to be understood and adapted to.

Capitalism.   We are a capitalistic nation. The accumulation of individual capital, whether this be in the form of money, goods, or property, is a common goal of all members of the society. The pursuit of capital is, however, regulated (or should be regulated) by certain rules. Accumulation of capital by theft or trading in illicit drugs, for example, is not an acceptable means of accumulating capital. The acceptability of other means of accumulating capital is more controversial. Is polluting or destroying the environment to gain capital acceptable? Is the use of potentially dangerous pesticides that increase crop yields allowable?

The spirit of capitalism, which is the dynamic power that drives our society and other successful Western societies, clearly has a dark side. And that dark side includes all of those areas in which the pursuit of capital clashes with humanistic and environmental values. The most clear-cut example of the conflict between capitalism and human values is to be found in the production, advertisement, and sale of cigarettes. Though a proven health hazard, cigarettes continue to be marketed. The capitalist rejoins that no one forces the smoker to smoke and that it is the smoker's choice to take the risk.

The role of children in capitalistic societies has evolved. At the beginnings of the Industrial Revolution, children were often exploited as workers in the service of the accumulation of capital. In England, children were employed in mines and factories. And in the United States young teenage girls were working in the sweatshops of New York. As industrial societies have become more automated, the need for lower level skills that could be provided by children has decreased. There is little exploitation of children as workers in modern industrial societies.

What characterizes contemporary capitalistic societies, particularly the United States, is the exploitation of children as consumers. Toy and clothing manufacturers and the music and movie industries now view children and youth as a vast market. Indeed, teenagers have the highest percentage of disposable income of any age group in our society. And as children and youth become markets, their health and welfare become secondary to the accumulation of capital as they did at the time of the Industrial Revolution.

For example, children have become a market for heavily sugared and salted foods from cereals to snacks like potato chips and popcorn. That these foods are not healthy for children is secondary to the fact that they cater to children's tastes and thus encourage children to get their parents to buy these products. The sale of war toys to children reflects the same subordination of child welfare by making a profit.

It is the contemporary capitalistic conception of children as a market that dovetails with the other social factors in making the individual concept of ability so congenial to our society as a whole. The notion of individual ability presupposes that the child is capable of choice and of making decisions. With that assumption, the capitalist has no scruples about selling to children. "Let the buyer beware" should hold for the child, as well as for the adult.

Yet the capitalistic exploitation of children today is every bit as harmful and pernicious as it was in the time of the Industrial Revolution, when children's physical abilities were exploited and their physical health was put at risk. Today children's psychological abilities are being exploited and their mental health is being put at risk.

Before closing this section I want to make it as clear as I can that I am not condemning any of the features of American society that I have described above. All of them are important and powerful sources for good and have contributed to our being the greatest society on earth. Yet it also has to be recognized that there are few, if any, unalloyed goods in this world. Negatives, as well as positives, are associated with each of the ideologies described above. We make those ideologies stronger, not weaker, by exposing and if possible correcting, those parts of the ideology that do not better human health and life.

Changing Characteristics of American Society

A number of recent changes in American society have also contributed to the acceptance of the individual over the group conception of ability in the United States today.

The women's movement.   Up until about the beginning of the 1960s, middle-class women in the United States were symbols of economic surplus. Most middle-class women did not work, not because they were unable to or didn't want to, but because their not working was a symbol of the husband's ability to support his family. More simply put, women did not work to show that their husbands earned enough to support their families. Women were thus in the anomalous position of being given credit for what they were not doing, namely, having a good time (playing cards, reading magazines, and eating candy) when they were in fact working very hard, fifty hours a week, not counting child care.

The women's movement was, in large part, a reaction against this position of being a symbol of leisure-class status. And that movement has been largely successful in that domain if not as much so in others. Today women can choose to work at home or by following a career without its being a symbol of anything. At the same time, however, a new symbol of leisure-class status has come to the fore, namely, children. In contemporary American society middle-class children become the symbols of their parents' economic surplus.

One way in which we demonstrate economic surplus is through what Thorstein Veblen called "conspicuous consumption." Many of the objects we use have both a utility function and a symbolic function. Clothing, for example, keeps us warm and protects us from the elements. Yet an inexpensive pair of slacks will do that as well as a pair of designer jeans. The difference between inexpensive slacks and designer jeans is conspicuous consumption. Likewise, we can drive a Ford or a Mercedes; both will get us where we want to go at the level of utility, but not at the level of status.

Accordingly, the current practices of dressing children in designer clothing, buying them expensive toys such as computers, and sending them off for costly private lessons are ways in which we demonstrate we have economic surplus. As symbols of economic surplus, children must not only wear the clothing, go to the lessons, and so on, but also must play a part. When she was a symbol of leisure-class status, the middle-class woman had to play the dutiful, loving, and, of course, appreciative wife.

Children, too, are expected not only to exhibit the evidences of economic surplus but also to play a complementary role to the parents' largess. In our society, this complementary role has become that of the "superkid." Just as the middle-class housewife had to be exemplary, so too must the middle-class child today. Parents today expect that their children will be "above average." Indeed, the contemporary concern with gifted children grows, in part, out of this notion that children who are symbols of leisure-class status must be exceptional.

Here again, the end result of this social change in the role of women has been a comparable change in the role of children. And that change, moreover, contributes to the acceptance of the individual as against the group conception of ability. The image of the superkid, who can do almost anything, is antithetical to the group conception of ability.

The civil rights movement.   The civil rights movement of the 1960s, like the women's movement, sought to redress the inequalities of educational and job opportunities of minorities in our society. One of these inequalities was clearly educational. Schools for minority children were demonstrably poorer in quality than those for mainstream children. One major thrust for redressing this situation was the provision of high-quality early childhood education for young disadvantaged children.

The most successful and well known of these programs is Head Start. Congress voted the funds for Head Start in 1964 and the first Head Start Centers were opened in 1965. At that time Head Start served close to a half million children, and it continues to serve that many children today. The Head Start Program was and is comprehensive. It not only provides an enriched intellectual environment but also fulfills the child's nutritional and health needs.

One of the original aims of Head Start was to improve the IQs and academic achievement of disadvantaged children. Although this was and is a laudable aim, it again focused on the individual difference rather than on group conceptions of ability. This focus became even more intense in reaction to the work of Arthur Jensen (1972), who argued for group differences in ability, but for race rather than age group differences. That heated debate, which lasted for years, tainted the group difference concept by associating it with racism.

So programs for disadvantaged young people, by focusing on individual differences and on the malleability of intelligence and academic achievement, worked against the acceptance of an age-limiting conception of ability. This focus on the individual dimension of ability was strengthened as a reaction to "Jensenism."

The American family.   Another change in our society that has contributed to the acceptance of the individual difference conception of ability is the restructuring of the American family. The so-called nuclear family of the post-World War II years consisting of a homemaking mother, a working father, and two and one half children is no longer the norm. Indeed it is said that in contemporary America, only 10 percent of families are nuclear.

The American family has changed in reaction to the women's movement and also to the sexual revolution. The women's movement made it possible for mothers to pursue careers without social censure. Sexual liberation, and the extreme individualism it spawned, helped change American attitudes toward marriage and divorce. In the past both men and women sacrificed personal happiness for the purpose of maintaining the family unit. The new values taught that this was not only morally wrong but also psychologically unhealthy for everyone involved.

This new image of marriage and interpersonal relations contributed to a soaring divorce rate, which thankfully has not continued to rise but still remains at much higher levels than was true in the early 1960s. In about 90% of the divorces, the mother retains custody of the children. And since child support and alimony are rarely adequate to maintain the family's previous lifestyle, the mother is often forced to work. This fact, together with women's liberation and its impact on women and careers, means that more mothers than ever before in our history are currently in the work force. In 1989 approximately ten million children under the age of six had mothers who worked either full or part time.

Unfortunately, the changes in the American family brought about by the women's movement and by the sexual revolution were not accompanied by adequate provision for child care. In 1972, President Richard Nixon vetoed the comprehensive child care bill on the grounds that it would destroy the American family. But Nixon made the same mistake many legislators are making today, namely, mistaking cause and effect. The child care legislation would not be a cause of the breakup of the American family. Quite the contrary, the legislation was needed to deal with the effects of the breakup of the American family that had already occurred.

In any case, the lack of high-quality, affordable child care for all those families who need it remains a crucial and still unmet need. In the meantime families are making do. Perhaps the largest percentage of children with mothers in the work force are cared for at home by relatives or in the relatives' homes. The next largest percentage are cared for in family day care homes, which are, for the most part, unlicensed. Day care centers, both private and public, still care for only a million of the ten million children in need of such care.

It is in the context of changed family pattern and the need for child care that the conception of individual ability comes into play. Today's parents have to assume that their children are capable of coping with all the disruption in their lives. They have to believe that the children will not be damaged by being cared for full time by nonparental figures and will not be harmed by the less than adequate facilities they are forced to put them into.

It is easier for parents to think in this way if they hold to an individual difference rather than to a group difference conception of ability. Parents need to believe that their children's ability to cope is more or less unlimited, just the opposite of what is implicit in the group difference conception.

The women's movement, the civil rights movement, and the changes in the American family have all contributed to the acceptance of an individual difference over a group difference conception of human ability. When the contribution of these changes is added to that of the abiding characteristics of American society, the forces against an age difference, developmental conception of ability appear formidable indeed.

THE NATURE AND IMPORTANCE OF PLAY

To understand why the individual difference notion of ability works against the acceptance of children's play as a legitimate activity, we need to look at play from a developmental perspective.

Piaget's Conception of Play

In his book entitled *Play, Dreams and Imitation in Childhood,* Jean Piaget (1951) discussed the various earlier conceptions of play and suggested that they were not sufficiently general to account for all aspects of play. The idea, for example, that play is a preparation for life leaves out of account the recreational play of adults. Likewise, Spencer's theory of play as a way of expending surplus energy does not really take account of activities such as imaginative play.

For Piaget, the only general explanation of play had to be tied to the fundamental functional invariants of intelligence. Put differently, it is only when play is viewed as a dimension of human intelligence, adaptive thinking, and action that it can be understood in the most general way.

In the Piagetian scheme, play is always the extreme of one of the invariant functions of intelligence, namely, assimilation. In its most pure form, assimilation is always a transformation of the world to meet the demands of the self. At the biological level this means that we transform foodstuffs into nutrients needed by our body. At the elementary level of mental functioning, the infant who sucks at any object is transforming all objects into objects to be sucked. At higher levels of intelligence, the artistic transformations of the human form by impressionist artists would again reflect almost pure assimilation or play.

At the other extreme from play, or pure assimilation, is pure accommodation, or work. Work is always the adaptation of the self to meet the demands of the world. At the biological level when the infant adapts the lips to the shape of the nipple, we have a beginning of accommodation. At the later age levels, the child's learning of a particular language reflects accommodation to the particular language of the environment. And at even higher levels, the lawyer who learns the law and established precedent is accommodating to demands of the real world.

Piaget also pointed out that play changes with age. In infancy play is primarily sensorimotor as the child transforms objects into things to be sucked, banged, or thrown. At the preschool level children acquire the ability to create symbols and begin to engage in symbolic play, which can range from the dramatic to the constructive play with blocks. In childhood proper when children attain concrete operations they begin to engage in games with rules. In such games the transformations are collective rather than individual. In playing Monopoly all the players agree that the cards represent property and the paper money, real money.

Play and Group Differences in Ability

It is now possible to understand in a little more nearly comprehensive way why play is being so ill received in contemporary American society. We have seen that the thrust of our history and the contemporary changes in our society are toward the individual difference conception of ability. That individual difference conception is essentially an accommodation conception of ability. The emphasis is on learning from the environment, maximizing ability, practicing acceleration, thinking earlier is better.

The earlier is better notion, which reflects the individual conception idea of human ability, is antithetical to play if this is understood as an assimilative rather than as an accommodative process. Put differently, many contemporary parents and educators, for all of the reasons I have outlined above, believe that it is most important for the child to adapt to the world that is, not spend time creating a world that is not.

Oddly enough, it is not play itself that is being opposed, but rather play in infancy and early childhood. In contemporary society, play is often seen as something you can do and enjoy only as an adult, not as a child. The recent movie *Big* reflects this theme but also the theme that children would prefer to play as children rather than as adults. Nonetheless, in Japan, where many children are pressured academically even during the early years, the college students take four years off to play. They join clubs and do not go to classes.

In summary then, many different forces are operating to favor a conception of individual ability over group ability as a way of understanding children's competence. This in turn gives rise to the earlier is better notion and to favoring the idea of early childhood as a period that should be focused on accommodation, or work, rather than on assimilation, or play.

REFERENCES

Catrecas, C. N., & Edwards, J. comp. (1952). *The new dictionary of thoughts.* New York: Standard Book Co.

Groos, K. (1914). *The play of man.* New York: Appleton Century.

Jensen, A. (1972). *Genetics and education.* New York: Harper & Row.

Montessori, M. (1967). *The absorbent mind.* New York: Dell.

Piaget, J. (1951). *Play, dreams and imitation in childhood.* New York: Norton.

Ripple, V. E., & Rockastle, R. E. (1964). *Piaget rediscovered.* Ithaca, NY: School of Education, Cornell University.

Rousseau, J. J. (1956). *The Emile of Jean Jacques Rousseau: Selections.* New York: Teachers College Press. (Original work published in 1762)

CHAPTER 2

Sociodramatic Play: Its Relevance to Behavior and Achievement in School

Sara Smilansky

This chapter presents material that is, in part, a report of research done by the author and in part a report of follow-up research done by others for which the author's original research served as a baseline.

The aims of this chapter are to

1. Provide solid research evidence on the effectiveness of appropriate adult interventions with regard to (a) the development and use of make-believe elements in dramatic and sociodramatic play and (b) the concomitant use of such elements in the development of and participation in dramatic and sociodramatic play activities
2. Present solid research evidence and empirical support for theoretical hypotheses about the significance of dramatic and sociodramatic play as a medium for developing cognitive, creative, and socioemotional abilities that will be useful within a school environment.

In order to present this evidence with clarity, it will be useful to define some of the terminology.

DEFINITION OF TERMS

Dramatic and Sociodramatic Play Activity

Most children around the world between the ages of two and eight engage in a form of voluntary social play activity we refer to as dramatic and socio-dramatic play.

Dramatic play consists of children taking on a role in which they pretend to be someone else. They imitate the person's actions and speech patterns, using real or imagined "props" and drawing on their own firsthand or second-hand experience of the imitated individual in various familiar situations.

When such activity involves the *cooperation* of at least two children and the play proceeds on the basis of interaction between the players acting out their roles, both verbally and in terms of acts performed, the dramatic play is considered "sociodramatic play."

Both types of play activity involve two basic elements. The most central element seems to be *imitation*, which, paradoxically, establishes a reality level for children. They try to act, talk, and look like some real adult person and recreate situations that are, in their perception, real. In most cases, they try to reproduce the adult world although they may act out other situations as well.

Because children's reality, identity, and surroundings limit the possibility of exact imitation, the second element enters here: that of *make-believe* or imagination. Make-believe allows children to project themselves into activities and situations that cannot actually be reproduced; thus, the situations are merely represented and are not exact. Children derive satisfaction not only from the ability to imitate but also from make-believe play, which provides unlimited access to the exciting world of adults.

Imitation includes both actions and speech patterns. Children pretending to be a bus driver will move their hands as though steering the bus, take money, give out tickets to the imagined passengers, and use expressions specific to a bus driver: "Move to the back of the bus," "Watch your step," etc. They may reproduce the noises of the bus even to accurate changes in the motor sound as gears are shifted and the noises of the mechanism that opens and closes the doors.

Make-believe depends heavily on verbalization. Words take the place of reality in the following ways:

1. Declarations to change identity: "I am the daddy, you are the mommy, and the doll is our baby."
2. Declarations changing the identity of an object or action: "I am drinking from the bottle," when the child is drinking from a fist. The drinking movement is imitative, but pretending the fist is a bottle is make-believe.
3. Substituting speech for action: "Let's pretend I already returned from work; I've cooked supper and now I'm setting the table." Only the last activity mentioned is actually imitated and acted out.
4. Setting the scene: "Let's pretend that this is a hospital and there are a lot of sick children here."

Make-believe in dramatic and sociodramatic play, as opposed to other circumstances where it serves as a means of escape from the real world, extends the scope of the imitative activity and provides a comprehensive and comprehensible context that increases the realism of the behavior.

Verbalizations evolving from imitation and make-believe in dramatic play occur in egocentric form, but the move to sociodramatic play brings about various changes. The verbalization becomes more developed and takes on the patterns and content of adult verbal interaction. Make-believe verbalizations are necessary now not only to set the scene for the one speaking but also to make the behavior understandable to the other children participating in the play episode and to provide proper interpretation and direction for the activity. Since sociodramatic play cannot proceed without cooperation between the players, verbalization also functions as a means of management and problem-solving reflecting child-reality and child interaction during the process of the play activity (for example, "Give me the doll," "Don't take the chair"). Although I have drawn lines between the different elements of dramatic and sociodramatic play activities, as well as between the different functions of the activities and speech, the play process contains all these elements in quick succession. But at least a minimum amount of make-believe, imitation, and play-related interaction must exist for sociodramatic play to have taken place.

Six elements may be identified that reflect the dramatic and the sociodramatic aspect of the play activity:

1. *Role play by imitation.* The child takes on a role and expresses it through imitative action or verbalization. The child enacts the character of a person or animal other than self in a different context.
2. *Make-believe with objects.* The child substitutes any or all of the following for real objects:
     Toys
     Unstructured materials, pieces of paper, pieces of cloth,
         boxes, pieces of wood or sticks
     Gestures and movements
     Verbal declarations.
3. *Make-believe with actions and situations.* The child substitutes verbal descriptions and gestures or movements for actions and situations.
4. *Persistence in the role play.* The child persists within the role for an episode lasting for a reasonable length of time—5, 10, 15 minutes.
5. *Interaction.* There is at least one other child involved and interacting within the framework of the sociodramatic play episode.
6. *Verbal communication.* There is some verbal interaction between members of the sociodramatic group related to what is going on within the episode.

Once a definition of the criteria and elements necessary for the evaluation of dramatic play and sociodramatic play activities was formulated, it was then possible to create an assessment and diagnostic tool with which to evaluate the dramatic and sociodramatic elements of play for children from ages four to eight. Observations of play activities of children were made to determine the degree to which each of the six elements could be found. Each element was scored from 0–3, where 0 means the element is not found at all, and 3 means the element is found consistently throughout various situations during the play activity. In addition, the ratings were made at 5-minute intervals and then averaged for an overall rating per 20- or 30-minute observation period. Children's play activity was evaluated as they played with the entire class, with self-selected playmates, and as assigned at random to groups in special rooms (Smilansky, 1968).

In order for play activity to be considered sociodramatic, elements 5 and 6 must be present. Consider the following situations:

- A little girl dresses up in a long dress, carries a shopping bag in one hand and announces: "I'm Mommy and I'm going shopping." Only elements 1 and 3 are clearly present, and, therefore, her role play is considered to be dramatic, not sociodramatic, play.
- Two children are playing in the nursery room corner called "the playhouse." One is ironing, the second is dressing and feeding a doll with a toy baby bottle. The only interaction between the children occurs when one says to the other: "Give me that dress for the doll." The interaction and communication is not within the framework of the various episodes they are enacting for themselves. In fact, there may not even be any make-believe at all. Only element 1 is clearly present—role play by imitation.

There does not seem to be an order of preference for the six elements; they are all necessary in order to develop into sociodramatic play activities and are interdependent to some extent. However, the richness of the play does depend on the extent to which the various elements are used and developed. There is, therefore, a difference between play episodes including a large group of children or just a pair; similarly, there is a difference if the child uses make-believe only occasionally or uses it very frequently during play with many imaginative creations. The scale described above takes all these differences into consideration. Thus, evaluation of richness depends, not on the content of the child's episode or on the type of role being played, but on the degree to which each of the six elements is developed and used as a play skill.

Relation Between Sociodrama and Other Terms

My choice of the term *sociodramatic play* reflects considerations of various other terms often used to describe the same or similar phenomena. *Symbolic play* and *representational play* are two such terms. But they stress the mental processes involved and not the children's observable behavior. Symbolism and representation deal with the cognitive and developmental conditions necessary in order for the described behavior to emerge. Furthermore, representational thought and play include a wide variety of behavior that cannot be defined as dramatic play as it has been defined. Thus, symbolic play and representational play are simultaneously overinclusive and inadequate.

Make-believe play and *pretend play* are more appropriate, for these terms express what the child consciously intends to do while engaging in dramatic or sociodramatic play activities. They are based on the behavior that manifests itself, as well as on the verbalizations of the children involved ("let's pretend . . ." or "let's make believe . . ."). They also convey the child's awareness of reality despite its transformation into make-believe and pretending. The problem arises when the terms refer to situations where children play roles in puppet productions or other representations of plots through the use of such materials as pipe cleaners or drawings, where the performing task is delegated to objects and the child acts as stage manager.

Role play is another term that is often used. It is, however, too narrow a description of what the children are really doing. It describes only one of the elements in sociodramatic play, that of taking on a role.

In deciding to use the terms *dramatic* and *sociodramatic play activities*, the following two general characteristics were considered:

1. Complex entity—a wide variety of mental processes and behavioral characteristics not included by all the other terms (i.e., representation, pretense plus reality orientation, organizational skills, reasoning and argumentation, social skills). The essence of sociodramatic play is the integration of these various elements into meaningful activities. The very complexity of the activity is its main characteristic.
2. Spontaneity and on-going improvisation; drama often implies fixed roles, plots, predetermined conclusions, but I do not include enacting such roles and plays as dramatic and/or sociodramatic play activity. The significance of sociodramatic play is the choice *the child makes* of which roles to take on and how the episode develops.

All this is not to say that the alternate terms are no longer valid. They simply are not specifically aimed at what I am trying to describe.

Dramatic and Sociodramatic Play in the Developmental Sequence of Play

Piaget (1962; 1964; 1966; 1971; & Inhelder, 1956; 1971) in his writings describes three different major play sequences:

1. Sensory-motor practice (functional play)
2. Symbolic play (our dramatic and sociodramatic play)
3. Games with rules.

Piaget does not relate in his writings to constructive, goal-oriented play behavior as a distinct type or stage of play development. Considering the dominance of such behavior in preschool children, it is surprising that it did not come under the scrutiny of one of the greatest observers of child behavior. It is possible that Piaget did not attach much significance to the difference between the functional pleasure a child derives from simple sensory-motor practice and that derived from a constructive play activity in which the child strives to accomplish a goal or to create a product according to a plan.

I have, however, concluded that constructive play activities are the developmental extension and elaboration of sensory-motor activities at the age level when the child already possesses some representational capacities. Therefore, the child can act according to play: instead of throwing sand or simply digging, the child "builds a castle" or "bakes cookies." This occurs parallel to the first stages of the development of symbolic play and often contains elements of pretend (neither the sand castle nor the sand cookies are real). Such activities are a transition from manipulation of material toward formation. In constructive play the materials are the focal point of attention; the child acts upon the materials and enjoys doing something with them. Satisfaction is derived from the qualities of the materials themselves; their properties determine what the child does with them.

However, sociodramatic play activities concentrate on roles and themes and not on materials. Such behavior begins as early as two years of age. Therefore, dramatic play cannot be a natural transition from sensory-motor practice play toward a more mature way of relating to the material world. In fact, dramatic play activities seem to be novel behavior expressing the child's growing awareness and understanding of the social milieu, which is made possible by the growth of representational thought and which makes possible, in turn, the further growth of representational capacity. As dramatic and sociodramatic play activities become more elaborate, the child also continues to participate in functional play that gradually becomes more goal oriented and constructive.

Furthermore, sociodramatic play activities seem to serve different needs than those served by functional and constructive play and activate a larger spectrum of dispositions, understanding, and abilities. Objects play a limited role in sociodramatic play: they are instrumental in acting out a make-believe role, for they are an integral part of the adult world. Symbolic role behavior is more dependent on objects at the early stages of pretend play, when gestural and verbal substitution for objects and activities has not yet developed.

Even at those early stages, however, there is a basic difference between "things" for a child involved in functional or constructive play and "things" used by the child in sociodramatic play activities. In dramatic and sociodramatic play, children are mostly interested in how adults use the things on which they are concentrating. They are interested, not in the object as a signifier, but in what it signifies in the context of social roles and interaction. Toy replicas and materials are important even at higher levels of sociodramatic play development as triggers for suggesting themes for enactment and role behavior. Therefore, a toy typewriter, for example, might increase the number of office episodes of dramatic and sociodramatic play activities or introduce the subject where it had not occurred before. After a while, however, more advanced players would abandon the toy typewriter and "type letters" on a box, a book, or on any other object vaguely reminiscent of the original typewriter. This does not seem to agree with the assumptions implicit in Piaget's play theory, whereby the use of objects emerges as an ontogenetic extension, continuation, and elaboration of the functional practice play period. It is probable that the developmental extension of functional practice play is in the realm of construct-creative goal-oriented activities (like building blocks) that also contain imaginative "as if" elements without the transformation of the self or of others into other people or beings. Neither functional nor constructive play activities cease with the appearance of symbolic-dramatic and sociodramatic activities.

Activities known as games with rules cannot be considered successors to symbolic-dramatic and/or sociodramatic play activities or as a transition from egocentric thought to a reality orientation. Some games with rules are widespread very early, specifically noncompetitive ones (puzzles or matching games), and competitive games are enjoyed at an only slightly advanced age (hide and seek, picture dominoes, card games). The question arises whether games with rules are more an extension and elaboration of constructive and sensory-motor activities with the added element of externally defined rules and success criteria, regardless of the competitive aspect.

It would seem that dramatic and sociodramatic play is based on different needs and serves a different function than any of the other three forms of play. Dramatic and sociodramatic play activities develop parallel to other forms of play and continue for a much longer period than has been described by Piaget. Dramatic play begins at about age two and develops most nearly fully during the age period between four and six. For many children it develops up to the age of ten and seems to cease upon the child's entrance into real-life responsibilities with the concomitant rewards and obligations rather than with the entry of the child into games with rules.

Relation Between Sociodramatic Play and Behavior in School

Sociodramatic play activates resources that stimulate emotional, social, and intellectual growth in the child, which in turn affects the child's success in school. We saw many similarities between patterns of behavior bringing about successful sociodramatic play experiences and patterns of behavior required for successful integration into the school situation. For example, problem solving in most school subjects requires a great deal of make-believe: visualizing how the Eskimos live, reading stories, imagining a story and writing it down, solving arithmetic problems, and determining what will come next. History, geography, and literature are all make-believe. All of these are conceptual constructions that are never directly experienced by the child. "Problems" are conceptual conditions into which children must project themselves in order to make decisions and take action to resolve the situation.

As we think about the relationship between sociodramatic play and school behavior, the following factors are offered for consideration:

1. Playing a role demands enough intellectual discipline to include only behavior appropriate for the role the child has taken on. The child must judge and select from a pool of possibilities.
2. In order to act within a sociodramatic episode, the child must grasp the essence of things—the major features of a character or a theme, the central characteristics.
3. Participation in sociodramatic activity teaches the child to concentrate on a given theme.
4. Participation in sociodramatic activity requires children to control themselves, to discipline their own actions with regard to episodic content, the themes, and the roles they have assumed.
5. The different, but successful, approaches to the story line that the other members of sociodramatic activities use teach the child flexibility—that there may be more than one right way to do things.
6. The different role definitions and theme development of the other players in sociodramatic activities teach the child new concepts as well as new approaches to problems. For example, the child may learn that there may be other behavior patterns for "father" than those with which the child is familiar.
7. Participation in sociodramatic play activities helps the child to move to-

ward advanced stages of abstract thought. We may observe the following procedure: the child begins with a toy that inspires imitative play—for example, a toy typewriter, and the child pretends to write a story. After a while, owing to the rapidity of spontaneous play and its growing complexity, the child substitutes a box or anonymous chunk of wood for the toy typewriter. Later, having misplaced the wood, the child uses a gesture, perhaps drumming the fingers in the air. Finally, dispensing with the actions altogether, the child simply announces the writing of a story.

8. The more sociodramatic play activities engaged in, the more accomplished the child becomes at sociodramatic play; the more children participated with, the more likely that the child will become acquainted with different interpretations of various roles and different definitions of various situations and themes.

The demonstrated inherently rewarding quality of learning within a sociodramatic activity framework and the preeminence of language as part of sociodramatic play activity cannot be overlooked in evaluating its significance for later achievement and success in school. I recommend further study of the relationship between the degree to which a child participates in sociodramatic play activities and the degree of that child's success and active participation in school activities. It is astonishing that games with rules have enjoyed such distinction in their use as learning tools, while sociodramatic activity has not.

Several studies have been carried out in the United States and in Israel on the relevance of sociodramatic play activities to other aspects of children's development (see Table 2.1). These are discussed in the following sections.

Relationship Between Sociodramatic Play and Cognitive Tasks

As shown in Table 2.1, three studies were designed to assess the relationship between sociodramatic play activities and cognitive tasks.

The study conducted by Helen Lewis (1974) in the United States considered 78 Appalachian children from families of low socioeconomic status. Their ages ranged from five years eight months to six years nine months. The hypothesis was that a child who demonstrated a high level of organized thought through action and language as expressed through sociodramatic play activity would show organized thought in response to image representation found in a picture-reading task. Sociodramatic activity levels were measured according to the Smilansky scale and a significant relationship was found between the child's ability to pursue a theme in the framework of sociodramatic play and the ability to look at picture content, organize it into a summary, and formulate a narrative so that it could be described verbally. It was clear that the child who could symbolize during sociodramatic play (make-believe with objects) could go beyond the literal level of picture interpretation, imagining and infer-

Table 2.1 Studies of the Relationship Between Dramatic and Sociodramatic Play Activities and School-Related Variables

Investigators	Age and Socioeconomic Status of Subject (yr)	Variables Related to Play
Marshall (1951)[b]	2.6–6.6, High SES	Acceptance of peers, friendly interaction with and independence from teachers
Lewis (1974)[a]	5.8–6.9, Low SES	Picture reading--language output and meaning
Rubin & Maioni (1975)[a]	4, Middle SES	Classification tasks, spatial perspective-taking
Johnson (1976)[a]	Preschool, Mixed SES	IQ and other cognitive tests; divergent thinking
Taler (1976)[b]	5–6, Low–High SES	Socioeconomic ratings; teacher ratings of adjustment
Tower et al. (1979)[b]	Nursery, Middle SES	Positive affect, concentration and persistence; interaction and cooperation; emotional indices
Smilansky & Feldman (1980)[c]	2nd Grade, Low & Middle SES	Reading comprehension, arithmetic

[a]One group of studies was designed to assess the relationship between dramatic and sociodramatic play activities and cognitive tasks.

[b]Another group of studies assessed the relationship between dramatic and sociodramatic play activities and socioemotional adjustment.

[c]One study assessed the relationship between dramatic and sociodramatic play activities and scholastic achievement.

ring details missing from pictures. In fact, the child who scored the highest level of sociodramatic play activity was found to have a higher level of syntactic maturity than the child who did not engage in sociodramatic play activity or who stayed at the level of dramatic play activity.

By measuring role-playing and empathy skills, a Canadian study on the play behavior of middle-class four-year-olds (Rubin & Maioni, 1975) tested the hypothesis that there is a positive relationship between the frequency of dramatic play and classification ability. The hypothesis stated that all these skills and abilities were grounded on an understanding of reciprocal relations. Each child was observed during free play and the behavior was classified according to four categories of play: functional play, constructive play, dramatic play, and games with rules. There was a small ($r = .20$) nonsignificant correlation between dramatic play and empathic role play. The authors did not differentiate between dramatic and sociodramatic activities. There was a correlation of .49 ($p < .06$) between dramatic play and classification tasks and of .55 ($p < .05$) between dramatic play and taking on spatial roles (taking n spatial perspectives).

A study conducted in the United States (Johnson, 1976) looked at the relationship between make-believe play and tests of cognition and divergent thinking. The 63-child sample was taken from various social and ethnic groups enrolled in a preschool program in a depressed area in Detroit, Michigan. The cognitive measuring tools used were the Peabody picture vocabulary tests (PPVT) and the picture completion subtest from the Wechsler Preschool and Primary Scale of Intelligence (WPPSI). The correlations recorded between nonsocial dramatic play and the other measuring tools were very low (.15 was the highest); sociodramatic play activity was found to be highly related to three of the four divergent thinking measures: $v = .35$ for picture completion, .35 for fluency, and .52 for fantasy subscores. Correlations of sociodramatic play activity with the cognitive tests were somewhat lower but still significant at the .05 level: .25 for the Peabody picture vocabulary tests and .25 for the subtest from the WPPSI. Interpretations of the results indicate that intelligence is necessary but by itself not sufficient for make-believe play. Divergent thinking ability seems to be an important component as well.

Since both intelligence and divergent thinking abilities are important for school, the evidence from the three studies would seem to indicate that sociodramatic play activity either uses these learning-relevant capacities or contributes to their development.

Relationship Between Sociodramatic Play and Emotional Adjustment

Although cognitive and academic achievement may be among the most important elements necessary for adjustment to a school situation, they are not the sole relevant dimensions. Social adjustment plays a very central role in school life. The happiness and ultimate success of a child in school rests to a very large degree on the ability to interact positively with peers and teachers on a person-to-person basis, as well as within group situations.

Accordingly, it would be helpful to evaluate the relevance of sociodramatic play activities in the field of social adjustment. A longitudinal study is best suited for such an investigation, but at present there are no such studies. There are, however, three cross-sectional studies on this topic, one done in Israel and two in the United States.

Marshall (1961) conducted the first study of the connections between dramatic and sociodramatic play activities and social skills and adjustment with a sample of 108 children aged two and a half to six and a half years from families of high socioeconomic status. The study results indicated a high correlation between sociodramatic play and the following social and language skills during free-play periods: acceptance by peers, frequency of language use during the sociodramatic activity, number of friendly interactions, and actions independent of teachers.

Tower, Singer, and Biggs (1979) studied the relationship between sociodramatic play activity and social and emotional adjustment in a study of 58 white middle-class nursery school children. They reported correlations between sociodramatic activity (extent of pretend behavior) and the following:

positive affect	0.70
concentration	0.65
interaction with others	0.52
cooperation with peers	0.45
fear	−0.51
sadness	−0.40
signs of fatigue	−0.41

Taler, in Israel (1976), studied the relationship between sociodramatic play activities (as measured on the Smilansky scale) and two social adjustment assessment tools: sociometric ratings by peers and teacher ratings on a standardized social adjustment rating scale. The sample consisted of 96 kindergarten children from families of low and high socioeconomic status. Taler found significant correlations between the social adjustment scores and those of sociodramatic play activity. Positive sociodramatic ratings seemed better related to sociodramatic play activity scores than negative sociometric ratings did.

Relationship with Scholastic Achievement

Only one study dealt with the relationship between sociodramatic play activity and scholastic achievement: a longitudinal study conducted in Israel

(Smilansky & Feldman, 1980). We traced Taler's (1976) group of kindergartners to their second-grade location and administered standardized reading
comprehension and arithmetic achievement tests. Their test scores were then
compared with Taler's scores of sociodramatic activity. The resulting correlations are shown in Table 2.2.

The correlations between the total sociodramatic play score in kindergarten and achievement scores in both reading comprehension and arithmetic in
second grade were higher than expected (.40 and .45) (Smilansky & Frenkel,
1980). Another Israeli study (Smilansky & Shefatya, 1979) showed a correlation of only .36 between the Stanford-Binet IQ score administered in kindergarten and reading achievement at the end of first grade. As one can see in the
Table, the breakdown of the play scores indicates that the ability to make-
believe with objects, as well as with actions and situations, appears to be most
highly correlated with scholastic achievement. We may conclude that high
imaginative representation in kindergarten is one of the most relevant skills
for school achievement. However, the other play elements are also highly correlated. A multiple-regression analysis of the reading scores with regard to the
six play elements showed that the two make-believe elements explained 23%
of the reading variations, while the other play elements were insignificant for
prediction purposes. Similarly, when the play elements were analyzed with
regard to arithmetic performance, the two make-believe elements explained
26% of the variation while the other play elements were insignificant. Such
findings over a three-year period are rare, and it is felt that a cross-cultural
replication study should be carried out to see if these results hold true.

Table 2.2   Correlations Between Sociodramatic Play in
            Kindergarten and Reading Comprehension and
            Arithmetic Achievement in 2nd Grade

Sociodramatic Play in Kindergarten	Reading Comprehension in 2nd Grade	Arithmetic in 2nd Grade
Imitative role play	.38**	.34**
Make-believe with objects	.41**	.41**
Make-believe with actions and situations	.32**	.30**
Persistence in the role play	.22	.33**
Interaction with co-players	.31*	.34**
Verbal communication with a role	.27*	.30*
Total Sociodramatic Play	.40**	.45**

* p < .05   ** p < .01

Summary

Additional empirical evidence (Fein, 1979) supports the contention that sociodramatic play activities are relevant for scholastic achievement in several areas. This evidence results from cross-cultural and cross-socioeconomic group studies using various evaluation tools. This in itself is a strong argument for the significance of this form of play activity in terms of the child's present and future school adjustment and success. None of the studies described have dealt with the causal relationship between sociodramatic play activity and cognitive, social, and emotional growth. The area of causal relationships between the results of adult intervention in children's play and their functioning in the cognitive, social, and emotional dimensions of their lives should be the focal point for testing in future studies. It is the focus of the next section.

EFFECT OF INTERVENTION IN CHILDREN'S PLAY ON BEHAVIOR IN SCHOOL

Beginning with the first experimental program (Smilansky, 1968), kindergarten teachers have intervened in children's play activity in many subsequent studies in order to improve the quality of dramatic and sociodramatic play activity. The majority of these studies investigated the transfer effect of the play activity to a large variety of related skills (see Table 2.3).

The first column of Table 2.3 shows that these experiments cover a 16-year period (1967–1983). The second column indicates that the children ranged from two years nine months to six years of age and from lower to middle socioeconomic levels and that they were from a variety of racial and ethnic groups.

The third column needs closer examination since it contains the variable of what was done with the children. All the studies included adult intervention in the make-believe play activities of the children with the aim of improving dramatic and sociodramatic forms of play. What the adults did varied from one study to another. Some discussed with the children possible topics that could be incorporated into dramatic or sociodramatic play activity. Others concentrated on play skills and did not intervene in the content. These adults encouraged the children to use nonstructured material, suggested partners and interaction within the framework of the theme episode, helped elaborate the theme, encouraged role adoption, and so forth. Still others not only introduced themes but also began to act them out, encouraged the children to use the play equipment with imagination, and suggested acting-out characters. Another group of adults dealt with dependence of children on ready-made toys, while

Table 2.3 Effect of Adult Intervention in Make-Believe Play on School-Related Concerns

Investi-gators	Subjects	Intervention	Gains in Play	Changes in School-Related Areas
Marshall & Hahn (1967)	2.9-5.6, Middle SES	Active participation of adults in children's play; discussed topics that might be utilized by the child in dramatic and sociodramatic play	*	More language used; more play with peers
Smilansky (1968)	4-6, Low SES	Active participation in child's play skills (not in content): encouraged children to use nonstructured materials, encouraged children to invite others to play as partners, helped to elaborate a theme, encouraged adoption of a role	*	Language criteria--quantity, quality of vocabulary; richness of vocabulary
Freyberg (1973)	5 Years Low SES	Simulation of plot with pipe cleaners, encouragement by adults: introduced the theme and began to act it out; encouraged the children to make use of the equipment imaginatively; encouraged to act out a character	*	Positive affect; concentration on imaginativeness in play activity
Feitelson & Ross (1973)	5-6, Low SES	Encouragement of fancifulness and inventiveness; decrease dependence on ready-made toys	*	Curiosity, innovative and original behavior creativity assessment tools

Study	Age, SES	Intervention		Measures/Outcomes
Rosen (1974)	5-6, Low SES, Black	Suggestions and active participation of adults, similar to Smilansky (1968)	*	Group problem-solving tasks; perspective-taking; prediction of others' preferences and wants
Saltz, Dixon & Johnson (1977)	3-4.5, Low SES; Mixed Ethnic	Enactment of fairy-tales; encouragement of sociodramatic play; encouraged children to describe and reenact visits to the doctor, grocery store, fire station, etc.	*	Cognitive tasks; impulse control; empathy, verbal intelligence; story interpretation
Smith & Syddall (1978)	3-4, Low to Middle SES	Encouragement and suggestions by adults imitated and maintained fantasy play in children; encouraged children to join in play with others	*	More group activity; equal gains on intellectual and socioemotional competence assessment tools as compared with skill-tutored group; language comprehension; basic concepts; creativity tests; group activity; attention span; cognitive ability and sociocognition
Golomb & Cornelius (1977)	4-4.6, Middle SES	Creation of pretend episodes, prompting child to explain pretense	Not tested	Conservation tasks
Burns & Brainerd (1978)	4-5	Active participation of adult	Not tested	Perspective-taking

Table 2.3 (continued)

Investi-gators	Subjects	Intervention	Gains in Play	Changes in School-Related Areas
Dansky (1980)	5, Low SES, Black & White	Active participation of adult encour-aging children to take on roles related to the general theme; inter-vention similar to that in Smilansky (1968); suggested the child do certain things related to role	*	Assessment of imaginativeness language-verbal comprehension production and organization cognitive tasks, thinking and sequential activity
Golomb & Bowen (1981)	5-6, Low SES	Intervention similar to Golomb and Cornelius (1977)	Not tested	Conservation tasks
Udwin (1983)	3-6, Normal & Institu-tionalized	Variety of techniques used by adults for encouragement	*	Assessment of creativity, verbal fluency; increase in imaginative play, positive emotionality; social interaction action and cooperation with peers; reduction in aggression; emotional and social adjustment

yet another looked outside the classroom for experiences that could serve as topics of dramatic and sociodramatic activities, such as visits to a doctor's office, a grocery store, or the fire station. Make-believe itself became the topic as children in some of the studies were encouraged to engage in directed, adult-initiated fantasy or to create pretend episodes and then explain the "pretending." Other studies described varied techniques used by the adults in order to encourage the children to take on roles or relate to certain general themes. Some investigators even made specific suggestions to children about what to do in order to carry out the roles more nearly completely.

Despite the variation in the processes of the studies and the experimental approaches, the active intervention of the adult in the affairs of the child is a characteristic shared by all the studies. The fourth column, "Gains in Play," indicates that all groups testing for this variable show significant gains in dramatic and sociodramatic play activity as the result of adult intervention.

The last column deals with the question of transfer effects of the adult intervention in children's play to related cognitive, social, and emotional skills necessary for success in school. The results point to dramatic and sociodramatic play as a strong medium for the development of cognitive and socioemotional skills. We could summarize these results as follows:

Gains in *Cognitive-Creative Activities*	*Gains in* *Socioemotional Activities*
Better verbalization	More playing with peers
Richer vocabulary	More group activity
Higher language comprehension	Better peer cooperation
Higher language level	Reduced aggression
Better problem-solving strategies	Better ability to take on the perspective of others
More curiosity	
Better ability to take on the perspective of another	More empathy
	Better control of impulsive actions
Higher intellectual competence	
Performance of more conservation tasks	Better prediction of others' preferences and desires
More innovation	Better emotional and social adjustment
More imaginativeness	
Longer attention span	
Greater concentration ability	

Our findings have confirmed that imitation of roles is not in itself instrumental in developing the child's abilities; rather, it is the make-believe process (verbal and nonverbal behavior), frequently supported by appropriate adult intervention, that is pivotal. Creating and coping with hypothetical situations—that is, removed from the here and now—and/or with abstract issues by means of dramatic and sociodramatic activity causes children to use specific skills that will be called into play during school. These include projecting oneself into imaginary situations called up in more or less rich detail and dealing with unexpected responses and development of the episode. Also, carrying the situation to its logical conclusion through sociodramatic play activities parallels school demands for the student to project the self into hypothetical problems and find and test possible solutions.

IS SOCIODRAMATIC PLAY PART OF PRESCHOOL CURRICULUM?

As the results of our studies (as well as other research studies) show, dramatic and sociodramatic play is a strong medium for the development of young children's cognitive and socioemotional skills. Our goal was to learn how these results are translated into educational practice, particularly in preschool and kindergarten classrooms. Therefore, we developed a questionnaire that would enable us to obtain information from classroom teachers on dramatic and sociodramatic play activities in their classrooms. (See Figure 2.1).

The questionnaire was submitted to a sample group of 120 preschool and kindergarten teachers: 60 American teachers (in Washington, D.C.; Boston, Massachusetts; and Columbus, Ohio) and 60 Israeli teachers (in Tel-Aviv, Netanya, and Petach-Tikva). Approximately half of the teachers in both countries taught children from families of low socioeconomic background, while the other half taught children from families of middle and high socioeconomic backgrounds.

The purpose was to analyze the teachers' responses in order to determine answers to the following five major issues, relating to sociodramatic play, which face preschool and kindergarten teachers:

1. Is sociodramatic play consciously included as part of the curriculum?
2. Are children's dramatic and sociodramatic activities assessed by teachers in the same way as other classroom activities are?
3. Is there active intervention on the part of the teachers in order to facilitate and develop dramatic and sociodramatic abilities?
4. What is the attitude of the teachers toward the role of dramatic and sociodramatic play activity vis-à-vis future success in school?
5. Are the universities, colleges, and inservice training programs preparing teachers to facilitate and assess the development of dramatic and sociodramatic play?

Figure 2.1   Questionnaire Regarding Dramatic and
             Sociodramatic Play in the Classroom
_____

Name of Teacher: _____
Address: _____
School Telephone: _____   Home Telephone: _____
Number of boys: _____   girls: _____   in your class.   Ages: _____

1. Is there a "playhouse" corner in your classroom?
2. List the type and quantity of equipment in your class
    "playhouse" corner.
3. List the time(s) of day when your children play there.
4. Give the number of boys: _____   girls: _____   who played in
    the playhouse corner during the last three weeks.
5. Do you expect all the children in your classroom to
    play in the playhouse corner at some time during the
    day or week?   Why or why not?   Please explain.
6. Should teachers help children learn how to play in the
    playhouse corner?   Why?   How?
7. Do you think the activities of the children in the
    playhouse corner help you prepare the children toward
    succeeding in school?   Why?   In what way?
8. During your training to become a teacher, was the
    importance of playing in the playhouse corner the
    subject of any of the courses you studied?
9. During your training to become a teacher, did you learn
    how to develop a child's ability to practice dramatic
    and sociodramatic play activity while in the playhouse
    corner?
_____

Results of the Survey

The results are summarized below and are arranged according to the five issues listed previously, based on the items in the questionnaire.

Issue 1. Is sociodramatic play consciously included as part of the curriculum?

1. All 120 teachers, without exception, reported that there is a "playhouse" corner in their classrooms.

2. There were no significant differences between countries or between classrooms in the types of toys and equipment available to the children in the playhouse. The major differences among the classrooms were in the quantity and quality of the toys they contained. For example, in some classrooms there were only one or two shabby, overused dolls, whereas in others there were up to 16 mostly new and high-quality dolls of all sizes and shapes. Toys found in all the classrooms included a sink, cabinets, a stove, table and chairs, pots and pans, a broom, a doll bed, clothing, an ironing board and an iron, a doctor's

bag, a telephone, purses and pocketbooks, some toy animals, empty food boxes, toy knives and forks, plates, and cups.

3. Sixty percent of the teachers reported that the children were able to play in the playhouse at any time of the school day—during the free-play period or when they had finished the directed work. Forty percent of the teachers reported an average of 30 minutes a day when children could play in the playhouse corner if they wished.

4. When separated according to sex, 10–25% of the boys and 25–50% of the girls played in the playhouse corner.

5. Ninety percent of the teachers did not expect all the children to play in the playhouse corner; 5% expected only certain of the children to play in the playhouse corner at some time during the week.

Some of their comments were, "Some children are not comfortable there"; "I like them to play there only when they like it"; "I like them to play there only when they feel really comfortable"; "The children have other options available"; "If the child doesn't feel like playing, it should be up to the child"; "Some children (mainly boys) are not interested in this type of playing."

Thus, we can see that preschool teachers in the United States and Israel do not consciously include dramatic and sociodramatic play as part of their curricula. Although they have environments suitable for such play, many do not devote specific times to it, nor do they expect all of the children to make use of the equipment, as they would in other areas of the curriculum.

Issue 2. Are children's dramatic and sociodramatic activities assessed by teachers in the same way as other classroom activities are?

6. None of the 120 teachers reported assessing their children's dramatic and sociodramatic play activity. They knew neither how to evaluate and measure nor what assessment tools were available to them.

Issue 3. Is there active intervention on the part of the teachers in order to facilitate and develop dramatic and sociodramatic play abilities?

7. Fifty percent replied: No, teachers should neither help nor intervene; 30% replied: No, teachers should not help but encourage; they should only demonstrate, not facilitate; 20% replied: Yes, teachers should help and intervene in order to facilitate and develop such abilities.

In response to why or how the teacher should facilitate such play abilities, the following answers appeared: the teacher may show the toys and equipment to the children, but the children must develop the skill to play with them on their own; the teachers may show the children how to play with the equipment, how to excel in play, how to use new toys and equipment appropriate to the different seasons, how to use the dress-up clothes; the teacher may show the children what toys are available.

How will the children learn to play? "Children will learn by watching other children;" "They will learn by themselves after a time;" "They should create their own play;" "They will learn by exploring the toys;" "They will learn by exposure to the toys at home;" "Play is a highly emotional experience, and therefore, the children should make their own choices—a teacher could harm the children by trying to help them."

Issue 4. What is the attitude of the teachers toward the role of dramatic and sociodramatic play activity vis-à-vis future success in school?

8. Ninety percent replied: Play does not really help prepare children for future success in school; 10% replied: Generally, it does not help, but it does make children happy, which is also important for future success in school.

Reasons given for why it does not help were as follows: "Play only helps develop the personality;" "Play helps emotional well-being;" "Play makes children happy;" "Play gives children satisfaction, joy, provides a relaxed atmosphere."

Issue 5. Are the universities, colleges, and inservice training programs preparing teachers to facilitate and assess the development of dramatic and sociodramatic play?

9. None of the 120 teachers remembered a course teaching them about the significance of playing in the playhouse corner.

10. None of the 120 teachers had taken a course during their teacher training that dealt with facilitating, developing, and assessing play activities in the playhouse corner. Only four Israeli teachers noted they had observed such activity during their practice teaching and had learned a small amount about developing more effective play activities.

The study results indicated that there were no significant differences between American and Israeli teachers.

Summary

It is clear from these results that all preschool and kindergarten teachers had the equipment and facilities in their classrooms appropriate for sociodramatic play. Such play was not, however, a conscious part of their curriculum. They did not expect each child to participate in such play during the day or even during the week; they did not feel that they should intervene in order to encourage or develop such play; they were neither taught about the significance of sociodramatic play nor taught how to intervene, facilitate, or assess such play. The teachers did not see sociodramatic play as preparation for future scholastic performance and assumed that children would learn to play on their own.

CONCLUSIONS

It would seem clear that the tendency of young children for imitation and make-believe play provides a unique opportunity for the child's enrichment and growth, as well as preparation for future school success. Yet, teachers in both the United States and Israel have consistently ignored this opportunity. Perhaps an explanation can be offered by the fact that most of the studies were conducted on small samples by academic researchers and educators. Unfortunately, there is a recognized gap between research findings and their application among the active teachers in the field. Advocates of structured curricula tend to overlook the cognitive learning potential of sociodramatic play activity and regard it as simply "relaxation." Followers of the classic developmental school believe that provision of a proper setting and environment plus encouragement is sufficient for the child to grow. They look on intervention in sociodramatic play activity with suspicion.

Basic attitudes clearly need changing; sociodramatic play activity, in all of its forms, should be seen within its developmental context. It is clear that play expresses the child's ongoing intellectual, social, and emotional development and growth. This growth, like any other, can be aided by teachers with sensitivity to the child's needs, wishes, and current status. The most appropriate forums for making needed changes in attitudes are the teacher preparation institutions.

Sociodramatic play should be presented from a theoretical, as well as practical, standpoint as part of the regular teacher education curriculum. The significance attached to sociodramatic play activity by most theoreticians of early childhood development would suggest a great deal more time should be devoted to its study than is presently allotted in most teacher preparation programs. The practical aspect of sociodramatic play should be taught, acquainting prospective teachers with observation and evaluation techniques and giving them practice in intervention methods. Significant positive changes in children's school adjustment and school success are anticipated when the recommendations culled from the research done during the last two decades are put into effect.

REFERENCES

Burns, S. M., & Brainerd, C. J. (1978). Effects of constructive and dramatic play on perspective taking in very young children. *Developmental Psychology, 15,* 512–521.

Dansky, J. L. (1980). Cognitive consequences of sociodramatic play and exploration training for economically disadvantaged preschoolers. *Journal of Child Psychology and Psychiatry, 21,* 47–58.

Fein, G. G. (1979). Echoes from the nursery: Piaget, Vygotsky, and the relationships between language and play. *New Directions for Child Development, 6,* 1–14.

Feitelson, D., & Ross, G. S. (1973). The neglected factor—play. *Human Development, 16,* 202–223.

Freyburg, J. T. (1973). Increasing the imaginative play of urban disadvantaged children through systematic training. In L. S. Singer (Ed.), *The child's world of make-believe.* New York: Academic Press.

Golomb, C., & Bowen, S. H. (1981). Playing games of make-believe: The effectiveness of symbolic play training with children who failed to benefit from early conservation training. *Genetic Psychology Monographs, 104,* 137–159.

Golomb, C., & Cornelius, C. B. (1977). Symbolic play and its cognitive significance. *Developmental Psychology, 12,* 246–252.

Johnson, J. E. (1976). Relations of divergent thinking and intelligence test scores with social and non-social make-believe play of preschool children. *Child Development, 47,* 1200–1203.

Lewis, H. (1974). *The relationship between sociodramatic play and cognitive performance of five year old children.* Unpublished doctoral dissertation, Ohio State University.

Marshall, H. R. (1961). Relation between home experiences and children's use of language in play interactions with peers. *Psychological Monographs, 75*(5), 509.

Marshall, H. R., & Hahn, S. (1967). Experimental modification of dramatic play. *Journal of Personality and Social Psychology, 5,* 119–122.

Piaget, J. (1962). *Play, dreams and imitation in childhood.* New York: W. W. Norton.

Piaget, J. (1964). Cognitive development in children. *Piaget rediscovered: A report of the conference on cognitive studies and curriculum development.* Ithaca, NY: School of Education, Cornell University.

Piaget, J. (1966). Need and significance of cross-cultural studies in genetic psychology. *Journal of Psychology, 1,* 3–13.

Piaget, J. (1971). Response to Brian Sutton-Smith. *Psychological Review, 73*(1), 111–112; republished (1971) in R. E. Herron & B. Sutton-Smith (Eds.), *Child's play.* New York: Wiley.

Piaget, J., & Inhelder, B. (1956). *The child's perception of space.* London: Routledge and Kegan.

Piaget, J., & Inhelder, B. (1971). *Mental imagery in the child: A study of the development of imaginal representation.* New York: Basic Books. (Original work published in 1966).

Rosen, C. E. (1974). The effects of sociodramatic play on problem-solving behavior among culturally disadvantaged preschool children. *Child Development, 45,* 920–927.

Rubin, K. H., & Maioni, T. L. (1975). Play preference and its relation to egocentrism, popularity and classification skills in preschool. *Merrill-Palmer Quarterly, 21,* 171–179.

Saltz, E., Dixon, D., & Johnson, J. (1977). Training disadvantaged preschoolers on various fantasy activities: Effects on cognitive functioning and impulse control. *Child Development, 48,* 367–380.

Smilansky, S. (1968). *The effects of sociodramatic play on disadvantaged preschool children.* New York: Wiley.

Smilansky, S., & Shefatya, L. (1979). Narrowing socioeconomic groups in achievement through kindergarten reading instruction. *Journal Studies in Education,* University of Haifa, *21,* 4–68.

Smilansky, S., & Feldrhan, N. (1980). *Relationship between sociodramatic play in kindergarten and scholastic achievement in second grade.* Tel-Aviv: Tel-Aviv University, Department of Psychology.

Smith, P. K., & Syddal, S. (1978). Play and non-play tutoring in preschool children: Is it play or tutoring, which matters? *British Journal of Educational Psychology, 48,* 315–325.

Sutton-Smith, B. (1977). Piaget on play: A critique. In R. E. Herron & B. Sutton-Smith (Eds.), *Child's Play.* New York: Wiley.

Taler, E. (1976). *Social status of kindergarten children and their level of sociodramatic play.* Unpublished master's thesis, Tel-Aviv University, Department of Psychology.

Tower, R. B., Singer, J. L., & Biggs, A. (1979). Differential effects of television programming as preschoolers' cognition, imagination, and social play. *American Journal of Orthopsychiatry, 49,* 265–281.

Udwin, O. (1983). Imaginative play as an intervention method with institutionalized preschool children. *British Journal of Educational Psychology, 53,* 32–39.

CHAPTER 3

The Role of Art and Play in Children's Cognitive Development

Elliot W. Eisner

Both art and play, like imagination and fantasy, are not regarded as a part of the serious business of schooling. To be serious requires clear goals, a well thought out plan for achieving them and, perhaps most of all, hard work. Neither play nor art is associated with work. On the contrary, play is considered the antithesis of work and in a society with Calvinist roots and a prevailing anxiety about school productivity, the idea that either play or art should be considered a part of the core of education is not particularly likely. Even cognitive psychologists interested in child development and curriculum theorists interested in programs for the young seem to neglect both art and play. Jerome Kagan's important book, *The Nature of the Child* (1984) for all of its virtues, has no entry in its index under either play or art and its only reference to the child's aesthetic sense is one sentence indicating that some scholars suggest "that a person's aesthetic sense is dependent upon early exposure to attractive toys." Kieran Egan's *Primary Understanding: Education in Early Childhood* (1988), like Kagan's book, has no entry under play, although he does devote two pages of his 287-page book to "the arts curriculum."

Given the importance of play—not to speak of art—in the cognitive development of children, it seems odd that scholars should neglect what virtually every one else regards as one of the characteristic features of childhood. If children do anything, they play.

My aim in this chapter is to explore just what it is that art and play do for the cognitive development of the young child and from this analysis to say something about their role in our schools. I begin with play.

WHAT DO WE MEAN BY PLAY?

At the outset it should be recognized that the term *play* refers, not to one, but to several related but distinct forms of activity. To play, as in to play around, suggests an exploratory activity through which children (and adults) discover the possibilities of experience. To play in this sense is to try to determine what a set of objects, events, qualities, or ideas can do. The child might, for example, play around with clay to discover what comes of it. An adult might play around with a set of ideas to determine their possibilities for solving a problem. An adolescent might play with peers to determine the limits of their tolerance. Play in this sense is related to being playful. It represents an effort to explore rather than to search. By exploration I mean that in play there is a tendency to keep oneself open for the unexpected, to act and then appraise in retrospect rather than to formulate a goal or objective and then to match the consequences of an action to it. To paraphrase Aristotle, "Play, like art, loves chance."

There is a second sense to which the term *play* refers and this sense pertains to the playing of a game. Playing does not require gaming, but gaming requires playing. To play a game, as distinct from simply playing, is to be guided by rules that are socially defined and shared by all players; no rules, no game. Thus, in playing hopscotch the child who steps on a line is counted out, while in playing with sand in a sandbox the child has no rules to which the activity with sand is inherently constrained. Of course, there may very well be rules against throwing sand, but those rules are not a part of, say, building a sand castle because a child building a sand castle is not engaged in a game. Games are defined by their ends and by their socially defined constraints. To play in the context of a game, a child needs to learn to adhere to its rules. *In this sense*, gaming is a form of human activity that occurs later than playing, although it should not be inferred from this remark that children give up playing once they have learned to play games.

A third use of the term *play* is related to its social features. Children play with each other. For young children we usually mean something like parallel play, that form of children's activity that does not require rule-governed forms of social interaction; children aged two to five may very well play "together" in the same room or area with little or no interaction. They may share the same space, they may be aware of each other, yet their activities are essentially solo. As children mature "playing with" means sharing a common framework of rules; the game emerges and one plays the game with others as, for example, a member of a team.

The term *play* also refers to a particular performance. A basketball team executes a play. A group of students put on a play. In the former, a routine that is shared by members of the team is exhibited. Professional football players and members of the Philadelphia Symphony Orchestra play for us. We see a play performed by first graders or by the cast of the American Conservatory Theater. What all of these groups have in common is their shared routines, which make possible a performance designed to delight, inform, edify, or in some other way, stimulate.

It takes no great psychological insight to recognize the importance of each of these forms of play in the child's cognitive development. The first form of play, that which enables the child to explore the possibilities of experience, is one of the primary means through which the child makes sense of the world. The phrase *making sense* is significant. What we know about the world is ultimately dependent upon our sensory experience, whether that experience is secured from contact with the qualities of the environment or from experience generated by our imagination. The qualities of the world are not, however, simply given; they must be construed. Although the infant comes into the world "well wired" and capable of differentiating many qualities in each sensory modality, the relationships among qualities that are often subtle and complex are not automatically given to the infant. They must be taken and the taking of such qualities is always a cognitive construction, a construe, a form of sense-making. To illustrate this point in its most refined form, consider the connoisseur of symphonic music. An individual who has listened long and hard to hear the music experiences auditory patterns that no novice can hear. Connoisseurship in music, as in any realm, requires one to learn how to *achieve* experience. Indeed, it is precisely the ability to experience what others miss and to appreciate its importance that distinguishes the connoisseur from the rest of us.

In the adult connoisseur we see manifestations of a process that begins at birth; learning to see, to hear, to feel the world around us or the world we create through our imaginative life. This is the process of *making* sense, not simply having or finding it.

This conception implies further that sense-making requires an active organism; *knowing* is a verb and always in a state of flux. Play is children's primary means of engaging the world, and precisely because play is not in its initial stages bounded by socially defined rules, it provides children with an open-ended situation through which they can explore the "world-as-it-is" or the world they imagine.

I have given equal time in my reference to playing with the "world-as-it-is" and to the world generated through an active imaginative life. Three-through six-year-old children frequently shuttle between the world-as-it-is and their own fantasy life with little difficulty and with great frequency. The ability to take leave of the world through day dreaming is, apparently, a source of satisfaction and, I believe, performs an important cognitive function. Yet pressures on teachers to increase children's time on task (Elkind, 1988) focus their efforts on the assignment of tasks set by the teacher rather than on those that children set for themselves. It may very well be the ability to take leave of the world-as-it-is that provides the space through which new possibilities for thought emerge. Relinquishing the constraints of convention in order to explore in the mind's eye the unconventional might provide one of the most important arenas in which creativity itself could be generated.

As a means of exploring the possibilities of experience the play process is displayed vividly in the ways in which infants use rattles and other devices that adults give them. They engage these devices through all their sensory modalities; they put them in their mouths so they can be felt and tasted, they look at and shake them for the sounds they create. The object is experienced in its multisensory forms through the processes of exploration I described earlier.

Play in the context of gaming also performs a significant role in the child's cognitive development. In this context the child must improvise within socially shared limits. If the game being played is school, or Hansel and Gretel, not every possibility the child can imagine is acceptable. Schools have certain parameters, so does Hansel and Gretel, and to violate these parameters is to void the game or, in special circumstances, to create a new one.

Improvisation within accepted conventions is, of course, one of the features of creative activity in art and science. Artists who work within a genre, say, pointillism or surrealism, must remain within the limits these genres impose if they wish their work to be identified with the genre. Those who break with an accepted genre risk the possibility of rejection from those who cannot read or do not accept the violation of its conventions. In music this was Stravinsky's early fate; his Firebird Suite was so repulsive to listeners when it was first heard in 1905 that he was booed off the stage during its initial performance. Van Gogh sold only one painting in his lifetime. The epithet *fauves* was assigned to those painters whose use of vivid color motivated critics to regard them as wild beasts.

Scientists encounter similar problems. What counts as science is defined by a set of shared conventions about method and evidence. Those who develop new methods and propose new forms of evidence risk rejection. Galileo is one vivid example. The point here is that games are performances played by rules. Innovation, even fantasy, is possible within some games as long as the rules of the game are not violated. Becoming social requires learning social conventions and working within their limits. This tension between the desire to invent and explore and the need to share and to work within social conventions permeates all of our social life. It is particularly evident in the way in which children are socialized. Consider the use of a fork as a catapult for a pea.

Young children often play with kitchen utensils while eating. During their activity some children discover that a fork can become a wonderful tool for catapulting peas across the room. They explore their newly invented catapult only to have it removed by one of their parents, often with a mild admonishment that forks are to be used for eating food, not for catapulting peas and carrots across the room. What occurs in this scenario is a process of socialization and in that process the development of what Dunker (1945) has called "functional fixedness." In this process the child is encouraged to think about an object or idea only with respect to its conventional function rather than to redefine it. Play is diminished as socialization to conventional expectation prevails.

An even broader example of functional fixedness is found in the consequences of language acquisition. The neologisms of the very young child constitute an incipient form of poetry, an exploration and invention of needed words, words that are expressively suitable for what they wish to say. "Icky" is such a word. Its auditory form is congruent with the child's sentiments. Poetic invention takes place in this and in the onomatopoetic devices young children use to enhance their fantasy life or to express the ineffable. Yet, one of the aims of socialization and clearly one of the dominant functions of schooling is to help children learn the socially accepted uses of words, punctuation, grammar, spelling, and other conventional forms. The acquisition of language is necessary in order to share conventions. Yet, as children acquire a vocabulary and see the world through the language they acquire, they learn not to see it as well, for a way of seeing is also a way of not seeing, and learning that there is a correct way to use language can suppress the tendency to violate the conventions that must be emphasized in the socialization process. By gradually relinquishing their tendencies toward play and invention children acquire what they need in order to survive as social creatures. One of the most important devices they use is language. Language prescribes a socially shared set of categories, and categories that are socially shared are conventionalized. In making speech social, we also risk diminishing the tendency toward conceptual innovation. Play is not simply a form of performance, it is a kind of attitude toward its object. The educational challenge is finding a way of helping children acquire the language they need while at the same time keeping a playful attitude toward language alive. The poetic use of language in schools and elsewhere may be one of the most important resources for doing this.

HOW DO THE ARTS RELATE TO COGNITION?

Like play, the arts also perform a variety of important functions in the development of children's cognition. My comments focus mainly on the visual arts, although much of what I have to say about the visual arts pertains to the other arts as well.

I have already indicated that the senses perform the primary function of allowing us to contact the qualitative world in and through which we live. According to some psychologists, Rudolf Arnheim (1969) for example, visual capacities are not only among our most important, they are essentially cognitive. He writes:

> By "cognitive" I mean all mental operations involved in the receiving, storing and processing of information: sensory perception, memory, thinking, learning. This use of the term conflicts with one to which many psychologists are accustomed and which excludes the activity of the senses from cognition. It reflects the distinction I am trying to eliminate; therefore I must extend the meaning of the terms "cognitive" and "cognition" to include perception. Similarly, I see no way of withholding the name of "thinking" from what goes on in perception. No thought processes seem to exist that cannot be found to operate, at least in principle, in perception. Visual perception is visual thinking. (p. 13)

The *achievement* of sight, as Arnheim indicates, is a cognitive event. Sight is more than mere sensation. It provides the content that is used in the creation of our imaginative life, for it is in the imagination that the visualization of events experienced is replayed and modified and where events experienced independently are related. Indeed, the conjunction of events that were once discrete for purposes of productive novelty is what Koestler (1964) refers to as bi-sociation, a process that resides at the roots of creative thinking. The point here is twofold: first, seeing as contrasted with looking is a form of cognitive achievement. Second, our *imagic store*, to use Broudy's felicitous phrase (1987), is made up of what we had once seen. Any activity that cultivates or refines our sense of sight not only escalates consciousness in its own right, it contributes to our imagic store. The visual arts make important contributions to both ends.

If the journey were so direct or simple, simply giving children art materials would do the job. It does not. Part of the reason it does not is that the visual arts perform different functions for children at different stages of their development. For children between two and four years of age, art materials provide opportunities for them to experience what Charlotte Buhler (1972) has called "function pleasure." Children pound clay, scribble, enjoy the texture of finger paint gliding over a smooth glossy surface for the sheer pleasure of the experience that these materials and activities yield. The children's aim is not primarily to create a preconceived image by converting the material with which they work into a medium, but to enjoy the process itself. It is not rare to observe two year olds playing with clay (in the first sense of the meaning of play) without looking at what they are doing. Their clay play is essentially a tactile rather than visual activity. As children get older, between three and five, they learn that some of the images they have can be named; this is a Daddy, this is my toy, this my doggie. In retrospect, the visual form not only gets a name, it becomes a symbol.

The realization that one thing can stand for another is also an important cognitive event, for it is through the assignment of names to images after they are made that children eventually become able to name and then make the image to which the name corresponds. In this development children formulate intentions and then draw what they intend to make.

The representation of the face or human figure, two of the most popular images preschoolers draw, constitutes an impressive form of inventiveness. The visual world is a world in flux; objects move, light and color change, nothing stays the same. What children must do is transform the flux of experience into its structural, but highly simplified, equivalent while working within the limits of a particular medium. The task is one of portraying distilled, but essential, elements. Children's early efforts at representation display a remarkable economy. If the medium is paint, a curve or a circle is sufficient to capture the head and the body, two lines take care of arms and legs. The children's aim is to simplify representation without attempting to achieve verisimilitude.

The ability to see the essentials in a visual configuration, or in an argument or essay, is, of course, one of the impressive functions of the intellect. Knowing what to neglect in order to make a particular point important and vivid is as critical in art as in conversation. Young children display through their drawings the roots of these significant cognitive abilities. As children learn and mature, the ability to differentiate perceptually continues to grow: more and more is seen and the desire to create images that display with verisimilitude the features seen becomes increasingly important. The cognitive task begins to shift from the simplified representation of essential features to the desire to make the drawing look like its subject. By age nine or ten, learning how to draw "accurately" becomes important.

With the desire to master enough technical skills to create drawings and paintings that look like their subjects, there is a tendency for children to tighten up, to diminish their inclination to play with materials or use them for the function pleasure they previously enjoyed. Further, there is a desire to want to make didactic use of their drawings and paintings to tell a story, to illustrate. When children's focus is on didacticism, there is a tendency to neglect attention to the formal or aesthetic aspect of the work. When the demands of accurate rendering are regarded by children as desirable yet formidable, it is hard to be playful with the image. The aim is to get it right and right for most children means making it look like what it is supposed to look like. "How do I get the road to stay on the ground?" "How do I make something look round?" "How do I make a horse look like a horse?" These are some of the questions children often ask. Between nine and twelve years old, children are concerned with mastery, and aesthetic matters are often a secondary consideration or not a consideration at all.

The creation of verisimilitude is made more difficult for children by their acquisition of certain schemata that are used as visual codes for common objects. Thus, a tree is drawn as a kind of lollipop, a bird is drawn as a V, the sun is almost always in the corner of the paper, a house is drawn having a slanted roof and a chimney, whether or not such houses exist in their neighborhood. These graphic devices function as didactic signs that keep children's attention away from the object. In fact, children between the ages of four and seven will pay little attention to a still life set up before them when they are asked to draw it. Fifteen year olds, however, look long and hard.

Because preoccupation with drawing skills is so important for so many children, it has been said that aesthetic concerns, considered as a developmental curve, have a U-shaped quality (Gardner, 1980). Both young children and adolescents attend to the formal or aesthetic aspects of the work, while children between nine and twelve often use their drawings for didactic rather than aesthetic purposes and are more concerned with drawing it right than drawing it artistically. This observation should not be interpreted to mean that aesthetic matters or matters of expressiveness do not emerge during middle childhood. Objects or events that are important to children at any age are often exaggerated in size and made vivid in color. Emotional significance emerges in their drawings, but these features are often the result of personal drives more than the result of reflective judgments about formal relationships. Indeed, children typically generate *local solutions* (Arnheim, 1954) to the objects they draw. That is, they focus on the object to be drawn as if it were essentially independent of the other forms on the paper. Children create relationships among objects drawn on the basis of logical, rather than aesthetic, criteria. One of the important forms of learning in the arts is learning how to consider formal and expressive qualities reflectively, that is, to bring them under the aegis of intelligent choice so that a satisfying visual composition can be treated.

The ability to pay attention to formal and expressive considerations in the context of drawing, painting, or sculpture is influenced by the skills with which children can manage a particular material. If children have difficulty managing that material, the material manages them. When children are in charge, when skills are well developed, confidence grows and attention can be redirected from the technical use of the skill to its aesthetic use.

The deep internalization of skills is often referred to as overlearning or *automaticity* (Bloom, 1986). Automaticity is achieved when skills are so overlearned that they can be called upon effortlessly, with virtually no thought to their use. Skilled cooks, athletes, experienced drivers display automaticity. We are able to enjoy the road from our car because we do not have to pay attention to the mechanics of driving. We are able to speak effortlessly in English because we do not have to reflect upon matters of grammar; French is another story!

The implications for educational practice that derive from the notion of automaticity is that sufficient familiarity with a medium so that its technical demands can be replaced by aesthetic and expressive possibilities is an important condition for the development of cognition. As children are able to focus on the formal, expressive, and inventive possibilities of a material rather than on matters of management, the kind of thinking they are able to do enlarges. Sensibilities are cultivated if students can afford to pay attention to unfolding visual qualities. Imagination is strengthened as confidence in being able to control a material is increased. The ability to control a material liberates the child to think about matters at the heart of art making.

There is one caveat that must be entered here. We see in the paintings of Japanese school children a remarkable display of technical virtuosity. The paintings, prints, and drawings of Japanese children are significantly more advanced than those of their American counterparts. Yet, their work often looks alike. The techniques they use and the schemata they display, as technically skilled as they are, are often so similar that one cannot help but wonder if technique has become formula and if inventiveness has been neglected. This is not to say that, on the whole, visual art of American children is more inventive. I do not believe it is, but this shortfall might be a function of the paucity of skills and the difficulty American children have in controlling the materials with which they work. The moral of the foregoing story is that while automaticity is important and while it might be a necessary condition for creative productivity in the visual arts, it does not ensure such productivity. Teachers have an important role to play in creating the conditions that invite, practice, and encourage such forms of cognition, in addition to those that develop technical skills.

WHY TEACH THE ARTS?

Given the complexities I have described, it does not seem unreasonable to ask, why teach the arts? Just what are their benefits in the context of schooling? My answer to the two questions that I have posed is based on certain ideas about the nature of the mind and the process and role of representation in its creation.

I do not believe that infants come into the world with minds. I do believe they come into the world with brains and that it is the process of socialization, maturation, and education that gradually converts brains into minds. Minds are made and brains are born. Brains are biologically given, minds are culturally acquired (Cole, 1985).

The kinds of minds that children come to own are influenced by the kinds of conditions and opportunities to learn that they encounter. Schools, those publicly supported institutions in which most children spend the major portion of their childhood, are intended to create minds (Eisner, 1982). Indeed, the curriculum and the teaching that children receive are the major resources for achieving this aim. Among the resources that schools employ are the forms used in culture by its inhabitants to represent what they have experienced. Thus, propositional language is one form for representing within its limits what humans want to express. Visual art and music are other forms. Literary language and poetry are still others, as are mathematics, dance, architecture, and the customs and ceremonies that have been invented to represent our ideas about life, death, and celebration. Becoming literate in the broadest sense means becoming able to encode and decode the meanings that these forms possess.

When schools provide children with opportunities to use materials to represent what they have experienced, they afford children opportunities to increase their literacy in the forms they are given an opportunity to use. Seeing, as I have indicated, is an achievement; it is not simply a task. Being able to paint or sculpt is an achievement, not simply a behavior. Thus, one important cognitive consequence of learning to see in and through the arts is the refinement of the visual and tactile sensibilities upon which consciousness itself depends. As children are encouraged to really look at the world, the probability is increased that they will actually see it. Seeing here is not simply an instrumental activity but one of perception (Dewey, 1934): the visual exploration and, in a sense, the "exhaustion" of the object's visual features. Visual art in this mode, is consummatory; the object is "consumed" for its own sake. In the process, the ability to see what is subtle but significant is increased.

But there is yet another consequence for perception that emanates from attention to the visual world, particularly attention to that visual world created by artists. I refer here to the fact that artists, like scientists, are makers of form and designers of schemata. The artists, like the scientists, know what to neglect and what to emphasize. The distillations that artists make of the world, or of some aspect of their experience, results in a powerful visual image. This image or schema is what children and adults who have learned to see incorporate in their cognitive structure. The artist's schema, like the scientist's, functions as a structure through which the world is appropriated (Eisner, 1991). Once we have seen a Monet landscape, landscapes remind us of Monet. Having seen Picasso's *Guernica,* we recognize the screams and cutting edges of war. Having encountered a sculptured figure by Rodin, we can look for sensuous surfaces and expressive comportment in people around us more easily. The "devices" created by artists and by scientists are tools that amplify our perception of the world. They provide the frames through which education aims to foster perceptivity and develop sensitivity to the visual world. The visual arts, for this particular function, are extremely potent resources.

The development of the perception of art and the world is not the only, and might not be a major, educational contribution of the arts in schools. For this we return to the process of representation and what it does for the child's cognitive life.

THE COGNITIVE BENEFITS OF REPRESENTATION

The major focus of my remarks thus far has been on matters of schema, imagination, and perception. All of these are processes that generate particular qualities of human experience, and although such experience might be important or satisfying to the child, its social value is nil unless it is transformed and made public through a form of representation. Among culture's major resources for this transformation are the arts. The process of representation has five major cognitive benefits for the child. First, representation allows the child to stabilize and make public what otherwise would be evanescent. There is nothing so slippery as an idea or an image. They come and go. They possess no physical embodiment. One of their most characteristic features is their elusiveness. When children are given the opportunity to work with a material that they can use to transform these elusive forms of experience into their public equivalent, the idea or image is stabilized and can be reflected upon and inspected.

The process of stabilization and inspection leads to the second important consequence of representation. Once the representation is stabilized, the editing process can occur. A child can alter the image that was made, it can be made more acute, it can be revised, it can be developed further, something very difficult to do in the imagination. The process of editing, and I use this term generically to apply to images, as well as to text, is a way of learning, not only of refining. The editing process allows a child to experiment and to discover what alterations of the work do for the work itself. In this effort the child has the opportunity to learn through the process of reconstructing the work.

The editing of the image is not a characteristic of what young children do with their art. Most teachers seldom encourage such activity, yet reflection upon what has been created is an important part of the process of painting and sculpting. Its neglect in classrooms results in lost opportunities in the course of children's art education.

A third function of representation is communication: the public representation of ideas and images is a way to share them with others. We usually take this function for granted, but unless the private is made public there is no way to participate in the experience of others. If Sir Isaac Newton had decided not to tell, Western science would not be what it is today. If Mozart had decided not to notate his music, our musical life would have been impoverished. The process of representation is a way to enter the lives of others and to begin to understand what others have thought and felt. Without representation, culture itself would not be possible.

A fourth function of representation is its contribution to invention. We tend to think of representation as a process that transforms images held in the mind's eye into the material that displays features of the original image in a public form whose structure approximates it. Indeed, the way in which I have been discussing representation so far is consonant with that view. The process is not, however, so straightforward nor is it so simple.

The process of representation is also an occasion for inventing images and ideas that were not a part of the initial idea (Collingwood, 1958). In the course of work unexpected qualities are created that the child can pursue. When this occurs, directions change, and the product created may have only a vague resemblance to the initiating image or intention. The work created becomes something of a surprise to its creator.

To be able to cope with and exploit such possibilities requires what Dewey (1938) called "flexible purposing," the ability to shift gears in midstream, to avoid rigid adherence to a predefined plan or script, to welcome unanticipated opportunities, and to exploit them for their potential. The process of representation provides opportunities that make the development of such abilities and attitudes possible *provided* they are encouraged in the classroom. Indeed, teachers could define tasks that encourage children to explore qualities and then to transform those qualities into images that they did not know they would have when they began. Flexible purposing helps children learn to be productively opportunistic.

The fifth and final contribution that the process of representation makes to a child's cognitive development centers on transformations of meaning and is, in a sense, the primary justification for including the arts in the education of the young.

There are many ways of transforming experience into a public form. Speech is one, text another, dance a third. Any particular form of representation an individual uses both constrains and makes possible what he or she is able to say. Thus, poetry was invented to convey what literal language cannot. Dance was created to express what visual images cannot represent. Music can represent what mathematics cannot describe.

Even within these forms there are different genres, each of which addresses unique aspects of human experience. Surrealist painters evoke aspects of human consciousness that a painter like Piet Mondrian neglects, and vice versa. The form of representation and each genre establish parameters within which meaning is developed and shared. Different forms of art call upon different aspects of being. The visual arts, for example, are a synchronic medium. Music is a diachronic one. Music, like gesture, unfolds over time and is better suited for describing some aspects of life than a painting that has no temporal dimension. Suspense, for example, is more easily represented in music than art. Painting is represented as an immediate visual field; music, like suspense, occurs over time.

Human beings have apparently felt a need to create forms that make it possible to convey particular aspects of experience. It is in these forms that meaning is embedded, and it is in the cultivation of multiple forms of literacy that such meanings are recovered. When such literacies are developed the child becomes a full legatee of the culture. Without them the meanings that are potential in such forms as art, music, and dance are destined to remain an uncrackable code or someone else's pleasure. Access to the arts, when it is well taught, develops those forms of cognition through which the unique meanings of the arts can become a part of the child's consciousness. Such an aim surely deserves an important place on our educational agenda.

And what of the relationship between art and play? The perceptive reader will note that both play and art have much in common. Both engage imagination, both require reflection, both profit from skill, both seek to generate new forms of experience, both lead to invention, and both are marginalized in the priorities of American education. In my view both children and the cultures within which they live would be better served if art and play had a more prominent place in our schools, and not only in the primary grades, but throughout the grades. Is it not time we provided such a place?

REFERENCES

Arnheim, R. (1954). *Art and visual perception*. Berkeley: University of California Press.

Arnheim, R. (1969). *Visual thinking*. Berkeley: University of California Press.

Bloom, B. (1986, February) Automaticity: The hands and feet of genius. *Educational Leadership, 43*(5), 70–77.

Broudy, H. (1987). The role of imagery in learning. Occasional Paper No. 1, Los Angeles: J. Paul Getty Center for Education in the Arts.

Buhler, C. (1972). *Introduction to humanistic psychology*. Monterey, CA; Brooks Cole.

Cole, M. (1985). Mind as a cultural achievement. In E. W. Eisner (Ed.), *Learning and teaching the ways of knowing, 84th Yearbook of the National Society for the Study of Education* (Pt. 2, pp. 218–249). Chicago: The University of Chicago Press.

Collingwood, R. G. (1958). *Principles of art.* New York: Oxford University Press.

Dewey, J. (1934). *Art as experience.* New York: Minton Balch.

Dewey, J. (1938). *Experience and education.* New York: Macmillan.

Dunker, K. (1945). On problem solving. *Psychological Monographs, 58*(5).

Egan, K. (1988). *Primary understanding: Education in early childhood.* New York: Rutledge.

Eisner, E. W. (1982). *Cognition and curriculum: A basis for deciding what to teach.* New York: Longmans.

Eisner, E. W. (1991). *The enlightened eye: On doing qualitative inquiry.* New York: Macmillan.

Elkind, D. (1988). *The hurried child: Growing up too fast too soon* (rev. ed.). Reading, MA: Addison-Wesley.

Gardner, H. (1980). *Artful scribbles: The significance of children's art.* New York:Basic Books.

Kagan, J. (1984). *The nature of the child.* New York: Basic Books.

Koestler, A. (1964). *The act of creation.* New York: Macmillan.

Part II
PLAY IN ITS HISTORICAL PERSPECTIVE

In the second part the authors explore how play has been perceived historically in the United States and in Israel.

Monighan-Nourot's approach is to define the qualities of play in each era since colonial times and to describe how play in the curriculum has been explained and implemented in the classrooms of the United States. She puts into focus the tug-of-war between "means" and "ends" and raises the question of whether play is preparation for adult life or a natural self-initiated activity. Each perspective, she finds, has challenged the other in different ways during each epoch. Monighan-Nourot uses richly detailed description including first-hand experiences of individuals who have lived through some of the more recent historical periods. Beginning with the eighteenth century, she highlights the work of some important individuals (e.g., Pestalozzi, Froebel, Blow, Hall, Gesell, Dewey, Freud, Erikson, Sprague Mitchell, and Biber) and some of the important educational movements (behaviorist, child study, psychodynamics) that have affected early childhood education and children's play.

What becomes clear is that with each new movement new insights into child development and children's play have been gained and earlier positions clarified. The question is raised of whether emphasis should be put on the mastery of isolated skills or on the maintenance of the long view of child development. The author leaves the reader to consider some of the dilemmas that are yet to be addressed, such as the fact that many teachers are unable to articulate a theoretical defense for the play aspects of early childhood curricula.

Monighan-Nourot points to the schism that seems to exist between the researchers and the practitioners in the field of early childhood education and urges a return to the early development of the child study movement, which saw teachers as researchers "with pen in the hand to jot down." In conclusion, Monighan-Nourot states that "childhood play is timeless, and its contribution to a changing society essential."

Michalovitz traces the shorter history of educational developments in the relatively young State of Israel. The reader can discern similar influences at work in each culture, although curricular decisions in Israel are made centrally, in contrast to the American decision-making process, which is usually to a greater degree decentralized.

Michalovitz uses Boring's conceptualization of "Zeitgeist" through which to analyze dramatic play throughout Israel's history. The activities carried on in the kindergartens of Israel, as in the United States, have been referred to historically as "work." Michalovitz attributes this to the fact that in Israel it was the Labor movement, with its socialist commitment, that initiated and originally ran the kindergartens. Israel's early childhood programs in their early stages (1940s) were influenced greatly by the psychodynamic school of thought, which focused on children's expression of emotions. The later period, which felt the effects of Sputnik, recession, and precarious national survival, began to place heavier emphasis on the products of the "learners." The focus of the school's efforts became achievement. Support for this approach is found both in developmental psychology and in the field of cognitive development, which have underlying philosophical commitments to making "better use" of the intellectual capacities of children. However, Michalovitz sees some hope that the benefits of dramatic and sociodramatic play will become more widely recognized and understood as cognitive psychologists translate into practice their new findings in imagery and imagination.

CHAPTER 4

The Legacy of Play in American Early Childhood Education

Patricia Monighan-Nourot

Dating from the time of Plato, play has had a place in the tradition of early childhood education. Drawing on the definition of "tradition" described by White and Buka (1987), I have looked at children's play in light of the shared beliefs, collective knowledge, and writings, research, and practices that have linked the community of early childhood education from colonial America to the present. Specifically, I have organized this examination of the role of play in the history of early childhood education around three questions: What are the defining qualities of play in each era? How was play defended in the curriculum? And how was play implemented in the classroom?

With regard to the first question, I have relied upon the following six characteristics of play identified by Rubin, Fein, and Vendenburg (1983) and summarized by Almy, Monighan, Scales, and Van Hoorn (1984) and Spodeck, Saracho, and Davis (1987).

1. Play is intrinsically motivated. This includes notions of self-directed activity and the ways in which exploration may lead to play.
2. Play involves attention to means rather than ends. Goals within play are flexible and self-imposed and may change over the course of play activity.
3. Play may be nonliteral or symbolic. Not all play is symbolic, but it may involve conceptualization of objects and roles that take on an "as if" frame of reference as children symbolically transform their current realities. Play may also be symbolic of unconscious desires and feelings.
4. Play involves freedom from external rules. Although play has implicit rules within an imaginary context, the freedom to create and change these rules differentiates play from games, where rules are externally imposed.
5. Play is self-referenced rather than object referenced and in this way is dis-

tinguished from exploration. The child imposes a personal organization on objects and situations instead of attempting to imitate. The balance of novel and familiar objects and the time allotted for play to evolve from exploration are issues here.

6. Play actively engages the child. This is evident in the concentration and enthusiasm children bring to play, as well as in the sense of mastery they derive from their play.

For the question "How has play been defended?" I drew upon Entwhistle's (1970) distinction between the moral and technical rationales for child-centered education. The philosophical or moral rationale for play rests on the belief in the inherent value of the childhood activity of play in and of itself and represents a humanistic attitude in protecting the rights of the vulnerable and malleable child. Instrumental rationales depend upon technical empirical evidence and are largely concerned with the future value that play accrues to the child and to society.

The final question regarding play in the curriculum is addressed by looking at the teacher's role in planning for and nurturing play and at the materials provided for play.

EIGHTEENTH CENTURY

The attitude of colonial America toward children was a legacy from earlier centuries in Europe. Play entered education only insofar as it represented the untamed, frivolous nature of childhood. The Church, dominating education, saw human nature as essentially evil. Hope of salvation from eternal damnation rested in the ability to know and read the Bible. So the "Dame Schools" in colonial America supplemented parental teaching by providing catechism and reading with hornbooks in the kitchen of an older woman. Once a child could read the scriptures, further education in writing, Latin, or a trade was optional and costly (Butts & Cremin, 1953). The plasticity of youth, although considered mainly a vehicle for salvation of the soul, was a common idea, one that was to gain popularity in the future with a qualitatively different view of human nature.

In Europe, seeds of future attitudes in America were sown through the legacy of Comenius (1592–1670) and the popular writings of Rousseau (1712–1778) and Pestalozzi (1746–1827). Major shifts that took place were a view of childhood from a focus on evil human nature to a focus on good and a recognition of play as a natural childhood activity. What were the qualities of play described by these early philosophers?

Qualities of Play

First, play involved the active engagement of the child. In *Emile*, Rousseau (1762/1964) writes of the young child: "Work and play are all one for him, his games are his work; he knows no difference. He brings to everything the cheerfulness of his interest, the charm of freedom, and he shows the bent of his own mind and the extent of his knowledge" (p. 126).

Motor play was regarded as valuable for its own sake as enjoyable, foreshadowing more contemporary ideas of play as attention to means rather than ends. Play was also intrinsically motivating to children, because it was the "natural" activity of childhood and was mediated through the senses. Comenius' writing had marked the beginning of the "sense realist" attitude toward play, a viewpoint substantiated later by Locke's belief that knowledge comes through sensation and perception. This idea was continued in the writings of Rousseau and Pestalozzi. In 1798, Pestalozzi wrote in *How Gertrude Teaches Her Children* (Anderson, 1931) "sense impression is the absolute foundation of all knowledge."

Although Pestalozzi did not address the role of play directly, he alluded to the idea that play involved representational symbols through his suggestion that materials be sequenced from concrete to abstract and that learning proceed from the particular to the general (Weber, 1984).

In *Emile*, Rousseau's (1762/1964) writing most clearly advocated the idea that play involves freedom from external rules: "Almost every method has been tried but one, and that the only one which can succeed, natural liberty, daily regulated. Give your pupil no kind of verbal instruction: he should receive none but from experience" (p. 396). In this he was supported by Comenius (1649/1953): "Every game is something more or less voluntary and therefore an exercise of freedom, whereas occupation with serious matters has the appearance of necessity and therefore of compulsion . . . that is why heavenly wisdom itself says that it plays with us" (p. 183).

Rationale for Play

At this time in Europe there was the beginning of a philosophical rationale for play in the education of young children. First there was the idea contained in the writings of Comenius, and later Rousseau and Pestalozzi, that the child's nature was particularly innocent and good, an idea that had not gained popularity since the time of Plato's idealism. The second feature of this rationale was the plasticity of youth; early education in a free and nurturing environment would foster the unfolding of innate human goodness, forming the character of the individual as the youth grew to adulthood. In 1649, Comenius wrote *The Great Didactic* (1649/1953).

> It is a property of all things becoming that they can easily be bent and formed as long as they are tender, but that they refuse to obey when they have hardened. Soft can be modeled and remodeled, hard wax will crumble. The young tree can be planted, replanted, trimmed and bent to any shape; not so the grown. (Braun & Edwards, 1972, pp. 31–32)

Although the philosophical arguments for play stand out in this period, it also marked the beginning of an instrumental argument for play as "preexercise" or preparation for activities of adult life. Comenius wrote that in pouring water and lifting buckets one could see the beginnings of an understanding of mechanics (Anderson, 1931).

Play in Practice

Motor play and play engaging the senses was thought to be the natural activity of children, and for Comenius and Rousseau the role of the teacher was minimal (Forest, 1927). Protection of the child from outside pressure and the provision of music, space to run freely, and materials attractive to the senses comprised the extent of the teacher's work in supporting play. Pestalozzi advocated, however, what we would call "teacher-proof curriculum," maintaining that the correct method and not the individual personality was the key to success (Entwhistle, 1970). The teachers' expertise rested in the ability to break tasks into the finest gradations possible. Implicit in this breakdown was a given sequence of materials that were to be presented in a specific order to children (Heafford, 1967). Pestalozzi was the only one who attempted to put his ideas into practice, raising the question of the contrasts between those who write about play and those who apply their ideas in classrooms, an issue still with us today.

NINETEENTH CENTURY

Concern for the nature of childhood as a distinct period of life found its way into American thought during the 1800s. The colonial emphasis on the Church and Calvinist doctrine of the inherently evil quality of human nature gave way to a notion of truth based on reason and logic (rationalism) and knowledge based on observation and experience (empiricism) (Spodek, 1988).

Social concerns shifted from the economically self-sufficient family unit to those created by increasing industrialization and urbanization (Lazerson,

1972; Strickland, 1982). Among these was the problem of children for working parents. Older siblings commonly brought the younger ones to school. There were often children as young as three in the rigid traditional environment stressing the 3 Rs and not conducive to the play of young children. By 1850, 15% of the elementary school enrollment consisted of children under the age of five (Strickland, 1982). Teachers and children were frustrated. As a result, public schools, which by the 1870s were compulsory in most communities, began to exclude children younger than six.

The nineteenth century saw the emergence of several new programs for the education of children considered too young for public school. These included infant schools and the fireside education movement, as well as the influential Froebelian kindergarten.

Infant Schools

The first half of the nineteenth century gave rise to the American version of the infant schools, begun in Scotland by Robert Owen, and popularized in England in the 1820s. There were two models of infant schools implemented in the United States. One was sponsored by Bronson Alcott, Owen's major disciple in the United States, and included opportunities for motor play, sensory experience, music, and dance. Alcott was heavily influenced by transcendental ideas concerning the closeness of children to divine wisdom and sentimentalized their responses to questions regarding the Bible, eventually leading to withdrawal of parental support for his Temple School in Boston. The second model was adopted from the writings of Wilderspin in England. The curriculum was rigid, didactic, and punitive. Because of the availability of Wilderspin's publications, this infant school model gained a footing in the United States.

But neither model was destined to remain long. By the 1840s, the infant school movement faltered from lack of financial backing. It had served the purpose of removing the younger children from public schools, and parents' fees were not enough to keep them going (Forest, 1927).

Fireside Education

Along with the demise of the infant school, another force gained momentum in the mid-nineteenth century: the fireside education movement. Strickland (1982) portrays this movement, which emphasized the sanctity of home and motherhood in the service of the vulnerable and malleable child, as a conservative response to the fear and anxiety engendered by the antebellum reforms of the day. Publications and discussions centered on the mother's influence in shaping the character of the nation through enlightened childrearing.

Discipline based on bonds of affection and activities that encouraged children's natural inclinations to play were encouraged. In this case the call to return to older fundamental values did not include a return to the harsh discipline and pessimistic view of the child held in colonial times. The philosophical rationale of play as natural activity and the plasticity of childhood were warnings concerning the dangers of academic pressure on young children. Pence (1986) credits Amariah Brigham with popularizing this perspective: "Early mental excitement will only serve to bring forth beautiful, but premature flowers, which are destined to wither away, without producing fruit" (p. 23).

Froebel and the Kindergarten

The mid-nineteenth century brought to the United States another movement transplanted from Europe: the Froebelian kindergarten. Froebel's methods were implemented in Europe, beginning in 1837, and came to the United States with the first German kindergarten in 1855. In 1860 the first English-speaking kindergarten was organized by Elizabeth Peabody. One of the stated purposes of the kindergarten was the "Americanization" of new immigrants (Forest, 1927).

Like the eighteenth-century philosophers, Froebel's ideas about play included early versions of many contemporary beliefs and practices in early childhood, in part because he drew heavily on his reading of Comenius and his experiences visiting Pestalozzi's school in Switzerland. Froebel (1896) saw play as a vehicle for unfolding the inner good of human nature. He called play the "purest most spiritual activity of man at this stage and at the same time typical of human life as a whole of the inner hidden natural alike in man and all things."

Qualities of play.   Qualities of play described in Froebel's philosophy included active engagement through motor play and concrete materials that were easily manipulated by young children. Mastery of the sequence of tasks prescribed was thought to provide its own reward to the child.

According to Forest (1927) and Weber (1984), Froebel's notion of "self-activity" is not as close to contemporary notions of self-directed activity and intrinsic motivation as it might appear on the surface. For Froebel, self-activity did not mean self-selection or free choice but instead reflected the teacher's interpretation of the child's outward form of inner tendencies, within Froebel's system. The teacher then prescribed the next step in the sequence of gifts or occupations. This issue of teacher-mediated play is one that reappears regularly in early childhood writings (Almy, 1966; DeVries & Kohlberg, 1987; Dewey, 1900; Fuller et al., 1947).

Froebel's "gifts" introduced the notion of symbolization to children's play but in a manner quite different from psychoanalytic or representational ideas of symbolic play. The symbols of the gifts were metaphysical. For example, the unity of God and man was represented by the first gift, a soft cloth ball, the divine sense of unity and diversity, by the small unit blocks arranged in a larger block (Froebel, 1896).

Froebel's method did not promote either freedom from external rules or attention to means rather than ends. The sequence of gifts and occupations and their specified activities had given goals. Even games were structured to form a curriculum of personal and civic morality. Play with songs and rhythms was a vehicle through which the child could be manipulated to learn patterns of social behavior and life skills (Troen, 1975).

Rationale for play. Froebel's ideas supported the philosophical rationale for play through the argument stressing the plasticity of early childhood. Unlike Rousseau, however, he explained that play in the schools was not a means for the child's innate goodness to unfold. He opposed early education that indulged sentimentalism by attributing educational value to "frolicking" in a juvenile "paradise" (Troen, 1975).

Susan Blow's initiative brought the first kindergarten into the public schools in 1871. At this point the arguments for play in the curriculum began to take on an instrumental nature; play was merely a vehicle for developing skills such as manual dexterity, measurement, modeling, and elementary notions of geometry, addition, subtraction, fractions, and division. Kindergarten play was an introduction and preparation for elementary school (Troen, 1975).

Play in practice. Although many educators applauded Froebel's ideas, those ideas in practice became even more rigidly teacher controlled as teachers uncritically adopted his methodology. Froebel's own rigidity about his ideas may have contributed to this trend. In 1843 at a conference in Rudolstadt, he was quoted in defense of his methods: "The child has intimations of these laws in his innocent aspirations; he expresses them symbolically in his daily activities and therefore the kindergarten reinforces the institutional law which stands to every human being as God's law" (H. Schroeder, niece of Froebel, cited in Forest, 1927).

Followers such as Susan Blow revered his work to the point of adoration. Writing in 1904, Blow suggests the dangers of allowing traditional games and toys in the kindergarten. She felt Froebel had culled what was educationally and spiritually sound from traditional play, embodied in the gifts and occupations and the finger plays or "motherplays" of early childhood. To modify these aspects of the play curriculum was to undermine educational quality.

Some kindergarten teachers did so, however. In 1900, at a meeting of the International Kindergarten Union (IKU), Patty Smith Hill and Anna Bryan organized a presentation entitled "The Letter Killeth" describing modifications made with Froebel's gifts that encouraged dramatic and constructive imaginative play. These modifications set the stage for the pedagogical battles between the radical and conservative kindergartners in the first decade of the 1900s as the child study movement lent credence to the questioning of Froebelian methods.

TWENTIETH CENTURY

The turn of the century saw the expansion of the kindergarten and an increasing emphasis on the scientific study of children. A new institution, the nursery school, emerged and, like the kindergarten, encountered new theories and confronted new social problems.

Expansion of the Kindergarten

As kindergartens became more common in both public and private settings, there were increasing battles between the radicals (Hill, Bryan, and Alice Temple) and the conservative Froebelians represented by Susan Blow. The radicals based their arguments on the scientific approach to child study emerging from the work of G. Stanley Hall and the work of Dewey and the Progressives.

The Progressives lauded many of Froebel's philosophical views on the nature of childhood and the value of play but took issue with the rigidly implemented curriculum of the gifts and occupations. Dewey (1900) writes in *The School and Society*:

> To state it baldly, the fact that "play" denotes the psychological attitude of the child, not his outward performances, means complete emancipation from the necessity of following any given or prescribed system, or sequence of gifts, plays or occupations. The judicious teacher will certainly look for suggestions to the activities mentioned by Froebel (in his Mother Play and elsewhere) and to those set forth in such minute detail by his disciples; but she will also remember that the principle of play requires her carefully to investigate and criticize these things and decide if they are really activities for her own children . . . the presumption is that in the worship of the external doings discussed by Froebel we have ceased to be loyal to his principle. (p. 114)

Instead of Froebel's metaphysical symbols, the Progressives sought to base the curriculum on pragmatics—Dewey's notion that the child's own experiences form the basis for learning. Another goal was to broaden the scope of the school to a concern for community life (Cremin, 1961). This included the social nature of learning in the classroom and the notion that children's play with others prepared them as citizens of a democratic society.

In 1903, the IKU charged a committee with a task of working out the differences in kindergarten philosophies. For nearly a decade the battle ensued. By 1909, separate reports from the IKU's "Committee of Nineteen" were issued for each position: Blow the author of the Froebelian stance and Hill the author of the Progressive stance. Both were at Columbia University where they jointly taught classes and aired their differences in the lecture hall. Snyder (1972) identified opposing notions of work and play and the relative merits of free and directed play as two of the major issues that emerged from these lectures.

Ultimately the Progressive view prevailed, and the kindergarten movement also encompassed the ideas of Hill's colleague E. L. Thorndike. This unique blend of Progressivism and habit training was publicized in Hill's *A Conduct Curriculum for the Kindergarten and First Grade*, published in 1923.

Child Study Movement

Under the influence of G. Stanley Hall, and under the stewardship of Lawrence K. Frank, the child study movement flourished in the 1920s. Although Hall's (1901) research methods were questioned by those who followed him, his influence in directing attention to the contents of "the young child's mind and not to his soul" was unmistakable. Interest in the scientific study of children was also propelled by concern for findings of widespread inadequacies in physical and mental health among World War I recruits.

One of Hall's students, Arnold Gesell (1880–1961) contributed to the popular interest in research, emphasizing scientific methods of observation to collect data concerning the child's physical and behavioral development. Knowledge of the norms established in Gesell's research eventually became crucial for nursery school teachers, and proud parents cited their children's accomplishments. Also influential in the popular press, and somewhat paralleling the connectionism of Thorndike, were the behaviorist ideas of John B. Watson (1878–1958).

The person who may have contributed the most to the scientific study of children was not a psychologist but an economist, Lawrence K. Frank. Frank's friendship with his colleague Wesley Mitchell and his wife, Lucy Sprague Mitchell, helped him to give form to the visions he had of social reform through early childhood education. In 1923 he persuaded the administrator of the Lucy Spelman Rockefeller Memorial to fund child study and parent education centers in universities across the country.

Among the centers funded by the Rockefeller money to conduct child development research was that directed by Gesell at Yale University and a number of others, including the University of California, Berkeley; Teachers College, Toronto; Columbia University; and the University of Minnesota. Observational studies of various aspects of children's play were conducted in many of the laboratory nursery schools established at these centers. Mildred Parten's research on social play, published in 1932, remains a central feature in many contemporary studies of play.

The major focus in the early days of the Rockefeller-funded centers was child study, research to find out, for example, the nature of children's behavior in a specified environment, the laboratory nursery school, and how it changed as the children grew. At the same time, however, the laboratory schools came to be regarded as models whose materials, equipment, and ways of teaching might be emulated as nursery schools became more widely accepted. There was accordingly some questioning of how the environment or the teaching strategies might be varied for greater effectiveness, but such questioning seldom led to research. The concern was for what was regarded as basic rather than applied research.

A major exception to this was the school of the Bureau of Educational Experiments (BEE) in New York City sponsored by Lucy Sprague Mitchell and taught by Harriet Johnson. Mitchell and Johnson's school exemplified the belief set forth in the *Twenty-Eighth Yearbook of The National Society for the Study of Education* (NSSE, 1929) that teachers ought to become researchers in their own classrooms. This was seen as the only effective way for curriculum needs to be addressed according to the interests and activities emerging from the children.

Although regular observations in the form of anecdotal records and detailed reports of artwork and physical activity were kept, the focus was always on the use of the information to enrich the curriculum (Antler, 1987). Play, was, of course, seen as central. Harriet Johnson (1928) writes in *Children in the Nursery School:* "To us the play activity of children is a dynamic process, stimulating growth and the integration of the entire organism as no system of training, however skillfully devised, could do" (p. 68).

Qualities of play.   The qualities of play at the BEE nursery school were much like those that later formed the cornerstone of the "traditional" nursery school, and were drawn from the experiences of The Play School opened by Mitchell and Caroline Pratt in 1916. Play was self-initiated and intrinsically motivating, and the time for exploration to evolve into play was consciously honored.

Dramatic play was valued as symbolic representation of adult activities that, with development, encompassed more detail. This reflected the "preexercise" theory of play seen in early writings on play, and can now be seen as an emphasis on the imitative accommodative aspect of representation rather than assimilative aspects later stressed by Piaget.

Attention to means over ends was supported in materials such as blocks. There was a conscious effort to avoid "static" material things that had a simple and limited use. Play with rhythms, sounds, and intonations of language was also encouraged, an interest that Mitchell expressed in her writing for children. Mitchell was before her time in describing children's developmental stages of language expressed in their play with sounds.

Mitchell also showed an intuitive understanding of the development of representational symbolism in her map-making activities that proceeded from block play, to develop spatial awareness, to icons, denoting geographical features. Like Dewey, she saw children's own experiences as points of departure for ideas that were distant in time and reality. This philosophy, evident in her *Here and Now* story books, pervaded her guidance of children's thinking in symbolically distanced ways throughout her curriculum (Antler, 1987).

Rationale for play.   Play was defended from the philosophical perspective as the natural activity of childhood and as reflecting the plasticity of youth. It was also defended from the instrumental viewpoint that play "enabled the child to advance in the direction of independence of attitude and self-invention of activity" (Johnson, 1928, p. x). Johnson valued the design elements such as patterning and symmetry in children's constructive play—a foreshadowing of the argument set forth years later by Sutton-Smith (1971) that play ought to be valued for its contribution to the aesthetic, noninstrumental aspects of living, as well as for its contribution to cognition and emotional harmony.

Play in practice.   The teacher's role was not only as a researcher and curriculum planner but also as a keen observer of the unfolding development of the individual and the group. Particularly important was the provision of materials with little comment or suggestions on the part of the teacher, in the belief that such verbalization encouraged overdependence on adults.

These attitudes toward the qualities, purposes, and practice of play in the early childhood classroom were to form the basis of Bank Street's program as it was later articulated through the work of Barbara Biber (1984).

The Nursery School

Influenced by the Child Study movement and by the popularity of the idea of education for young children, nursery schools gained footing in the United States in the early 1900s. These early programs took several forms in establishing traditions in early childhood education.

Drawing on the McMillan sisters' "open air" nurseries in England, "traditional" American nursery schools emphasized spontaneous motor play with ample opportunities for children to run and climb. Unlike the nurseries for poor children in England, American nursery schools served primarily the children of well-off families and reflected an articulated curriculum. In contrast were the day nurseries, established in the United States in the 1850s for poor children and concerned more with custodial care than education.

Qualities of play. Play in the nursery, as exemplified in the descriptions of the *Twenty-Eighth Yearbook of the National Society for the Study of Education* (NSSE, 1929), was considered the means by which children "attain their fullest development," particularly in motor coordination.

Play was considered intrinsically motivated, in that it invited motor activity and experimentation. It allowed children to test their powers and extend exploration to their entire environment.

Play was also actively engaging. In the NSSE *Yearbook* the authors write, "It is only in his play that the child's whole power is called forth, that he gets himself entirely into what he does" (NSSE, 1929, p. 701).

Dramatic play was seen as symbolic as children reproduced and elaborated their own experiences and those they witnessed in the lives of adults. Imagination was deemed important in augmenting the properties of materials available for dramatization.

Play was also characterized by attention to means rather than ends. "The stirring experience comes to the child through the process of doing, not so much through the product, which may be the more tangible result" (NSSE, 1929, p. 695). There was accordingly an emphasis on creative activity with blocks, wood, clay, and paints. The child's "patterning impulse" was thought to be satisfied by opportunities for both exploration and play.

Freedom from external rules was encouraged insofar as it was safe for children. Games with rules were not to be introduced before the age of six and teachers were encouraged to appreciate games spontaneously organized by the children themselves.

Rationale for play. Both philosophical and instrumental rationales were employed to defend play in the curriculum. Play was seen as the natural manifestation of childhood impulses and fully integrated activity. Its contribution to the "normal biological development of the young child's organism" was seen as "fundamental to his future success and happiness" (NSSE, 1929, p. 693). In addition to the full development of motor coordination, play was also thought to be a valuable contributor to children's social development in the form "of sharing toys, of adapting to varying personalities, and of entering into activities in which there is an increasing demand for cooperative effort" (NSSE, 1929, p. 695).

Play in practice. The teacher's role in the traditional nursery school was to provide unobtrusive guidance, to ensure that "success crowns the child's effort often enough to encourage a questioning attitude toward his environment" (NSSE, 1929, p. 698) and to provide for physical safety and appropriate play materials.

"Raw materials" (NSSE, 1929, p. 696) that encouraged constructive, creative activity were considered the most valuable, and apparatus for climbing and jumping were considered preferable to sandboxes and swings, which were thought to encourage more sedentary activity.

Other Models for Nursery Education

The "traditional" play-based nursery school was pervasive in the United States in the 1920s and was extended to parent cooperative settings where parents supervised children's play. Other models gained popularity as well. Montessori schools and schools stressing habit formation reflected different views of children's play.

Montessori's influence. Maria Montessori (1870–1952) developed a preschool program for working class children in Rome. She introduced it to the United States in 1915. Although she included provision for children's selecting their own activities, and those activities were thought to be intrinsically motivating because of the emphasis on sensory experience, Montessori actively discouraged fantasy and imaginative play. She wrote, "in the life of the child, play is perhaps something of little importance which he undertakes for the lack of something better to do" (Kohlberg & Colleagues, 1987, p. 268). In addition, Montessori felt that art activities and fantasy might actually harm children, leading to chaotic thinking and mental instability.

For Montessori, attention centered on the goals of activities rather than the alternative products that attention to means might create. Rules governing the proper use of materials were strictly enforced. Her notion of self-directed activity was similar to that of Froebel. For Froebel, the selection of impulses to be followed by the child was determined by the teacher's interpretation. For Montessori, the selection rested in the self-correcting nature of the materials.

Montessori's rigidity about her curriculum undermined the acceptance of her ideas into American nursery education. Lazerson (1972) writes that early childhood education was just recovering from the battles over Froebelian rigidity, and the religious fervor associated with Montessori's movement came too close on its heels for wide acceptance of her ideas.

Schools based on habit training. In addition to Montessori's structured program, there were other schools where play was not at the center of the curriculum. Schlossman (1976) portrays the post-World War I nursery school movement as one dominated by the behaviorist ideas of Watson and Thorndike. At this point the Progressives dominated kindergarten education, and in many places also influenced the primary curriculum. Middle-class parents enrolled their children in nursery school to teach them habits of compliance and conformity as a hedge against what they perceived to be the permissiveness of the public school kindergartens. Schlossman speculates that there was a popular perception that teenagers were out of control, and the public reasoned that conditioning for proper behavior needed to be started early. As Schlossman (1976) puts it, there was an implicit warning, "do it right, do it early, or else!" (p. 461).

The Psychodynamic Influence

In the 1930s and 1940s the normative frame of reference used to describe typical sequences for development expanded to include more emphasis on language, social, and affective development. Common childhood fears and behaviors such as shyness and aggressiveness were described in stages for young children with recommendations for teachers on how to handle them. Concepts derived from Freud's work gained acceptance among researchers. For example, Forest (1927) documents the appearance of psychoanalytic phrases like "complexes" and "anxiety" in personality studies of children at the Iowa preschool laboratory.

Millie Almy (personal communication, June 1988) recalls that nursery educators, like the early developmental psychologists, read the work of Freud and other analysts. It was widely discussed but not formalized at first in nursery school methods. Many teachers were, however, influenced by Susan Isaacs' *Intellectual Growth in Young Children* (1933/1966) and *Social Development in Young Children* (1933).

As an example of the early schism between behavioral and psychodynamic views Almy (personal communication, June 1988) notes that at Yale University's clinic of Child Development, directed by Gesell (who was quite hostile to psychoanalytic thought), the staff of the nursery in 1936 received regular psychiatric guidance regarding its work with children. The next year, when the psychologist responsible for the nursery retired and was replaced by a physician, such consultation ceased.

Qualities of play. From the psychoanalytic viewpoint, the primary feature of play was symbolic expression of unconscious emotions, performing the functions of catharsis, with fulfillment and resolution of conflict and frustration. Freedom from rules of any sort often gave rise to a permissive attitude that was not always guided to become ego strength or resolution.

Attention to means over ends was seen in the spontaneous, self-initiated nature of play, where goals were self-imposed and free to vary. Play was thought to be intrinsically motivated, not so much by the features of the activity itself, but by internal impulses seeking release from the unconscious. Children were also actively engaged in their play, the intensity of which would lead them to gain mastery over the situation and their inner selves.

Rationale for play. The purpose of play was primarily preventive mental health. "Play as prevention" and "educational therapy" are phrases used by Hartley, Frank, and Goldenson (1952), in their book *Understanding Children's Play*. Although the philosophical rationale stressing the vulnerable nature of young children, and hence, their right to play without interference from adults, was in the background, instrumental rationales concerning the future consequences of a childhood filled with free play were emphasized. Isaacs wrote in 1929: "How large a value children's play has for all sides of their growth. How great an ally the thoughtful parent can find it? And how fatal to go against this great stream of healthy and active impulse in our children" (Smith, 1985, p. 116).

As Erik Erikson's work gained importance in the 1940s (the 1950 White House Conference on Children was based on his work), play acquired another purpose—that of an "ego function" independent of the child's need for conflict resolution. In Erikson's view, play reflects an impetus toward mastering reality. The child fantasizes mastery over the world and at the same time practices mastery directly in play (Erikson, 1963; Kohlberg & Colleagues, 1987). Play is, therefore, the earliest form of the ability to master situations through experimentation and planning, a feature common to Dewey's ideas, but from a different standpoint.

Play in practice. Play in practice informed by psychoanalytic views differed from previous eras in that the teacher's role was much more passive. Teachers were to watch but not interfere lest they inhibit the full expression of feelings. Freud's admonition not to "smother" children in fear that they become "fixated" resulted in a hands-off approach to children in classrooms. This was not only in contrast to traditional nursery practice but also inconsistent with the natural inclinations of many teachers. Docia Zavitovsky recalls her first job, in 1936:

> This was a psychoanalytically oriented group. Most of the members of the board were analysts, and the thing that was interesting was that we were supposed to have distance from the children; we weren't supposed to hold them or in any way be that close to them. But, when the supervisor or person in charge would go away, we would join in and play with the children. It seemed much more natural to us. It seemed wrong not to have that kind of contact with them. Then when someone would see the supervisor coming back, they would give us a high sign and we would more or less man our

stations, and we would blend in with the sandbox or blend in with the shrubs. (Bothman, 1976, p. 22)

Raw materials such as clay and sand and blocks were preferred, but "finished" materials that carried potential meaning for children (e.g., baby dolls) were also suitable (Biber, 1984).

Perhaps the most direct example of psychodynamic views in early education was The Walden School, established as a Progressive school in the 1930s, differing from other Progressive schools of that era in the role of the teacher, whose job it was to adjust both curriculum and teacher-child relationships according to their insights regarding the unconscious processes of children (Biber, 1984).

The psychodynamic influence gradually undermined the emphasis on habit training, which was replaced by unobtrusive introduction of routines based on observation of the child's needs. Landreth (1947) writes: "eating/sleeping take place between other interesting activities and are to be accepted as incidental in relation to the daily schedule. No emphasis is placed upon them, and the child is considered to be responding poorly in school if undue feeling is associated with them" (Landreth, 1947, p. 128).

Emergency Programs and Early Childhood Education

Two events, the Depression and World War II, were to change the field of nursery education dramatically. One change was the rapid growth and subsequent popularization of nursery school education for all children (Anderson, 1947). Another was the relaxation of standards for teachers. By 1927, Forest reported that there were more Ph.D.s in the field of nursery education than in any other field outside university teaching (Stewart, 1990).

The popularization of the nursery school movement was first accomplished through the establishment of nursery school and teacher training through the Works Progress Administration (WPA) in 1933. The National Association of Nursery Educators (now the National Association for the Education of Young Children) initially met the news of this project with trepidation. Such rapid expansion would surely undermine the standards of quality for nursery education. Despite the short training periods for "any warm body" interested in working with young children, optimism remained high during the 1930s for the future of nursery education in promoting self-realized, socially adapted human beings (Frank, 1937).

As the WPA nurseries closed, the second set of emergency measures were enacted with the passage of the Lanham Act used to fund child care for mothers working in the World War II effort.

Although the major focus of these centers was on physical care for children, the well-developed ideas for provision of play in the curriculum were implemented insofar as centers had equipment or creative teachers willing to provide it. Mary Alice Mallum, first Director of the Santa Monica (California) children's centers (1943–49), recalls children's play:

> The children's play was so much a part of the times. A lot of the dramatic play was "standing in the cigarette line" or "standing in the stocking line" or in the playhouse, "tearing paper for food stamps." "Go get some meat," all that sort of thing. We didn't have a lot of equipment in those days, but we had a lot of great experiences for the kids. . . . We made all the playhouse furniture and had a ball on Saturday repainting it. . . . We made all of our table toys too. (Bothman, 1976, p. 11)

James L. Hymes, Jr. (1944), writing about the Kaiser Program in Oregon, also pointed to the need for teachers to be aware of the social and emotional needs of children evidenced through their play, particularly those children whose family lives were greatly stressed by the war effort.

At this point in this history the philosophical rationale of the humanists and the "heart culture" common to early childhood educators since the days of Lucy Sprague Mitchell's grand experiments (Antler, 1987), fueled efforts not only on behalf of children but also for adults unemployed and those in need of child care during the war. Could the field do it all—and do it well?

The Waning of the Progressive Movement

The humanistic attitude that marked the efforts for early education to serve both children and adults was undermined in the late 1940s as the Progressive movement, which had grown to influence nursery school, as well as kindergarten education, began to lose ground. According to Cremin (1961), owing to schisms and fragmentation of ideals, phrases like the "whole child" and "creative self-expression" became nothing more than clichés. Teachers were not sufficiently trained to combine individualization and curriculum integration in their classrooms. Progressive education done poorly was chaos.

After the war there was also a decline in social reform initiatives and a general return to conservatism. Immigration was less intense and new information jammed the curriculum. There was an effort to separate education from other forms of social reform and to define its place in society.

Unfortunately, as Cremin (1961) notes, the proliferation of knowledge only increased the need for humanism in education. It remained for early childhood education to continue the humanistic legacy of the Progressives as the launching of Sputnik and the creation of Head Start reified the instrumental rationale for education and threatened the role of play.

The Concern for Cognition

Sputnik, symbolizing the scientific triumph of the Soviets over the Americans, mobilized concerns about the quality of American education that had been increasing throughout the 1950s. In some universities and school systems concerns for the low achievement of children living in poverty had already led to the formation of experimental early childhood programs designed to provide children with skills they seemed to be lacking. The possibilities for the success of such programs were underscored in the early 1960s when publications by Bruner (1960), Hunt (1961), and Bloom (1964) came out.

The next several years saw the expansion and proliferation of experimental compensatory education programs, some involving only modifications of earlier nursery schools, by then referred to as "traditional." Others bore little resemblance to the nursery school. Eventually, as Head Start came into being, as money became available under other federal programs, and as evaluation of the effectiveness of programs received increasing emphasis, the various programs came into direct competition with one another. Which program could best promote cognitive skills?

The Influence of Piaget

In the 1960s, owing largely to the influence of the theorist Jean Piaget and his early contemporary Lev Vygotsky, who give central importance to play in the intellectual development of children, the behaviorist focus on cognition as the acquisition of specific skills was complemented by a strong argument in favor of a constructivist view of child development. Sara Smilansky's work, published in 1968, organized Piaget's work into a system that teachers and researchers could put to practical use in studying children's play.

Qualities of play.   From the Piagetian perspective, play is the basis of young children's self-initiated activity, from which they construct characteristic ways of acting and thinking. The intrinsic motivation derives from satisfaction inherent in the activity and leads to both active engagement and mastery. Opportunities for both exploration and play are ample.

Play is also the manifestation of the developing semiotic function of the young child. The ability to transform objects, roles, and situations is thought to be central to the growing ability to use symbols.

Another quality is attention to means rather than ends. Children's goals are self-imposed and may shift according to their understanding of the situation. There is also freedom from external rules. In both Piaget's (1962) and Vygotsky's (1967) writing about play, rules are seen as generated within the play rather than adhered to from an outside source.

Rationale for play. Instrumental justifications for play abound in the research literature generated by Piagetian notions of the contribution of play to development. Play is thought to support the development of such cognitive qualities as curiosity; exploration; divergent thinking; symbolic transformation; representation of physical, logicomathematical, and social knowledge; temporal sequencing; conservation; spatial reasoning; seriation; classification; and perspectivism (DeVries & Kohlberg, 1987).

Another instrumental justification for play involves play as a precursor to intrinsically motivating work. Rather than emphasize the contrast between children's play and adult work, common qualities are addressed (Csikszentmihayli, 1979).

Play in practice. Two models influential in preschool programs specifically drew on Piaget's formulation of play for their curriculum: the Cognitively Oriented Curriculum/High Scope, developed through Head Start, and the Kamii and DeVries Program. Both programs relied heavily on the traditional nursery school's notion of teacher-child interaction, scheduling, and materials but emphasized changes in children's thinking as they construct knowledge.

In addition, High Scope also used Smilansky's (1968) system adapted from Piaget as a basis for intervening in children's play and designated specific cognitive objectives for aspects of play (for example, matching two labels when playing store). High Scope curriculum has drawn criticism for teachers' insertion of cognitive goals not directly related to children's concerns (DeVries & Kohlberg, 1987). In this sense, the quality of self-activity in play was similar to Froebel's and Montessori's techniques. White and Buka (1987) characterize High Scope curriculum as contemporary versions of Froebel's gifts and occupations.

In the Kamii and DeVries model, group games, a common feature in nursery education, were expanded beyond the realm of socioemotional development to consider their implications for Piaget's stages of cognitive and moral development (Kamii & DeVries, 1980).

A third program that incorporated not only the Piagetian cognitive perspective but also the psychodynamic view of play was the "developmental interaction" approach at Bank Street (Biber, 1984). Added to the instrumental arguments regarding play's contribution to cognition was the goal of facilitating ego strength and conflict resolution in ways described by Erikson (1963) and Isaacs (1933/1966) and White (1963).

Bank Street's legacy was the BEE school of Harriet Johnson and Lucy Sprague Mitchell, a program that incorporated what was known about children's physical, social, and emotional development and foreshadowed many of the qualities of play added by the emphasis on cognition. As the technical knowledge base and theoretical rationale for play grew, Bank Street looked to these sources to corroborate the practices and assumptions held over from earlier days (Day & Parker, 1977).

Head Start

Head Start emerged as a program of social•reform aimed at the children of poor families, based on research designed to investigate the role of the environment on human development, growing by the late 1960s to serve 500,000 children. Several of the Head Start models, such as High Scope and Bank Street, incorporate play into the curriculum. Some used game-like techniques and others incorporated play in ways more typical of the "traditional" nursery school.

The "traditional" model (Miller, 1979) incorporated an emphasis on the development of the "whole child" with primacy afforded to social and emotional development. Cognitive skills were not to be isolated from other kinds of development and the idea that "play is the child's work" predominated. Children were thought to learn through a wide variety of experiences that afforded opportunities for their innate tendencies toward growth to unfold.

Programs that emphasized play were based on "context-free" theories such as Piaget's that focus on the universals of development and are designed to account for individual development. In contrast were the "context-sensitive" theories, emphasizing the role of the child's family and culture in determining cognitive abilities. These programs focused on the deficiencies of poor children and their remediation through specific skills training (Bruner, 1972). Bereiter and Engelmann (1966), for example, believed that selectivity of skills to be trained was considered more relevant to the Head Start goal of "catching up" than to "whole child" play-based programs. In addition, the traditional programs emphasized positive self-concept as a foundation for learning cognitive skills, while Bereiter and Engelmann emphasized self-concept as a result of success in learning cognitive skills.

A third difference was the focus of the technical rationale for programs. The traditional models and the Montessori and Piagetian models took a long-range view of development, rather than stress the mastery of isolated academic skills. The Bereiter-Engelmann model emphasized academic skills and behavioral objectives that would prepare the child for success in a structured public school classroom. Play was consistent with the goals of the former but not the latter. This issue of nursery school and kindergarten education as preparation for a school system fundamentally opposed to the tradition of early childhood in philosophy is one that continues debate today (Keliher, 1986).

Those Head Start programs that emphasized play did not, however, fare well with the measured goals of Head Start. Part of the goal structure for Head Start, ideas such as "social competence" and "daily effectiveness," was not amenable to standardized evaluation measures. Programs emphasizing academic skills and specific behaviors were more easily measured by these means. Philosophical differences that had been brewing in early childhood education for many years came to a head, resulting in little consensus among early childhood professionals regarding goals, curriculum, and assessment procedures (Omwake, 1979).

This lack of focus on program quality had another effect besides the diversity of programs; broad, undefined goals led to an emphasis on paraprofessionals as teachers. Community employment within Head Start was a major goal, based on the rationale that children's home and community environments needed to be strengthened and that members of their own community might better communicate with them. There were few standards for either personal or professional competence. Experienced teachers fled Head Start, frustrated by power struggles inherent in the arrangements of staff. Efforts to educate staff through extensive inservice programs undermined budgets for children's programs. Thus, the issue of the preparation for teachers to implement a child-centered curriculum continued from the years of WPA and Lanham Act nurseries into the 1960s.

In the 1970s, under Zigler's leadership, coherence of goals and curriculum was sought. Child development principles were taught and the role of play in the classroom was stressed (Omwake, 1979).

Despite these efforts, Omwake reported in 1979 that there was little evidence of spontaneous play in many Head Start classrooms:

> Descriptions of classrooms suggest a picture of thousands of children spending half or full days in a relentless round of identifying shapes, matching colors, repeating the alphabet, and counting to ten. Such activities as dramatic play, block building, painting, and water play tend to be viewed by many teachers as special rewards for good behavior instead of important learning experiences. (p. 225)

Omwake attributes this largely to the rigidity of Head Start teachers who gained seniority before Zigler's emphasis and training; many were reluctant to let newly trained staff implement play-based techniques. Joffe (1977) also points to the attitudes of poor parents in seeing the child as "scholar" and their goals for tangible skills that will serve their children well in the public school system. Teachers who hope to defend play in their classrooms must address these concerns.

Renewed Interest in Play

Almy, in her 1966 article, highlighted many of the issues that now concern early childhood educators in their efforts. In this article she synthesized the psychoanalytic views of play with Piagetian views and provided guidance for teachers in analyzing cognition as it is revealed in spontaneous play. She also discussed once again the differences between teacher-initiated play and self-initiated play, an issue that has haunted such discussions from the time of Froebel. Her article illustrates what has become the central concern of those interested in children's play: how to bridge theory and practice effectively.

Whereas practice was at the forefront of encouraging play in previous decades, followed by efforts to research play in child development, the reverse relationship has come to predominate today.

Play at Risk in the Curriculum

Perhaps it was the skills emphasis in the publicity on Head Start; perhaps it was the influence of technology on adults' sense of security (Elkind, 1981; Keliher, 1986); perhaps it was the public outcry for educational accountability in the wake of failed open classrooms. For whatever reasons, play began to lose ground rapidly in the early childhood curriculum of the 1970s.

As a kindergarten teacher with a preschool background I argued with administrators and parents about the importance of spontaneous play in my classroom at this time. Rather than succumb to the growing array of workbooks that I was expected to "get through" during the kindergarten year, I left the public schools and returned to nursery education.

I encountered the parental attitudes that Elkind so vividly describes in *The Hurried Child* (1981) and *Miseducation* (1987). As a beginning doctoral student I found myself delving into the child development literature on play in an effort to defend its place in the curriculum—a battle I mistakenly believed I escaped when I left the kindergarten.

My impression then, and one that continues, is that research in play by developmental psychologists has far outstripped the understanding of teachers of young children. I see two major reasons for this. The first is that the phrases "play is the child's work" and "children learn through play" have become mere clichés and lost the meaning they carried when coined by teachers who were educated to understand the play they saw in their classrooms. Like the Froebelians and Progressives before us, many teachers of young children have adapted traditional practices without questioning their origin or meaning in the lives of the children they teach. Hence, many teachers are unable to articulate a defense of play in their curriculum and are vulnerable to pressures to conform to the behavioristic standards of the elementary school—a battle many early kindergarten teachers fought.

The second reason is the schism between researchers and practitioners of early childhood education. Teachers rarely seek information from research; if they do they have difficulty understanding it. Much research on children's play is carried out without regard to its practical consequences or efforts to make it accessible to practitioners. Few early childhood teachers have continued the tradition born in the child study movement and exemplified by teachers such as Harriet Johnson and Lucy Sprague Mitchell, where "pen in the hand to jot down" always accompanied the teacher. This is, in part, due to the poor grounding in developmental theory that most kindergarten teachers and many preschool teachers receive in their preparation for teaching (Spodek, 1982). It may also be, in part, due to an abdication of the philosophical rationale for play in the early childhood classroom arguments that were upstaged by defenses of play based on a concern for cognition. Signs of a rebirth of this rationale are Almy's "The Child's Right to Play" in *Young Children* (1984) and the recent Association for Childhood Education International position paper entitled *Play: A Necessity for All Children* (Isenberg & Quisenberry, 1988).

We have now a grand opportunity to articulate the philosophical rationale with the instrumental rationales for play, drawing on current research in cognitive, social, and moral development much as the nursery school of the 1920–1940s drew on psychodynamic clinical studies to support their arguments for the long-range benefits of play.

But in doing so, we challenge ourselves more than ever before to formulate a preparation program for teachers that can impart to them the knowledge base in early childhood development and techniques for using that base through their own research to improve practice (Bowman, 1986; Monighan-Nourot, Scales, Van Hoorn, with Almy, 1987).

The efforts of the National Association for the Education of Young Children (NAEYC) to do this through accreditation procedures and publications describing developmentally appropriate practice are commendable (Bredekamp, 1986). I think at this point in time they serve a useful purpose in articulating links between theory and practice, but I fear that they will be implemented without regard to the depth of meaning and flexibility needed to create classrooms that are truly centered on children's spontaneous activity and teachers' sensitive facilitation. Without the knowledge to understand the "why" of the curriculum, the "how" loses meaning, and I fear current efforts to restore play to early childhood will suffer the fate of Froebel's techniques, the ideas of the Progressives, and the legacy of the traditional nursery school.

I should like to see early childhood educators build more bridges between theory and practice and use that information to educate the public about the role of play. Parents are a powerful lobbying force and want what is best for their children. It is our job to articulate our position to them and to reinforce our professional authority by reference to our knowledge base and our commitment to young children (Silin, 1985). Finally, we need to use both philosophical and instrumental arguments to convince policy makers of the importance of play in the early childhood curriculum—play is an integral part of our tradition and we cannot afford to let it go by the wayside. Instead, we must carry it proudly into the twenty-first century, for the preciousness of childhood play is timeless, and its contribution to a changing society essential.

REFERENCES

Almy, M. (1966). Spontaneous play: An avenue for intellectual development. *The Bulletin of the Institute of Child Study, 28*(2), 2–15.

Almy, M. (1984). Reaffirmations: Speaking out for children: A child's right to play. *Young Children, 39*(4), 80.

Almy, M., Monighan, P., Scales, B., & Van Hoorn, J. (1984). Recent research on play: The perspective of the teacher. In L. Katz (Ed.), *Current topics in early childhood education* (Vol. 5, pp. 1–25). Norwood, NJ: Ablex.

Anderson, J. (1947). The theory of early childhood education. In *The forty-sixth yearbook of the National Society for the Study of Education: Part II.* Chicago: University of Chicago Press.

Anderson, L. F. (1931). *Pestalozzi.* New York: AMS Press.

Antler, J. (1987). *Lucy Sprague Mitchell: The making of a modern woman.* New Haven, CT: Yale University Press.

Bereiter, C., & Engelmann, S. (1966). *Teaching disadvantaged children in the preschool.* Englewood Cliffs, NJ: Prentice-Hall.

Biber, B. (1984). *Early education and psychological development.* New Haven, CT: Yale University Press.

Bloom, B. (1964). *Stability and change in human characteristics.* New York: John Wiley.

Blow, S. E. (1904). *Kindergarten education.* Albany, N.Y.: J. B. Lyon.

Bothman, A. (1976). *Reflections of the pioneers on the early history of the Santa Monica Children's Centers.* Unpublished master's thesis, California State University, Northridge.

Bowman, B. (1986). Birthday thoughts. *Young Children, 41*(2), 3–8.

Braun, S. J., & Edwards, E. P. (1972). *History and theory of early childhood education.* Belmont, CA: Wadsworth Publishing Company.

Bredekamp, S. (Ed.). (1986). *Developmentally appropriate practice.* Washington, DC: National Association for the Education of Young Children.

Bruner, J. S. (1960). *The process of education.* New York: Vintage Books.

Bruner, J. S. (1972). Poverty and childhood. In R. K. Parker (Ed.), *The preschool in action: Exploring early childhood programs* (pp. 7–35). Boston: Allyn & Bacon.

Butts, R., & Cremin, L. (1953). *A history of education in American culture.* New York: Holt, Rinehart and Winston.

Comenius, J. A. (1953). *The analytical didactic of Comenius* (V. Jelinek, Trans.). Chicago: University of Chicago Press.

Cremin, L. A. (1961). *The transformation of the school.* New York: Knopf.

Csikszentmihayli, M. (1979). The concept of flow. In B. Sutton-Smith (Ed.), *Play and learning.* New York: Gardner Press.

Day, M. C., & Parker, R. K. (1977). *The preschool in action: Exploring early childhood programs* (2nd ed.). Boston: Allyn & Bacon.

DeVries, R., with Kohlberg, L. (1987). *Programs for early education: The constructivist view.* New York: Longman.

Dewey, J. (1900). *The school and society.* Chicago: University of Chicago Press.

Elkind, D. (1981). *The hurried child.* Reading, MA: Addison-Wesley.

Elkind, D. (1987). *Miseducation: Preschoolers at risk.* New York: Knopf.

Entwhistle, H. (1970). *Child-centered education.* London: Methuen.

Erikson, E. (1963). *Childhood and society.* New York: W. W. Norton.

Forest, I. (1927). *Preschool education: A historical and critical study.* New York: MacMillan.

Frank, L. K. (1937). The fundamental needs of the child. *Mental Hygiene, 22,* 353–379.

Froebel, F. (1896). *Pedagogics of the kindergarten* (J. Jarvis, Trans.). New York: D. Appleton.

Hall, G. S. (1901). The ideal school as based on child study. *Journal of Proceedings and Addresses of the National Education Association,* pp. 474–488.

Hartley, R., Frank, L., & Goldenson, R. (1952). *Understanding children's play.* New York: Columbia University Press.

Heafford, A. (1967). *Pestalozzi: His thought and its relevance today.* London: Methuen.

Hill, P. S. (Ed.). (1923). *A conduct curriculum for the kindergarten and first grade.* New York: Charles Scribner's Sons.

Hunt, J. M. (1961). *Intelligence and experience.* New York: Ronald Press.

Hymes, J. (1944, May). The Kaiser answer: Child service centers. *Progressive Education,* pp. 222–223.

Isaacs, S. (1933). *Social development in young children.* London: Routledge & Kegan Paul.

Isaacs, S. (1966). *Intellectual growth in young children.* New York: Schocken Books. (Original work published 1933.)

Isenberg, J., & Quisenberry, N. L. (1988). Play: A necessity for all children. *Childhood Education, 64* (3), 138–145.

Joffe, C. E. (1977). *Friendly intruders: Child care professionals and family life.* Berkeley: University of California Press.

Johnson, H. M. (1928). *Children in the nursery school.* New York: John Day.

Kamii, C., & DeVries, P. (1980). *Group games in early education: Implications of Piaget's theory.* Washington, DC: National Association for the Education of Young Children.

Keliher, A. U. (1986). Back to basics or forward to fundamentals. *Young Children, 41*(6), 42–44.

Kohlberg, L., & Colleagues. (1987). *Child psychology and childhood education.* New York: Longman.

Landreth, C. (1947). Practices and resources in early childhood education. E. M. Fuller, H. Christianson, N. Headley, C. Landreth, A. Peterson, S. L. Wood (Eds.), *The forty-sixth yearbook of the National Society for the Study of Education* (pp. 101–171). Chicago: University of Chicago Press.

Lazerson, M. (1972). The historical antecedents of early childhood education. In *Early childhood education: The seventy-first yearbook of the National Society for the Study of Education: Part II.* Chicago: University of Chicago Press.

Miller, L. (1979). Development of curriculum models in Head Start, In E. Zigler & J. Valentine (Eds.), *Project Head Start: A legacy of the war on poverty.* New York: MacMillan.

Monighan-Nourot, P., Scales, B., Van Hoorn, J., with Almy, M. (1987). *Looking at children's play: A bridge between theory and practice.* New York: Teachers College Press.

National Society for the Study of Education. (1929). *Twenty-eighth yearbook of the National Society for the Study of Education: Preschool and parental education.* Bloomington, IN: Public School Publishing.

Omwake, E. B. (1979). Assessment of the Head Start preschool education effort. In E. Zigler & J. Valentine (Eds.), *Project Head Start: A legacy of the war on poverty.* New York: MacMillan.

Osborn, D. K. (1980). *Early childhood education in historical perspective.* Athens, GA: Educational Associates.

Parten, M. B. (1932). Social participation among preschool children. *Journal of Abnormal Psychology, 27,* 243–269.

Pence, A. R. (1986). Infant schools in North America, 1825–1840. In S. Kilmer (Ed.), *Advances in early education and day care* (Vol. 4). Greenwich, CT: JAI Press.

Piaget, J. (1962). *Play, dreams, and imitation in childhood.* New York: W. W. Norton.

Rousseau, J. J. (1964). *Emile.* In S. E. Frost, Jr. (Ed.), (R. L. Archer, Trans.), *Emile, Julie and other writings.* New York: Barron's Educational Series. (Original work published in 1762)

Rubin, K., Fein, G., & Vendenburg, B. (1983). *Play.* In P. H. Mussen & E. M. Hetherington (Eds.), *Handbook of child psychology: Vol. 4. Socialization, personality and social development* (pp. 693–774). New York: John Wiley.

Schlossman, S. L. (1976). Before home start: Notes toward a history of parent education in America. *Harvard Educational Review, 46*(3), 436–467.

Silin, J. G. (1985). Authority as knowledge: A problem of professionalism. *Young Children, 40*(3), 41–46.

Smilansky, S. (1968). *The effects of sociodramatic play on disadvantaged preschool children.* New York: Wiley.

Smith, L. A. (1985). *To understand and to help: The life and works of Susan Isaacs (1885–1948).* Cranbury, NJ: Associated University Presses.

Snyder, A. (1972). *Dauntless women in childhood education 1865–1931.* Washington, DC: Association for Childhood Education International.

Spodek, B. (1982). The kindergarten: A retrospective view. In L. Katz (Ed.), *Current Topics in Early Childhood Education* (Vol. IV, pp. 173–193). New York: Ablex.

Spodek, B. (1988, April). *Early childhood curriculum and the definition of knowledge.* Paper presented at the Annual Meeting of the American Educational Research Association, New Orleans.

Spodek, B., Saracho, O., & Davis, M. (1987). *Foundations of early childhood education: Teaching three-, four-, and five-year-old children.* Englewood Cliffs, NJ: Prentice-Hall.

Stewart, D. (1990). *The history of California's children's centers.* Unpublished doctoral dissertation, University of California, Berkeley.

Strickland, C. E. (1982). Paths not taken: Survival models of early childhood education. In B. Spodek (Ed.), *Handbook of research in early childhood education* (pp. 321–340). New York: Free Press.

Sutton-Smith, B. (1971). A syntax for play and games. In R. E. Herron and B. Sutton-Smith (Eds.), *Child's play* (pp. 298–310). New York: John Wiley.

Troen, S. K. (1975). *The public and the schools: Shaping the St. Louis system 1838–1920.* Columbia, MO: University of Missouri Press.

Vygotsky, L. (1967). Play and its role in the mental development of the child. *Soviet Psychology, 12,* 62–76.

Weber, E. (1984). *Ideas influencing early childhood education: A theoretical analysis.* New York: Teachers College Press.

White, R. W. (1963). *Ego and reality in psychoanalytic theory.* New York: International University Press.

White, S., & Buka, S. (1987). Early education: Programs, traditions and policies. In *Review of research in education* (Vol. 14, pp. 43–92). Washington, DC: American Educational Research Association.

CHAPTER 5

Academic Pressure and Dramatic Play in the Israeli Early Childhood Educational System

Rina Michalovitz

The growing pressure on very young children for academic achievement is, in Israel, largely a development of the past two decades, finding expression in the curriculum and scheduling requirements for kindergartens throughout the country. It is difficult for the reader to relate to what is likely to become the prevailing educational trend in Israel without an understanding of the system in which it operates.

Preschool in Israel is national, and not only free of charge, but also compulsory from the age of five. Although three- and four-year-olds are not obliged by law to go to kindergarten, fees for this age group are massively subsidized. As a result, 98 percent of all five-year-olds currently attend kindergarten. The whole system, including kindergartens run by private individuals, is under government supervision, and all staff in the public kindergartens are civil servants.

The system is national in organization and essentially centralized. The Ministry of Education determines not only standards and methods but also the syllabus and program. Thus, preschool education is informed by the outlook of those who frame educational policy at all levels of the system, according to their views of the possibilities and limitations of this stage of child development, as interpreted by preschool educators in the field. In this situation, the classic Tylerian model (Tyler, 1964) could provide a satisfactory framework for analyzing the broad goals of preschool education in Israel. The relative importance of these goals changes from time to time, influenced both by the needs of the child and those of society, as expressed in the prevailing philosophy of education and in educational and developmental psychology. These influences are the guidelines for what it is desirable and possible to teach in any discipline, within a given knowledge structure. The Tylerian model is most effective, however, in analyzing situations at one given time and is less useful in the understanding of a continuous process. Hence, a different model, one that does not originate in education, is used here to follow the development of early childhood education in Israel. Reexamining concepts at different periods with the aid of this model, an attempt is made here to explain ongoing changes in the attitudes of the system toward academic achievement as a goal, and toward dramatic play as a means toward the ends of Israeli preschool education.

It was E. G. Boring (1950), the father of the history of psychology, who developed the concept "Zeitgeist" to explain how psychology had developed as a science. This concept is adopted here to help explain the inevitable changes that have taken place in 40 years of early childhood education in Israel. Boring sees Zeitgeist as the sum total of the influences on change and development. He includes prevailing world views, developments in related sciences, new tools and technologies, and the influence of historical events on those who have experienced them.

HISTORICAL DEVELOPMENT

There was a certain conceptual contradiction inherent in the development of kindergartens in the prestate days. Educational thinking was based on the progressive-pragmatic ideas of John Dewey (1902). The approach to education subsumed Dewey's educational approach, which maintains that active learning takes place when the child meets real-life situations and becomes interested and responsive to them. In putting this approach into practice, however, the Israeli system also made use of Freudian psychology as a means of understanding and relating to the child. In effect, this dualistic approach introduced a contradiction. The child is seen simultaneously as an initiator who learns as the result of actively seeking solutions to problem situations of his or her own conscious choosing and also as one whose intellectual activity is predetermined by inborn needs and impulses, whose ego acts simply to find legitimation for these drives.

The kindergarten of 40 years ago provided a free educational setting designed to enable the child to experience everyday situations. Playing at cooking, washing, gardening, or woodwork provided both learning experiences taken from daily life and the basis for the child's developing dramatic play. This play started as a game of imitation, moving into the second stage as a game of identification, and had a recognized place in the child's daily schedule.

Although the learning value of play was recognized, its main importance was perceived to be its contribution to the child's emotional development. In the psychoanalytic tradition, moreover, it was seen as a means of sublimation. Play was an area in which the child could express forbidden desires and emotions such as fear, jealousy, anger, and hate. It was an area in which the child could elaborate emotional difficulties, particularly those of oedipal origin.

Thus within this framework dramatic play was perceived to be an immanent force in the child's development, a universal and necessary characteristic of childhood, and as such required no adult involvement. In fact, teacher intervention in play was taboo. It was not only superfluous, according to Dewey, but also interruptive and damaging, according to Freud.

The kindergarten of the 1940s offered activities such as drawing, painting, coloring, and pasting. In kindergartens run by the labor movement with its socialist commitment, these activities were called "work." The teacher would call the child to "come and work at the drawing table." Modeling the clay was similarly termed "work."

The teacher's role in the kindergarten of the 1940s was to encourage any activity the child chose in the belief that, because the child chose it, the activity itself, without intervention, would provide a learning experience. The teacher's job was mainly to encourage and to stress values. Surveying the tower a child had erected out of building blocks, the teacher would emphasize the work involved in the comment: "Here's a fine, hardworking builder." Dramatic play was perceived, in essence, as "the mirror of the child's soul," for the teacher to observe but not to touch. The motto of the time was very much "the educator on the sidelines," in the Bank Street tradition.

The historical developments of the early 1950s, which saw the mass immigration of Jews from many different parts of the world right after the establishment of the State, of necessity brought new tasks to the entire educational system, preschool education included. Compulsory education started with kindergarten. The children who trooped in came from all over the world, speaking in many tongues. All had to learn Hebrew. Along with the language, they had to acquire some common systems of habits and values.

These were strenuous years, as the system struggled with its problems. There was no time to inquire whether accepted concepts were still valid in the new situation or what changes in practice were in order, in view of the new reality. Hence, we still saw the doll corner and the other standard equipment designed to provide the children with learning experiences in the context of their daily lives and to afford a chance for emotional self-expression.

But this equipment did not reflect the immigrant children's experience and was unrelated to their daily lives. Kindergarten teachers found themselves waiting, as the children dragged the play material around the room, for some kind of dramatic play; usually, this failed to emerge.

In the late 1950s, Israel became aware of the problem of culturally deprived children. What is known as the Intensive Method was brought into the kindergarten in an attempt to help these children to advance. It was the result of a local need on one hand and of developments in psychology with the adoption of the Piagetian approach on the other. In 1960 for the first time, kindergartens in Israel developed a curriculum that attempted to give the children a knowledge of their own physical and social environment, to instill basic concepts including mathematical concepts and those of time and space, and to guide language development. The idea behind the Intensive Method was to use the children's daily experience to intensify learning and the acquisition of knowledge about their surroundings, while enlarging the resources of language and ideas.

Piagetian theory did not, however, gain sole control of the system. Rather, it was integrated into the previously held concepts. Thus kindergartens developed an integrated view in which new educational content found expression in the familiar play corners. This was done by introducing new props to stimulate the children to use newly acquired knowledge in play. At the same time, there was tenacious adherence to the approach that a teacher had no need, and indeed no right, to intervene in the process of learning through play.

The Intensive Method was adopted, then, throughout the early childhood education system in Israel. It was, in effect, the beginning of the effort to direct this stage of education toward achievement. It was also the beginning of a concerted attempt to close the gap between the groups of culturally deprived children and other groups, an attempt that has continued for three decades. This gap showed itself in a lack of information, in language development, in cognitive capacities, and in the inability of culturally deprived children to make effective use of dramatic play as a learning tool.

In 1969, Sara Smilansky presented the outcomes of her 1968 study of Israeli kindergartens. As a result of her findings, an attempt was made to establish the status of sociodramatic play both as a means of acquiring skills and as a learning tool. The teacher was now to play an active part in the process. These findings encountered, however, an educational system that was not conceptually ripe for them. The system continued to view dramatic play only as a means of expressing the child's emotions and, as such, an area where there was no place for teacher intervention. This attitude continued, even though, among culturally deprived children, dramatic play did not live up to the expectations of educators that it would serve as a means of emotional expression and release.

There had been another historical event. The Soviets had launched their Sputnik, which proved to be a turning point in the educational thinking of Western countries. It forced Western educators to give more thought both to the development of scientific thinking and to the nurturing of creativity. Preschool education in Israel was affected in two distinct ways:

1. The creative arts were emphasized strongly. The kindergarten teacher no longer invited the children to "work" in clay. Instead she asked, "Have you created anything in clay today?"
2. Curriculum plans included science education at all levels, including kindergarten.

This may have been the beginning of the strong emphasis now placed on academic achievement in Israeli kindergartens.

Both in addition and parallel to these historical developments, the early 1970s saw the weakening of the psychoanalytic approach, while both Piagetian and behaviorist theories gained prominence in educational thinking. Teachers in early childhood education discussed habit formation, along with the acquisition of concepts from mathematics and the natural and social sciences, language development, and basic skills. The demand to teach reading in kindergarten was reiterated but rejected by psychologists and sociologists alike. Following the work of Sigel (1971) and others, there were also experiments in developing the intellectual processes of classification, ordering, seriation, and reasoning in preschool children.

The increasing demand for academic achievement in the late 1980s appears to arise from several sources. Some of these are common to American and Israeli society, while others are peculiar to Israel. The demand appears to express the Zeitgeist of our time, since all the factors Boring (1950) enumerates unite in this contemporary attitude.

It is hardly necessary to go into the factors that led to the Bell report, *A Nation at Risk* (National Commission on Excellence, 1983), and to some 30 other reports published in the United States, all of which pointed toward educational factors leading to danger on one hand or opportunity on the other, as far as national security was concerned. In Israel there were parallel demands for achievement on a national level. But besides the fear of economic recession and a lower level of well-being that awoke such deep fears in the United States, there was an additional fear in Israel, the immediate fear for national survival. Survival was perceived to rest on superior efficiency, achievement, and "human quality." While most of the pressure was exerted on the universities, it worked its way down through the secondary schools, which pressured the elementary schools to produce more competent pupils. The pressure continued down to the kindergartens. The entire system was required to produce learners who would be more competent at the next stage of their education.

CURRENT EDUCATIONAL OUTLOOK

The educational outlook that was once child centered is now mainly society oriented, and this latter outlook is now gaining pride of place in educational activity. It has given rise to a series of educational objectives such as "Nurturing Involvement in the State," "Strengthening National Unity," "Education for Democracy," and "Israel's Declaration of Independence as a Basis for Israeli Life." This year's objective is "Respect for Law and Legal Process." Preschool education too is required to consider what can be done to educate children toward these values, besides dealing with all the areas generally considered to be part of school readiness.

These increasing demands on young children have found support in psychology. Gelman (1979) and her group, and others too, have cast doubts on basic concepts that have long been the foundation stones of developmental psychology: egocentrism and personification, for example. Two-year-olds have been found to perform conservation, to make one-to-one correspondences, and to display orientation in space. Sydney Strauss (1982) and his group discovered the U-curve characteristic of development. They suggest that young children can function appropriately in many areas, depending both on the complexity of the function and on whether or not a mode of representation is available to the child: the possibility, for example, that a given problem can be solved by practical and motor means rather than by verbal-conceptual means.

Atari games have opened to question ideas long accepted about the limits of eye and hand coordination among young children. Children's use of the computers that have been introduced into kindergartens in Israel has illustrated the ability of young children to anticipate and to plan.

All this supports the claims of those who maintain that the new demands made on young children simply enable them to realize their full potential, untapped until now.

Neither the educational reform in Israel that introduced a junior high school unit, nor the change in the structure of the matriculation exams, nor the struggle for improved reading comprehension in the elementary schools has brought about a change in the kindergarten syllabus. Notwithstanding, there is much more pressure for academic achievement at an early age, a pressure augmented by achievement-oriented parents concerned for their children's future success in school, which is perceived as a condition for attaining satisfactory social status.

The preschool system has, in fact, adopted a hidden curriculum. Under present conditions it is small wonder that dramatic play has been pushed aside as something that makes no immediate or clearly defined contribution to the child's achievements in fields esteemed by parents.

It is possible, however, that factors other than parental desire for achievement have contributed to the downgrading of dramatic play in education. For one thing, though early childhood educators have found themselves engrossed in the improvement of the children's cognitive skills, they have never shaken off their obligation to the child's emotional well-being. In this field, too, education has absorbed some of the approaches and clinical methods of modern psychology. In the wake of various group therapy trends, kindergartens have been offering structured programs like the one called "The Charmed Circle" to encourage the children to talk about their feelings. Possibly some educators have seen this to be a substitute for dramatic play, a procedure that might fill the need for sublimation, self-expression, and the release of feelings.

Another substitute for dramatic play may be what Hurlock (1972) calls "active television viewing." She is one of the people in the field who include TV viewing as a latter-day version of dramatic play, an activity that, as it were, has gone underground as the result of adult expectations that children should "act more grownup." It is maintained that the child viewers imagine for themselves roles in the drama and that their scenarios are not necessarily the same as the one on the screen. It is, nonetheless, reasonable to assume that children whose dramatic play skills are weak will also be passive and nonconstructive viewers of television. In any case, whether or not one accepts TV viewing as an update of play activity, the fact remains that watching TV occupies many hours that young children once devoted to play, particularly active dramatic play. In making this substitution, the children enjoy the support of their parents, who consider TV viewing to be a pastime that offers varied educational opportunities.

CONCLUSION

In conclusion, I want to offer some remarks about the present status of sociodramatic play in Israel, a status that appears to be a product of our own Zeitgeist in all the respects that Boring (1950) has pointed out.

Israel's educational philosophy now is society oriented. In determining the goals of education, Israel allots a legitimate and highly prominent place to the needs of society. To be sure, the needs of the child are considered, and there is an increased level of sensitivity to these needs in preschool education. Perhaps this is the source of the agreement—even the convention—regarding the importance of dramatic play in early childhood. But how important is dramatic play, and in what sense is it important? It is held to be important as a means of self-expression for the child and, this being so, the teacher is not to intervene.

Nevertheless, historical and existential conditions in Israel today are seen as focusing a concentrated effort toward maximum intellectual development and the promotion of excellence. Thus, despite the generally expressed agreement on its importance, play takes second place in the kindergarten setup, while the educator concentrates on didactic, "learning-oriented" activities.

Recent research in developmental psychology in general, and in cognitive development in particular, supports the view that with suitable intervention, better use could be made of the intellectual capacities of young children. This legitimizes pressure for academic achievement, making this the central goal of early childhood education. Furthermore, with new clinical procedures based on group dynamics, play is not the only means whereby the young children of today can express emotions.

New technologies such as television and the computer, so readily available to adults and children alike, have greatly affected the way other media of expression are used. Whether television and computers are used as a teaching tool or to facilitate learning, we find that they now usurp both the place and the time that teachers once allotted to children's play.

These points indicate the relation between didactic activities and socio-dramatic play as components of the kindergarten curriculum during the past decade in Israel.

Can one see in the movement away from play a sign of things to come, as Postman (1979; 1982) claims in several of his books? Is it a sign that childhood is about to disappear? This does not appear to be the case.

A more acceptable, and indeed a more accepted, view is to place the various stages of dramatic play, from the simplest imitation to the most elaborate forms of this activity, among the means of representation and among the learning tools inherent in all human beings. The use made of the potential that lies in these forms of expression depends on the physical circumstances and on the human environment of the child. Favorable environmental factors include sympathetic adults and cultural norms that recognize and encourage play as a means of representation and as a learning activity. Will adults, now so interested in the child's intellectual development, start to encourage play once again? Boring's guess would have been that this is, in fact, what will happen, if only because of the impact of a body of new knowledge in psychology. This relates to cognitive psychology, where theories are now being translated into programs and applications, and particularly to the body of knowledge relating to imagery and imagination. Psychology has recognized the role and function of imagery and imagination as part of cognitive activity and their importance when it comes to realizing full human potential. If we agree that sociodramatic play is, among other things, one of the most effective means of activating children's imaginations to the fullest, it follows then that encouraging this type of play once more, nurturing it and supporting it, is in keeping with the needs and ambitions of Israeli society and with its desire for educational achievements even for children who are at a tender age. Indeed, this is what the Zeitgeist of the future has in store.

REFERENCES

Boring, E. G. (1950). *A history of experimental psychology.* New York: Appleton-Century-Crofts. (Original work published in 1929).

Central Bureau of Statistics. (1987). *Series of education and culture statistics.* Jerusalem, Israel.

Dewey, J. (1899). *The school and society; being three lectures.* Chicago: The University of Chicago Press.

Dewey, J. (1902). *The child and the curriculum.* Chicago: The University of Chicago Press.

Gelman, R. (1979). Cognitive development. In D. W. Porter & M. R. Rosenzweig (Eds.), *Annual Review of Psychology, 29,* 297–332, Palo Alto, CA.

Hurlock, E. (1972). *Child development.* New York: McGraw-Hill.

National Commission on Excellence in Education. (1983). *A nation at risk: The imperative for educational reform.* Washington, DC: Author.

Postman, N. (1979). *Teaching as a conserving activity.* New York: Delacorte Press.

Postman, N. (1982). *The disappearance of childhood.* New York: Delacorte Press.

Sigel, I. E. (1971, January). The development of classification skills in young children: A training program. *Young Children.*

Smilansky, S. (1968). *The effect of sociodramatic play on disadvantaged preschool children.* New York: John Wiley and Sons.

Strauss, S. (1982). *U-shaped behavioral growth.* New York: Academic Press.

Tyler, R. W. (1964). *Basic principles of curriculum and instruction.* Chicago: University of Chicago Press.

Part III
PLAY IN TEACHER
EDUCATION

It is essential to know what teachers colleges are providing in the preparation of teachers in order to understand the actual practice within a given country. Part III focuses on teacher preparation in the United States and in Israel, particularly as it pertains to children's play. Bowman examines the perspective of the United States while Glaubman examines the Israeli perspective.

Bowman chose to assess the level of commitment to "play education" in teacher education through a study of selected catalogues, professional standards, requirements for certification and licensing, and the extent to which play appeared in professional journals. Her assumption is that since the "centrality" of play has been recognized by such theorists as Dewey, Erikson, Froebel, Piaget, and others, play could be expected to be a focal point in other aspects of early childhood teacher preparation. What she found was dramatically to the contrary. College catalogues list few courses with focus on play. In fact, she discovered that play seldom appears in early childhood teacher education course descriptions. She concludes that while faculty are sometimes committed to play as an important aspect of early childhood curriculum, they are reluctant to use the word *play* in writing about their courses and programs. Bowman found that it may be a widespread inability to articulate what play is, and what it means in the lives of children, that stands in the way of communicating about this very necessary, legitimate, and widespread method of learning.

One of the difficulties in the design of teacher preparation programs, she states, is that early childhood program differences are found across the following three dimensions: the ages of the children served, the goals and purposes of the services, and the delivery system in use. Closely related to these issues is the disharmony of certification and licensing requirements for early childhood teachers in given age groups, even within the same state. Bowman asserts that all teachers of young children should have received the same level and quality of professional preparation. Play, she emphasizes, must be viewed within the broad context of which teacher preparation is a part.

Bowman finds that the issue of play needs to be addressed within the differences found in child care settings, various age groups of children, and diverse program types. She states that the content of the various levels of teacher preparation must be addressed through a deepening of concepts rather than through repetition. In conclusion, she urges more school/university collaboration at the school site, both for the enhancement of joint research and to assist in deepening the understanding of the important role of play in children's classrooms across the United States.

Glaubman gives a general, historical overview of teacher education in Israel. She reports on a study of attitudes toward play as reflected in teacher preparation programs in Israel. She examines college course syllabi, finding them to be representative of what is taught in the colleges. Glaubman's study included the results of a questionnaire that she had developed and administered to the faculties of the Israeli teacher preparation institutions. Glaubman's review of the play literature, like Bowman's, led her to believe that knowledge about play and its development and enhancement is central to the professional preparation of early childhood teachers. Her findings partially support this contention since individuals responding to the questionnaire indicated that they, too, believed play to be very important and that it contributed substantially to child development. Yet, only one tenth of the teacher education courses Glaubman analyzed allotted course time to play. She speculates that in the last two decades, programs have emphasized cognitive skills as the most distinctive and important goal in working with young children. Play, she finds is not the most efficient vehicle for achieving this purpose.

However, since she had found the declared attitude of college and university teachers toward play to be positive, Glaubman finds fertile ground in which to develop the field of play in teacher preparation. Her chapter concludes with some suggested ways for college faculty to work with teachers in this area.

CHAPTER 6

Play in Teacher Education: The United States Perspective

Barbara Bowman

The importance of play in early childhood is well known. In play children explore and master emotional, social, cognitive, and physical domains of experience and practice the skills that presage their participation in the activities of their community. It is not surprising that play is central to the best known theories of early childhood development and education (Dewey, 1938; Erikson, 1950; Froebel, 1974; Montessori, 1964; Piaget, 1962; Rousseau [1762/1911]; Vygotsky, 1976) and is prominent in research (Fein & Rivkin, 1986) and in recommendations for early childhood curricula (Biber, Shapiro, & Wickens, 1970; Hohmann, Banet, & Weikart, 1979; Read, 1966).

In view of the dominant role of play in theory and practice, one would expect it to be a significant aspect of teacher education. A sample of college catalogues suggests this is not the case. Colleges list few courses entitled "Play," and in most, the word *play* does not even appear in course descriptions. Professional standards also fail to mention play as an essential aspect of teachers' competency. The National Association for the Education of Young Children's Professional Standards and Guidelines (NAEYC, 1982, 1985) do not use the term *play* in either the Objectives or Standards section.

Why does play receive so little attention if it is critical to the learning potential of young children? In some instances, rather than ignored, play is hidden, subsumed under other words and phrases. Play is covered in such topics as "creative activities," "selecting toys and materials," "planning for self-initiated activities," and "observing children's activities," in courses entitled Curriculum, Cognitive Development, Classroom Methods, and Learning Environments. Apparently, faculty are committed to their students' studying children's play but are reluctant to use the word. Evidently, they believe that emphasizing play would be misunderstood.

While all children play, many adults believe that play is wasting time and the teacher's responsibility is to limit play in favor of more serious pursuits (Shepard & Smith, 1988). The notion that teachers need to attend college to learn about an activity as natural to children as play seems to be counterintuitive and requires explanations to potential students, their parents, and even to other colleagues in professional education. So, while play is valued by many early childhood teacher educators, they are hesitant to use the word because of its connotation.

   This professional ambivalence is not new. Lawrence K. Frank said, "Part of the confusion arises from the old distinction between work and play, with the feeling that while work is good, play is somewhat questionable, if not bad or sinful" (Leeper, 1968, p. 311). In order to help adults better understand the importance of play to the development of children, Maria Montessori compared it with adult's work. Her intent was to dignify children's playful interaction with people and things by equating it with the serious things that adults do—work. Unfortunately her message is not yet understood. Today, early childhood professionals continue to try to make play more credible by calling it by other names.

   Even given the frequency with which play is covered under other topics, its emphasis in teacher education is often less than one would expect considering its importance in development. Conflicting beliefs regarding the proper role of play in programs for young children undoubtedly contribute to this. In many programs young children are viewed as candidates for educational practices similar to those used with older children. Direct instruction has become popular as a way of making up the educational deficits of disadvantaged children and accelerating the development of more advantaged ones. According to this view, instead of places to play, nursery schools, kindergartens, and the primary grades should be hotbeds for "real" learning. Advocates justify this approach to teaching and learning by noting the vast increase in how much there is to be learned, that children start school earlier and spend more time there, and that young children are indeed prodigious learners.

   Martin (1987) eloquently described how these changes in thinking about young children have affected kindergarten. She wrote, "Kindergarten used to mean brightly colored paintings, music, clay, block building, bursting curiosity, and intensive exploration. Now the kindergarten's exuberance is being muted, its color drained and spirit flattened, leaving us with stacks of paper and teacher manuals" (p. 22).

   The eclipse of play is by no means complete. Many writers, professional organizations, schools, colleges, and universities are active proponents of play. Many leaders in the field have taken strong positions against formalizing the curriculum in the early school years (Elkind, 1988; Howes, 1988; Katz, 1987).

   The National Association for the Education of Young Children (NAEYC) is a persistent advocate of play in programs for young children. The index of their journal, *Young Children*, gives 15 references to play from November 1984 to September 1985, and 16 under the heading "Learning Through Doing, Choosing, and Playing" in 1986–87. *Developmentally Appropriate Practices in Early Childhood Programs* (Bredekamp, 1987), the NAEYC handbook for programs for children from birth to age eight, has more references to play than almost any other topic. The *NAEYC Guide to Accreditation* (1985) includes references to play materials, outdoor play, creative, and self-selected activities.

Other early childhood professional organizations, such as the Association for Childhood Education International (ACEI) and the Southern Association for Children Under Six (SACUS), have been similarly strong in their advocacy of play, and their journals frequently have articles about play.

Schools also give support to the notion of using school time for play. The New York City Public Schools (1983) recommend in their curriculum guide, Getting Started in All Day Kindergarten, that play (called Work Period) be scheduled for an hour each day and Active Play (indoors or outdoors) be planned for another half-hour. Many colleges and universities are committed to a developmental perspective and include course work on play. They are training teachers to value play and build time for it into the curriculum (Erikson Institute, 1989).

EARLY CHILDHOOD PROGRAM DIFFERENCES

Teaching about play is made more complex because of the diversity of programs in the early childhood field. Spodek and Saracho (1982) have pointed out that these differences make designing teacher preparation curricula difficult. Programs vary according to the ages of children being served, the goals and purposes of the service, and the delivery system for the program. How much and what kind of play is considered desirable differs across all these dimensions.

Age of the Child

While many professional organizations define early childhood from birth to age eight, programs usually serve each of three age groups separately: infants and toddlers, preschoolers, and kindergarten/primary, most often in separate schools or centers. The program characteristics considered appropriate for each age group vary to the extent that NAEYC has different "appropriate practices" for each age (Bredekamp, 1987). The Child Development Associate Program (CDA, 1986, 1987) has different competencies for caregivers of infants/toddlers and preschoolers. A review of texts and curriculum manuals for each group revealed that the younger the child the more appropriate play was considered to be and the more active teachers were expected to be in supporting it.

Type of Service

There are many different kinds of early childhood programs. Day care, nursery school, preschool, at-risk, special education, early intervention, compensatory education, home visitor, before and after school, and summer day camp are some of the varieties. Each program type has distinct goals and objectives, and there is no single definition of quality. Indeed, the various program types often have disparate goals and objectives and conflicting conceptual frameworks and belief systems. For instance, day care may be considered a service to parents without significant responsibility for the education of children, and educational programs for children may disregard the needs of parents and family life. Programs subscribing to a maturationist perspective, whether in an educational or day care setting, are less willing to intervene in the "natural" activities of children than programs driven by a behavioral orientation are.

With the caveat that there is apt to be as much difference within each program type as there is between programs, the literature in the field supports the following generalizations: intervention programs for high-risk children are less likely to focus on play than nursery programs for average, middle-class children. Teachers in day care and school academic programs are not as active supporters of play as those in traditional half-day "developmental" programs. This means that the fastest growing segments of the early childhood field—day care, school-based academic and special programs—tend to be least supportive of play.

Delivery Systems

A number of formal and informal institutions operate all types of programs for children. Private, social service, religious, and public institutions maintain full- and part-day programs for children in centers and schools. Few have a system-wide position on play, and there is great diversity within each. Head Start Performance Standards (1984) do not specifically require programs to provide opportunities for children to play, yet their film, The Creative Curriculum, promotes play as an important dimension of good programming. Montessori schools encourage self-directed activities but exclude sociodramatic play from their program objectives. The emphasis on play in many public schools differs from classroom to classroom as teachers make their own decisions about how much and what kind of play to encourage. The ideological biases of program leadership, teachers, and parents probably predict curriculum better than administrative auspices.

TRAINING REQUIREMENTS

Just as schools and centers have various purposes, their requirements and regulations for teacher training are different.

State Licensing

Most day care and preschool programs are regulated by state licensing standards. The number of states that require some training for center-based teachers has expanded rapidly in the past few years, but 27 states still do not require all teachers to have any early childhood training before being given responsibility for a classroom (Phillips, 1988). Since low pay, poor working conditions, and high turnover are characteristic of day care, the training of day care practitioners in most states is apt to be minimal.

Program Requirements

Head Start and some day care centers require the Child Development Associate (CDA) Credential for teachers to be in charge of a classroom. CDA (1986, 1987) explicitly demands that teachers be competent in the use of play as a teaching technique. One would expect teachers with CDA credentials to have had some training about play and to have been judged on their ability to supervise and plan for play in the daily program. It is impossible to know, however, how extensive their knowledge and competence are.

Many early childhood programs require teachers to have a two-year or four-year degree in early childhood education or child development. Colleges may offer a course in play or include play in their curriculum methods course, but, as in the case of CDA, it is difficult to assess how extensive this training is.

WHERE ARE TEACHERS TAUGHT?

Preservice and inservice training are provided in two-year colleges, four- and five-year university programs, and by professional groups.

Preservice

Teachers in four-year college programs are trained in a variety of different departments. Phillips (1988) has listed 21 departments offering courses for early childhood caregivers and teachers: Early Childhood Education, Home Economics, Elementary Education, Family and Child Studies, Family and Environmental Resources, Child Care, Child Development, Allied Health, Occupational Home Economics, Social Sciences, Health Occupations, Education, Human Development, Teacher Education, Behavioral Sciences, Vocational Arts, Psychology, Human Ecology, Public Service, Family and Consumer Education, and Education and Family Day Care.

In general, teachers in baccalaureate programs receive little formal training in understanding and supporting children's play. Most colleges and universities do not offer a course in play, as such, or make it clear that play is being covered under other courses. Programs for teachers of preschool-age children located in Education Departments target their professional education requirements toward academic subjects, particularly reading, social studies, and mathematics. Students in Human Development and Home Economics Departments are somewhat more likely to find courses on play. The bias against play in education-oriented programs is borne out by the dearth of articles on the subject appearing in educational journals. The *Education Index* from 1986 to 1988 lists only a few articles written on play, and the *American Educational Research Journal* had only one article in all of 1987. In 1987, *Child Development Abstracts Bibliography* gives only one abstract on play under Educational Processes and 12 in the other disciplines.

Teaching certificate programs that include preschool have more courses that include play and creative activities than teaching certificate programs found in K-6, K-8 Elementary Education programs. Phillips (1988) reports that only 19 states have certification standards that include preschool, 3 have certificates that extend from birth to grade 3 (age eight), and 9 certify teachers for preschool and primary grades. The remainder of the states have no special certification for early childhood education. Most public school teachers have not, therefore, had a course in play during their undergraduate career.

Many two-year colleges offer Associate Arts degree programs in early childhood education as well as in day care. Certificate programs of 12 to 22 credit hours are commonly found in these institutions as well. Child Development Associate training, with its stress on developmentally appropriate curriculum, is often woven into both degree and certificate programs. The two-year colleges are in the forefront, therefore, in educating teachers about play.

Inservice

Professional groups offer sessions on play at their meetings. The two largest early childhood organizations, NAEYC and ACEI, typically have such presentations at their annual and affiliate group conferences. Unfortunately, NAEYC reports that for their conference in 1988, only 35 of approximately 2,600 program proposals clearly dealt with play, and in recent years sessions on play have not been well attended.

WHAT IS TAUGHT ABOUT PLAY?

Two bodies of material seem to dominate the professional literature on play. The first is theories of play, particularly the relationship between play and cognition (Fein & Rivkin, 1986). The second theme is the uses of play in classroom programs.

Theories of Play

During the early part of this century, interest in children's play was inspired by the psychoanalytic movement and focused on emotional causes and effects. Erikson's book, *Childhood and Society* (1950), was the major theoretical effort in this genre and profoundly affected how early childhood educators viewed play. Peller's work (1952), applying theory to practice, reflects this tradition. She stressed the value of play as release of feelings, the opportunity to remold past experience in order to master it, and as practice for future action. She focused on the inherently personal aspect of play and its self-curative power. Since the 1960s, as Piaget's work aroused interest in children's cognitive development, the significance of play to the emotional development of young children has received less attention. But it continues to be integral to much of the child development theory and to the theoretic allegiance of a few teacher-training institutions (Biber et al., 1970).

Piaget's ideas on play are covered widely in courses and written materials. Stages of children's play, sensorimotor, symbolic (constructive and dramatic), and games with rules are generally mentioned, and the relationship of play to assimilation is explained. More recently, Vygotsky's idea of the zone of proximal development has found its way into the early childhood literature (Monighan-Nourot, Scales, Van Hoorn, & Almy, 1987). Phenomenological approaches, which try to discover how children create meanings, will undoubtedly again broaden the interest in the field to include the affective component in play.

In both psychoanalytic and the Piagetian theories, emphasis is on the self-directed nature of children's play rather than on the role of the adult in changing children through play. Play is described as having self-curative or self-development power the child would "normally" use with little adult direction needed. Piaget (1971) contended "the essential property of play to be the deformation and subordination of reality to the desires of the self" (p. 338). Erikson and Piaget have both stressed the need of children to control their own play if it is to serve its purpose in cognitive development and mental health.

Most textbooks on early childhood education present a number of different theories of play. These theoretical descriptions are usually quite brief, and seldom is an effort made to tie them to practice in a meaningful way. They seem more likely to provide students with an orientation toward and an appreciation of play for young children but not to give them a tool with which to think about it in their classrooms. Superficial coverage of theory is characteristic of much of the training available to teachers. While students may be familiar with the major ideas of various theorists, they have difficulty applying them to classroom practice. This is particularly a problem in the preparation of paraprofessional teachers, who are apt to be uninterested in abstract learning as taught in traditional academic courses. How and what theory is appropriate at each step on the training ladder continues to be an issue.

Role of Play in the Classroom

Texts and curriculum guides suggest three uses for play in classrooms. Free play is a way for children to act on their environment according to their own understanding. By observing play, teachers are able to assess children's cognitive and emotional social development and personal concerns. Through planned play activities, teachers can achieve their own goals and objectives.

Free play. Many early childhood texts and journals recommend that teachers provide preschool children with constructive materials and daily life articles and arrange ample time for free or spontaneous play (Seefeldt, 1980; Hohmann, Banet, & Weikart, 1979). Despite this advocacy for play, there is still considerable disagreement about how much emphasis should be placed on free play in classrooms. A number of factors push early childhood programs away from play and toward more recitation and pencil-and-paper activities. The "effective schools" movement, has focused attention on other aspects of the learning environment, such as time on task and group instruction. Much of the early research on disadvantaged children stressed their need for instruction (Bereiter & Engelmann, 1966) rather than the traditional play program of nursery schools. Since teaching to the test leads more directly to testable achievement, concern with teachers' accountability has made direct instruction attractive. The larger group size characteristic of classes in public schools makes free play less easily organized and controlled. And finally, the school reform movement has stimulated parents, administrators, and legislators to push for early acquisition of academic skills and the elimination of play in favor of work sheets.

These approaches have been hotly contested by many developmental psychologists and early childhood educators. Schweinhart (1987) writes that High Scope follow-up data suggest that poor children, whose early experience contained opportunities for self-directed play, developed more prosocial and problem-solving behavior in later life than children who had been in more adult-directed programs. Howes (1988) contends that the push-down curricula (formal/academic) characteristic of many schools in California is developmentally inappropriate and harmful to the further educational success of children. Kamii & DeVries (1978) recommend learning logical/mathematical concepts in the context of group games as a more developmental and effective educational strategy. They are joined in the approach by a number of reformers in mathematics education (Bell, 1988; Henniger, 1987).

The pendulum swing of educational practice seems to be moving in the direction of greater emphasis on developmentally appropriate activities that include play. A number of states are developing program guidelines that call for an emphasis on play during the preschool years (Michigan, 1988), and professional groups, such as the National Association of State Boards of Education, are taking a strong stand on developmental appropriateness in early childhood programs from preschool through the primary grades (NASBE, 1988).

Observing and interpreting play. Play is a window on a child's understanding of the world. Since young children are frequently unable to tell adults of their thoughts and feelings, other ways of understanding them are essential. Play provides one such way. By observing the child's play, the teacher has "a substitute for spoken language" (Wallach, 1988) through which to gain insight into the child's cognitive and affective life. It is suggested that children's house play, for instance, can shed light on their understanding of object relations, social interaction, category systems, and other such cognitive achievements.

Although teachers are urged to observe children's play, one suspects that much of its meaning escapes them. While play provides a window on the child's intrapsychic life, it is a cloudy and distorted one. Observations are as apt to mislead as to inform; in this way play is like dreams. It is difficult to interpret as children merge fantasy and reality. In view of the meagerness of teachers' formal and clinical training, it is unlikely that they become very skillful interpreters. Nevertheless, there are a number of assessment instruments and strategies designed to help teachers make use of their observations of individual children, including their play (Carini, 1982; Cohen, 1978).

Observing and interpreting sensorimotor play of infants and handicapped children is less problematic and can provide considerable insight into their developmental status. Instruments and schedules are available that translate normative patterns of play into an assessment system (Fenson, Kagan, Kearsley, & Zelazo, 1976; Nicolich, 1977; Wagner, 1985).

Guided play.   The most frequent message to teachers about play is to use it to further their own agenda. By planning play centers and activities, "formal" learning objectives can be achieved. Seefeldt (1980), for example, writes about specific equipment and materials that encourage children to play in ways that reinforce particular learning goals.

Smilansky (1968) and others have extended the notion of using play to teach skills by pointing out the positive effect when adults intervene in children's play. Teachers in infant programs are encouraged to engage in playful interactions with them, though most warn teachers to take their clues from the infant in pacing play episodes (Segal, 1985). Lekotek and Toy Lending Libraries recommend play to reinforce educational objectives for disadvantaged and disabled children.

A new trend toward incorporating subject matter skills into play is apparent in emergent literacy programs where children are helped to enact stories they have written using their classmates as actors and audience (Paley, 1981). Children are also encouraged to include in their pretend play the various uses of literacy, such as writing shopping lists in the housekeeping corner.

ISSUES IN TEACHER EDUCATION

Despite more than a century of research on play and its value for young children's learning, it is still not fully appreciated and remains in the shadows of teacher education. This is reflected in professional ambivalence about the use of the term *play*, the superficial and often conflicting coverage of play in educational materials and courses, and the downgrading of play in programs for young children.

What can be done to make play a more important component in teacher preparation so that teachers can value it, use it constructively in their programs, and advocate for it professionally? Following are some issues to address as the basis for discussion and action.

Nomenclature

The question of what to call play is an important one. Should it be called by some other name more easily explained and defended? Calling play "work" makes it seem a more serious pursuit and is consistent with current educational usage—home work, seat work, school work, and group work. The other alternative to avoid the stigma of the word "play" is to describe the various characteristics of play and use them to label activities—creative, self-selected, perceptual-motor activities. Both of these options are tempting. There is, however, a danger that by avoiding the word, the essence of play may be lost.

Certainly play is serious and can be useful to foster specific concepts and skills. But when it is thought of as simply joyless activity designed to achieve teacher objectives, it may lose its special quality. For instance, when the players cannot bend the activity to their own needs and perceptions, it is not play. The personal and highly motivating aspects of play are sacrificed if teachers override the child's preferences with their own. Play blends cognitive, emotional, physical, and social concerns; it merges reality and fantasy, time and space, concrete and symbolic. Play that is directed toward a series of narrowly defined school objectives, without "playful" fusion of the properties of the personal, social, and physical world, denies its basic structure and the holistic nature of children's learning.

When play is called work and teachers create learning objectives to justify its presence in the curriculum, there is a chance that play will become a casualty to its justification. Early childhood professionals need to reassure parents and the general public that children's play is a legitimate method of learning. Rather than blur the differences between work and play, between activity objectives and playing, perhaps it would be better to clarify them. Teacher education could accept as its challenge to prepare teachers to be advocates of play because they understand and can explain its value.

Play in Children's Programs

Another issue is the proper place of play in early childhood settings. The purpose of play in various programs is different, and the opportunities to play must reflect those differences. Children in day care need a broad range of play opportunities. Benham, Miller, and Kontos (1988) pointed out that in their assessment of child care centers, teachers rarely incorporated play into their plans nor did they promote creativity in play, even though they provided play materials and time to play. Children struggling with stressful or constricting environments require greater support and stimulation to use play both as a cognitive and mental health activity. But, unless there is a reason to the contrary, it should be assumed that poor children, children with special needs, also need the same opportunity to learn through play as other children do.

Children of different ages have different play needs. The professional literature suggests that the younger the child, the more important it is for them to engage in self-directed play. Vygotsky (1976) makes a special case for the importance of play during the preschool age and sees play as an ideal way to scaffold upward a child's abilities, as the teacher has access to the child's zone of proximal development (Monighan-Nourot et al., 1987).

While there are some differences in the play needs of young children in various programs, these differences should not be exaggerated. For instance, a false dichotomy has been created between the training of teachers for education and for day care settings, play being considered irrelevant for teachers intending to work in schools. In order to end this, teacher-training institutions will need to work with state departments of education and state licensing agencies to synchronize their training requirements and to identify the appropriate content for teachers of all young children in whatever setting.

Career Ladders

The appropriate content for the various levels of teacher training is also an issue. Because early childhood programs employ high ratios of teachers to children, the economic realities demand differentiated staffing patterns. Career ladders need to be established with clear delineation of the content of each phase of teacher preparation. Currently, course descriptions in community colleges are similar to those provided at both the baccalaureate and graduate levels. Little work has been done on delineating the differences between these levels. Senior and junior colleges, as well as graduate schools, need to spell out the training content appropriate to their level so that students deepen their understanding at each stage rather than simply repeat the same content.

School/University Collaboration

Teachers need inservice training and consultation from developmental specialists and therapists if they are to use play as a diagnostic tool. The meaning of children's play is not readily apparent and teachers need help to understand a child's intentions in play. Wallach (1988) notes the difficulty in making use of the observations of children's play, particularly children who are traumatized or highly stressed, or children from chaotic or severely disorganized families. The teacher observing a child putting a doll in the toy oven may not know whether the child is expressing anger with a new baby, imitating violence observed at home, or using the doll, symbolically, as a roast to be prepared for a pretend dinner. And even if the teacher is fairly sure that hostility or violence is being expressed, there is a potential danger in interpreting children's unconscious thoughts and feelings. Wallach (1988) writes, "If the ideas or feelings expressed are unconscious and the child is unaware of them, making them explicit without preparation and in a non-supportive context can interfere with a child's attempts to cope with a difficult situation" (p. 21).

Universities have resources to assist teachers in their understanding of children, but they are usually unavailable where the teacher needs them: in the classrooms. University professors need time and encouragement to work with teachers in their classrooms, helping them improve their understanding of children's behavior and find supportive practices. This is as essential in the domain of play as in any other.

Additional research on play in early childhood programs also is essential. Much of the theory and research on play that is available is of limited use to practitioners. Questions posed by Carlsson-Paige and Levin (1987) regarding how teachers should respond to children's "war play" are examples of ones needing to be investigated. Research should focus on play as it occurs in the daily lives of children in group settings, making use of the insights of teachers, as well as of researchers. Collaboration between training institutions and the schools and service agencies where teachers work can help make play a legitimate component of high-quality early childhood programs.

REFERENCES

Bell, M. (1988). Math Project, University of Chicago School of Education. Testimony for National Association of School Boards of Education.

Benham, N., Miller, J. T., & Kontos, S. (1988). Pinpointing staff training needs in child care centers. *Young Children, 43*(4), 9–16.

Bereiter, C., & Englemann, S. (1966). *Teaching disadvantaged children in the preschool.* Englewood Cliffs, NJ: Prentice-Hall.

Biber, B., Shapiro, E., Wickens, D. (1970). *Promoting cognitive growth: A developmental interaction point of view.* Washington, DC: National Association for the Education of Young Children.

Bredekamp, S. (1987). *Developmentally appropriate practices in early childhood programs serving children from birth through age 8.* Washington, DC: NAEYC.

Carini, P. (1982). *The school lives of seven children: A five year study.* Grand Forks, ND: University of North Dakota.

Carini, P. (1975). *Observation and description: An alternative methodology for the investigation of human phenomena.* Grand Forks, ND: University of North Dakota.

Carlsson-Paige, N., & Levin, D. (1987). *The war play dilemma.* New York: Teachers College Press.

CDA National Credentialing Program. (1986). *Family day care providers.* Washington, DC: CDA.

CDA National Credentialing Program. (1987). *Infant/toddler caregivers in center-based programs.* Washington, DC: CDA.

Cohen, D. (1978). *Observing and recording the behavior of young children.* New York: Teachers College Press.

Dewey, J. (1938). *Education and experience.* New York: Collier Books.

Elkind, D. (1988, July). Play. *Young Children*, p. 2.

Erikson, E. (1950). *Childhood and society.* New York: Basic Books.

Erikson Institute Bulletin. (1989). Chicago, IL: Erikson Institute.

Fein, G., & Rivkin, M. (1986). *The young child at play: Reviews of research* (Vol. 4). Washington, DC: National Association for the Education of Young Children.

Fenson, L., Kagan, J., Kearsley, R., & Zelazo, P. (1976). The developmental progression of manipulative play in the first two years. *Child Development, 47,* 232–236.

Froebel, F. (1974). *Mother's songs, games and stories.* Salem, NH: Ayer Co.

Head Start Performance Standards. (1984). U.S. Department of Health and Human Services, Office of Human Development Services, Administration for Children, Youth and Families, Head Start Bureau. Washington, DC: US Department of Health, Education, and Welfare.

Henniger, M. (1987). Learning mathematics and science through play. *Childhood Education, 63,* 167–171.

Hohmann, M., Banet, B., & Weikart, D. (1979). *Young Children in action.* Ypsilanti, MI: High Scope Press.

Howes, C. (1988). *Here they come; ready or not!* Sacramento, CA: California State Department of Education.

Illinois Department of Children and Family Services Licensing Standards, 1985. Springfield, IL: State of Illinois.

Kamii, C., & DeVries, R. (1978). *Group games in early education: Implications of Piaget's theory.* Washington, DC: NAEYC.

Katz, L. (1987). What should young children be doing? In L. Kagan & E. Zigler (Eds.), *Early schooling* (pp. 151–167). New Haven, CT: Yale University Press.

Leeper, S., Dales, R., Skipper, D., & Witherspoon, R. (1968). *Good schools for young children.* New York: Macmillan.

Martin, A. (1987). Back to kindergarten basics. In M. Okazawa-Rey, J. Anderson, & R. Traver (Eds.), *Teachers, teaching, and teacher education* (pp. 22–25). Cambridge, MA: Harvard Educational Review.

Michigan State Board of Education. (1988). Standards of quality and curriculum guidelines for preschool programs for four year olds. Lansing, MI: Department of Education.

Monighan-Nourot, P., Scales, B., Van Hoorn, J., and Almy, M. (1987). *Looking at children's play: A bridge between theory and practice.* New York: Teachers College Press.

Montessori, M. (1964). *The Montessori method.* New York: Schocken Books.

NAEYC. (1985). *Guidelines for early childhood education programs in associate degree granting institutions.* Washington, DC: NAEYC.

NAEYC Guide to accreditation. (1985). Washington, DC: National Association for the Education of Young Children.

NASBE. (1988). *Right from the start.* Alexandria, VA: National Association of School Boards of Education.

National Academy of Early Childhood Programs. (1987). NAEYC (1982). *Guidelines for early childhood education programs in four and five year college programs.* Washington, DC: NAEYC.

New York City Public Schools. (1983). *Getting started in all day kindergarten.* New York: Board of Education of the City of New York.

Nicolich, L. (1977). Beyond sensorimotor intelligence: Assessment of symbolic maturity through analysis of pretend play. *Merrill-Palmer Quarterly, 23*(2), 89–99.

Paley, V. (1981). *Wally's stories.* Boston: Harvard University Press.

Peller, L. (1952). Models of children's play. *Mental Hygiene, 36*(1), 66–83.

Pepler, J. (1982). *The play of children: Current theory and research.* New York: Karger.

Phillips, C. (1988). Briefing paper for the National Association of School Boards of Education (Draft). Washington, DC: Council for Early Childhood Professional Recognition.

Piaget, J. (1962). *Play, dreams and imitation in childhood.* New York: W. W. Norton.

Piaget, J. (1971). Response to Brian Sutton-Smith. In R. E. Herron & B. Sutton-Smith (Eds.), *Child's play* (p. 238). New York: John Wiley & Sons.

Read, K. (1966). *The nursery school.* Philadelphia: W. B. Saunders.

Rousseau, J. (1911). *Emile.* New York: Everyman's Library. (Original work published in 1762)

Schweinhart, L. (1987, Spring/Summer). *Child-initiated activity: How important is it in early childhood education?* Ypsilanti, MI: High Scope Press.

Seefeldt, C. (1980). *A curriculum for preschools.* Columbus, OH: Charles E. Merrill.

Segal, M. (1985). *Your child at play: Birth to one year.* New York: Newmarket Press.

Shepard, L., & Smith, M. (1988, Fall). Escalating academic demand in kindergarten: Counterproductive policies. *Elementary School Journal, 89*(2), 135–146.

Smilansky, S. (1968). *The effects of sociodramatic play on disadvantaged preschool children.* New York: Wiley.

Spodek, B., & Saracho, O. (1982). The preparation and certification of early childhood personnel. In B. Spodek (Ed.), *Handbook of research in early childhood education* (pp. 399–426). New York: The Free Press.

Vygotsky, L. (1976). Play and its role in the mental development of the child. In J. Bruner, A. Jolly, & K. Sylva (Eds.), *Play: Its role in development and evolution* (pp. 537–554). New York: Basic Books.

Wallach, L. (1988). Play and stories. In J. Gabarino & F. Stott (Eds.), *What children can tell us* (pp. 154–169). San Francisco, CA: Jossey-Bass.

CHAPTER 7

Play in Teacher Education: The Israeli Perspective

Rivka Glaubman

There are two major goals of this chapter. The first is to review and analyze attitudes toward play that are reflected in Israeli programs for early childhood teacher education. The second goal is to present a comparison between those attitudes and the attitudes toward play, particularly sociodramatic play, held by college faculty in Israeli early childhood teacher education programs. This study is based on a recognition of the central role of play in childhood and the importance of teachers to its enhancement.

Children's play has been extensively studied over the last two decades. One of the most striking phenomena of childhood is the consistency of playful activity. The child starts playing very early in infancy and continues playing from then on, albeit with changing structural properties in the play behavior that reflect changes in children's development. Children's play has been categorized into four main types, representing a four-stage model of play development: functional-practice play, constructive play, symbolic-dramatic (or fantasy-pretense) play, and games with rules (Piaget, 1962; Rubin, Fein, & Vandenberg, 1983; Smilansky, 1968; Smith, Takhvar, Gore, & Vollstedt, 1986). A number of factors have been shown to be of immediate importance in the study of play. These include the sequential structures of play development, individual differences, social-cognitive-emotional correlates and outcomes of play, and the particular significance of pretense and sociodramatic play.

Parents and educators appear to have a special role in enhancing play. Although a certain amount of make-believe develops intrinsically, as can be seen in the dramatic and sociodramatic play typical of early childhood (Piaget, 1962; Rubin et al., 1983), children do not automatically learn how to play.

Adults can help children achieve flow in play and encourage, model, and stimulate their play activities. They can also actively give guidance and match tasks to children's skill levels to help develop their sense of control (Christie, 1986; Hutt, 1979; Johnson, 1988; O'Connell & Bretherton, 1984; Smilansky, 1968). As O'Connell and Bretherton (1984) note: "Activities conducted with the assistance of capable collaborators enable children to achieve more than they might on their own" (p. 343).

Although there is general agreement that play is important for the healthy growth of the child, the question arises whether intervention is necessary to enhance play. Furthermore, the question emerges of whether intervention is equally necessary in all types of play, or only for certain types. Brainerd (1982), Johnson and Ershler (1981), Singer (1973), and others claim that programs in formal education should include the deliberate development of play, especially sociodramatic play. They also note, however, that it is particularly important to know when not to interfere. Some children will need to be encouraged to play whereas others will need enrichment of their play. It is the task of the teacher to diagnose children's play functioning and treat each child accordingly (Christie, 1986; Smilansky, 1968).

In light of all this, one would expect that teacher education programs in early childhood would be designed to instruct prospective teachers about children's play and ways to guide it effectively. This is especially true for dramatic and sociodramatic play, the play most typical of children in nursery schools and kindergartens and most correlated with a broad variety of developmental gains (Johnson, 1988; Rubin et al., 1983; Smilansky, 1968; Smith et al., 1986). Despite the accepted theoretical importance of play, the extent to which the subject has received encouragement in teacher preparation is not clear.

The study reported on in this chapter consists of two parts. The first part is an analysis of the 1975 Ministry of Education recommendations for initial training in early childhood teacher education, as expressed in its official publication. Also included in the first part is a survey of college programs in early childhood education. This survey covers 33 courses in teaching methods offered by 16 colleges. In addition, the survey covers 66 courses in early childhood education that include methodology and are taught in 11 of these colleges. The data are reflective of the written syllabi issued only by these 11 colleges. The syllabi of the other 5 colleges were not available. The programs were analyzed by the method of content analysis (Borg & Gall, 1971; Sax, 1979).

The second focus of analysis was a questionnaire soliciting information about attitudes toward play held by college teachers in the field of early childhood education. Owing to the reluctance of some teaching staff to respond to questionnaires, the data base is relatively small (22 of 50). In general, this part of the study focuses on the level of importance these teachers of teachers attribute to play, the types of play they consider to be important, and the degree to which they suggest teacher intervention in children's play should occur.

The rationale for analyzing course syllabi is that the course syllabus represents the culmination of a substantive planning process. It is the peak of an "iceberg" of beliefs, knowledge, and experience relating to the education of children. It can be assumed that the program reflects the emphasis that the college places on a given subject. Since information gathered through this method is indirect and inferred, it is thought that the opinions of the instructors themselves, expressed through a questionnaire format, would help to validate and substantiate the course content analysis. The questionnaire was designed to provide direct and differentiated information about instructors' views of the importance of play and play intervention.

FORMAL EARLY EDUCATION AND THE CURRENT STRUCTURE OF TEACHER PREPARATION

Since the special structure of early childhood education in Israel has direct implications for teacher preparation, a historical overview of practice in the country is useful. Formal compulsory free education for children in Israel starts at age five. Municipalities provide kindergartens that charge a fee for all four-year-olds. In underprivileged areas they subsidize kindergartens for three- and four-year-olds. Age groups in kindergartens may consist of either four- and five-year-olds or three- and four-year-olds. At present there can be no group that combines children from all three age groups. These grouping arrangements are based on local community needs.

Nursery schools and day care centers for children of three or younger are either private or managed by voluntary women's organizations. The latter used to provide mainly for the underprivileged. With the expanding demand of working mothers, the number of day care centers all over Israel cannot match the needs. Private nurseries for children beginning as young as a year-and-a-half or two years of age up to four years of age can be found anywhere and run by any person interested in doing so. Although nursery schools are inspected by official Ministry of Education superintendents, there are no regulations concerning the structure of the physical plant and equipment of the center, nor are qualifications specified for the private nursery school teacher.

Early childhood teacher education in Israel is conducted in special teacher preparation colleges rather than in the universities. Some of these colleges accredit their graduates with a Bachelor of Education (B.Ed.) after four years of study, but most offer certification as a Senior Teacher after three years of study. Prospective teachers of young children can choose from two options: specialization as nursery and kindergarten teachers for children three to six years old or specialization as kindergarten and elementary school teachers for children five to eight years old.

Not all of the colleges in Israel have early childhood programs. Rather, most emphasize preparation of primary school, junior high school (grades 7–9), and special education teachers. The preparation of day care staff for work with infants and toddlers lasts only one year and is done in special training institutes managed by the Ministry of Labor and Welfare. It became the responsibility of this ministry because day care centers were originally established mainly for the care of underprivileged children. Currently, most care givers in private nurseries and in day care centers have had no special training at all.

Recently, a new department for the education of children less than one to three years old has been introduced in the Ministry of Education. This is part of an ongoing reorganization of the whole structure of education in Israel. One expected result is that teacher education for the very young will improve as more formalized and improved institutional practices are introduced. At present, there is no clear trend or policy concerning early childhood teacher education other than the brief guide of recommendations produced in 1975 by the Office for Teacher Preparation in the Ministry of Education, which has never been reprinted (*Proposition of Outlines*, 1975).

The programs for early childhood teacher education vary. There are no common curricular standards. Syllabi produced by college teachers differ markedly, therefore, in content, form, and style. Nevertheless, commonalities can be found. Most three-year programs specify the aims of each annual course and outline the course content. The first year in teaching methods consists mainly of early childhood theory and basic principles of implementation. The second year emphasizes teaching principles, practice, and methods for the kindergarten. The third year consists mainly of broadened field practice and student projects that combine studies of theory and practice and are focused on the central ideas and problems of early childhood education. Many colleges do not, therefore, print course plans for the third year of teacher preparation. Most printed syllabi are in the form of lists (detailed in varying degrees) of teaching subjects and are meant for distribution both within and outside a given college.

The current state of play in early childhood teacher education programs in all 16 of the Israeli colleges that have such programs is of interest. In some colleges the numbers of hours allotted to each subject are specified in the course content. In others, the themes with detailed subtitles for each subject are stated. Some colleges list the course themes with no additional specifications of time, course requirements, or subtitles.

Ministry of Education Recommendations

The Ministry of Education recommendations for initial training in early childhood teacher education were published in 1975 on a one-time basis. The recommendations booklet includes content and time allocation; actual training recommendations; curricula recommendations; methods, means, and aids recommended for teaching; and directions for the final test to qualify as early childhood education teachers.

Analysis of the four major parts of the Ministry of Education recommendations offers the following picture:

1. Yearly hours recommended for specializing in early childhood teaching are allocated to three areas: training, teaching methods, and field practice. Three annual hours are recommended for training and are taught in two consecutive years, two hours in the first year and one hour in the second year. Two annual hours are recommended for teaching methods, one annual hour in the first year and one in the second year. In each of the three preparation years field practice is recommended, 20% of which is recommended for the student teacher's actual field experience. Only in the area of teaching methods was play mentioned. It appears in 25% of the course content themes and indicates that out of the total programmatic time recommended for specialization in early childhood teaching by the student teacher, *only* 5% is allocated to play. The specified play content divisions are introduction and importance of play; aims and goals of teaching play; observing and reporting on play observations; and play types with or without instruments.
2. In evaluating student teacher performance, only 8% of the citations (3 of 36 items) refer to the student's behavior in regard to play. Two items appear in the first part. They are (a) evaluating organizational qualifications—organizing centers for play creativity and experimentation and (b) cultivating proper habits for work and play. One item appears in the second part, evaluating communication qualifications, by which is meant the creation of a balance between free activities and directed activities. Note that play is inferred here to be a free activity. In the third part, content mastery, there is no mention of any play item.
3. There was no mention of play in the recommendations for curriculum content for all other courses in early childhood programs.
4. Under the topic, teaching methods, means, and aids, only in 1 of 7 subgroups of methods (14.3%) was a brief mention made of play in teaching aids and strategies. Of 14 methods mentioned, 3 (21%) referred to play (e.g., sociodramatic play, educational games, and puppet shows).

A more recent document, recommendations for education in Israel in the 1980s (Peled, 1976), contained a section referring to early childhood education, but no mention was made of play.

Course Content Analysis

The content analysis of college courses on methods of teaching in early childhood was done by calculating the percentage of play themes in each course as compared with the total number of themes in that course. Figure 7.1 presents the portion of course content relating to play in educational programs focused on teaching methods in early education as reflected by syllabi or course descriptions.

As Figure 7.1 shows, two thirds (64%) of the early childhood teaching methods courses include play themes rarely or not at all. A full third of the courses do not mention play at all. Only one tenth of the courses allot more than a third of their programmatic time to play.

Figure 7.2 provides the data from 11 colleges regarding time allotted to play in the 66 early childhood education courses other than teaching methods (e.g., geography, science, language, literature, etc.). These courses include some aspects of teaching methodology. Figure 7.2 provides the total number of hours allotted to each subject and the specific number of hours allotted to play.

The greatest number of hours devoted to any aspect of play is in puppetry courses. As in the creative education and drama grouping, the puppetry courses also address play mainly in its theatrical form. Play occurs with the second highest frequency in the grouping of art, design, and graphics courses where creating and designing educational games is the major effort. Other types of play are physical movement in physical education and in the rhythm, music, and movement grouping and language play and play-songs in language and literature studies. As can be seen, play is only a minor part of the overall program of studies.

Analyzing the play themes contained in the syllabi of early childhood teaching courses brings to light the conceptualizations of play held by the instructors in those colleges. Figures 7.3 and 7.4 specify the proportion of various play themes in the syllabi of early education teaching methods courses.

Figure 7.3 groups play themes into different areas of focus. Focus 1 is a miscellaneous grouping of the themes related to play that have not been included under the four remaining areas of focus. Focus 2, play and development, represents the importance and meaning attributed to play within early education teaching methods courses. Focus 3, theory and categorizing, relates to the theoretical sorting and understanding of play structure and rationale.

Figure 7.1   Distribution of Early Childhood Teaching Methods
                Courses by Frequency of Reference to Play

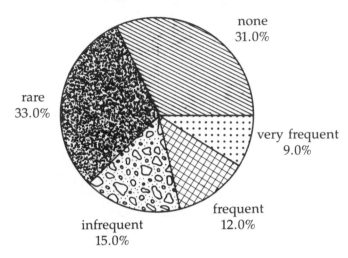

CHART KEY: Frequency of play reference

Note. N of colleges = 16; N of courses = 33

Focus 4, organizing play, deals with procedures and the physical management
of play. Focus 5 represents types of play and includes all types of play that were
included as separate subjects. Figure 7.4 breaks down the references to play in
the syllabi as a function of eight different play types.

    Review of Figure 7.3 shows that the category, particular play types, in-
cludes the highest percentage of play themes. Approximately one third of the
play themes appear in the course Teaching Methods in Early Childhood Education. As Figure 7.4 indicates, educational games are of highest concern to
the college teachers surveyed. Educational games receive nearly half of the
references in the syllabi, over and above those allotted to the creating and designing of educational games (see Figure 7.2 on play allotment, grouping Art,
design, and graphics).

    The types of play specified are varied and frequently refer to individual

Figure 7.2 Portion of Class Hours Dedicated to Play in Other Early
Education Courses

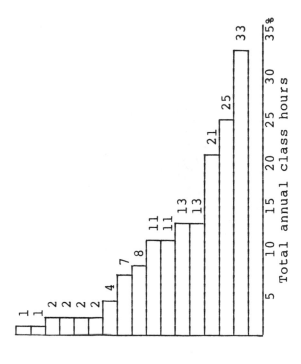

☐ = 1 hour alloted to play

Health
Human study
Geography
Science
Computer
Special education
Curriculum development
Bible and Judaism
Creative education and drama
Physical education
Rhythm, music, and movement
Mathematics
Nature studies
Puppetry
Language and literature
Art, design, and graphics

Total annual class hours

Note. N of colleges = 11; N of courses = 66

Figure 7.3 Proportion of Play Themes in the Syllabi of Early Education
          Courses of Teaching Methods (N=23 Syllabi)

Focus of Play Themes

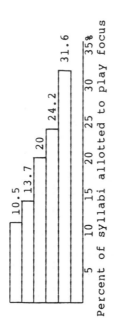

Percent of syllabi allotted to play focus

Figure 7.4 Distribution of Play Types in Syllabi (N=23 Syllabi)

Play Types

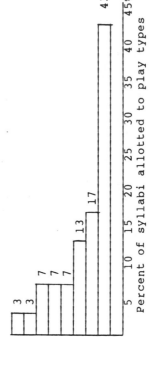

Percent of syllabi allotted to play types

conceptualizations of play types. These types of play do not refer to the theoretical categorizations of play found in the literature (Piaget, 1962; Rubin et al., 1983; Smilansky, 1968; Smith et al., 1986). Some of the types of the specified play types may overlap in part or completely (e.g., sociodramatic play and social play, free play and toddler play, constructive play and junkyard play, games with rules and educational games, play-songs and social play). These titles are those used by the college teachers in their individual syllabi.

Figure 7.3 shows that although a number of other activities related to play were mentioned in the programs (e.g., creative work, experimentation, and drama), these took up a minor part of the program (10.5%). College teachers' explanation of the rationale for play and its contribution to child development took up one fifth (20%) of the time used for teaching about play. This includes the teaching of the definitions and the characteristics of play, play theories, developmental stages, and the theoretical sorting of play types. Figure 7.3 also shows that a quarter of the play themes in the syllabi (24.2%) were concerned with the organizational aspects of play. This included organizing play corners, preparing materials, and developing behavioral expectations and general organizational aspects of play activity and material.

Additional information was available in printed materials that the colleges issued about the teaching of play within the context of their inservice education courses. In the lists of these inservice courses offered by 7 colleges, there was a total of 12 courses devoted specifically to the topic of play: 2 courses on mathematics and reading games, 2 on theatrical play, 3 on centers of play and games, and 5 on dramatic workshops, movement, and creativity. Although these courses were devised to promote understanding of play by practicing teachers, their themes are identical to the themes found in the early childhood education programs (see Figures 7.2 and 7.3).

ATTITUDES OF EARLY CHILDHOOD EDUCATION INSTRUCTORS TOWARD PLAY IN THEIR PROGRAMS

To validate and further substantiate the findings drawn from the analysis of 16 early childhood education colleges, a questionnaire (see Appendix) focused on attitudes toward play was distributed to all 50 early childhood education instructors. The questionnaire consisted of three parts: (1) the importance of play in early childhood education (11 items); (2) the extent to which play should be included in the construction of early childhood education programs (13 items); and (3) the actual steps the college teacher would be willing to take in order to improve the current program (6 items).

Table 7.1 presents the overall importance teachers attributed to play. The first part represents the importance teachers attributed to play in enhancing child development. The second presents the extent of the contribution to child development that teachers attributed to various types of play and the importance of active intervention by the teacher in the enhancement of each type of play. Instructors were asked to rate importance on a 5-point scale with the following values: 5 = highly important, 4 = important, 3 = partly important, 2 = slightly important, and 1 = not important.

As can be seen from Table 7.1, play is considered to be very important in general and specifically to all developmental aspects of the child. All types of play are seen as contributing very highly to children's development. Since the mean for functional and constructive play is slightly higher and its standard deviation is smaller, it would seem that there is agreement that these types of play make the greatest contribution. It is significant that teachers' active intervention was seen as "highly important" for enhancing educational games and "important" for enhancing games with rules. Intervention is considered "least important" for functional and constructive play and "partly important" for enhancing sociodramatic play.

In question five, responding college teachers were asked to specify additional contributions made to children's development through their participation in play. The respondents suggested that in addition to what was specified in the questionnaire, play also makes contributions to children's psychophysical development and personality development (e.g., "independence," "self-study capability," and "preparation for life by learning rules and the practice

Table 7.1 Importance of Play (N=22)

Play	M	SD
in general	4.86	0.47
to academic enhancement	4.71	0.45
to social competency	4.86	0.34
to emotional state	4.73	0.54

Play Types	Contribution to Child Development[a]		Importance of Active Intervention[b]	
	M	SD	M	SD
functional	4.77	0.52	2.68	0.63
constructive	4.77	0.42	3.00	0.90
sociodramatic	4.55	1.12	3.23	1.00
games with rules	4.23	1.13	3.90	0.73
educational games	4.50	1.08	4.55	0.58

[a] $F = 1.71$ no significant differences between means

[b] $F = .28.5$ significant differences between means $p < .01$

of democracy"). Other additional contributions listed by the respondents might be considered as specifications of cognitive or emotional contributions (e.g., cognitive learning in general, language, problem-solving, development of expression, and remediation of cognitive areas requiring further development).

Under question five in the questionnaire, emotional expression was suggested by some college instructors as a contribution to children's emotional health that is made through their play. When asked to specify other types of play contributing to child development, structured social play, computers, and electronic games were mentioned.

Table 7.2 presents the college teachers' opinions about what is needed to improve the current status of play in the college curriculum. The first part presents the college teachers' opinions about the changes that are needed in order to support the status of teaching about sociodramatic play in the college. The second shows the college teachers' actual readiness to make those changes.

Table 7.2 shows that the present proportion of play in the overall program is estimated at an average of 29% (*SD* 14%, range 10–70%) and should be 33% on average (*SD* 11%, range 10–50%). This would seem to imply that on the average, college teachers are quite satisfied with the current proportion of time devoted to play in their programs.

The college teachers were asked to state their opinions about the study of sociodramatic play in the colleges. They were asked whether the emphasis should be changed and if so, what changes they would be ready to make. Table 7.2 also shows that the college teachers thought that the study of sociodramatic play in the college curricula should occur mainly in field practice and in theoretical studies. It appears that college teachers believe that sociodramatic play should receive less emphasis in methodology courses and in the programmatic hours already allocated to the study of play in the program.

However, the college teachers' actual readiness to make the changes is shown to be significantly less than what they themselves have indicated should be changed. In the case of field practice, where the college teachers stated that changes should be made to incorporate sociodramatic play, their readiness to change was the highest. This suggests that the most meaningful and feasible area of change relevant to sociodramatic play is in the area of field practice. An approach of "learning by doing" in sociodramatic play seems to be suggested.

The college teachers were asked to add other important fields in teaching that require greater emphasis and support. More than half, 55%, of the teachers mentioned areas other than play as being equally important and in need of more curricular emphasis. In regard to play, they specified that additional time was necessary in three areas parallel to those specified in the questionnaire. These include teaching of various types of play, teaching the methodology of play, and teaching about the theory of play. Among the various types of play

Table 7.2 College Teachers' Opinions About What is Needed To Improve Current Status of Play

Percent of Time for Teaching About Play in Program

Actual Current State of Teaching			Changes Needed		
N	M	SD		M	SD
22	29%	14%		33%	11%

Proposed Changes in Program To Incorporate Sociodramatic Play

Enlarge Proportion of Play in	Should be Changed			Readiness to Make Changes	
	N	M	SD	M	SD
hours in program	21	2.95	0.90	3.00	1.20
theoretical studies[a]	20	3.95	0.92	2.15	1.24
methodology[b]	20	3.40	1.40	2.55	1.40
field practice	21	3.90	1.50	3.67	1.40

[a]significant difference between interest and readiness to make changes by t-test: t = 4.1 p < .05

[b]significant difference between interest and readiness to make changes by t-test: t = 1.72 p < .05

requiring more time, the following headings emerged: sociodramatic play, educational games, constructive play, free play, puppetry, games with rules and social games, communication games, computer games, movement, individual and group play, and play centers. Workshops for analyzing and constructing play and games were specified for the teaching of play methodology. So, too, were methods of intervention and enhancing play, play environments, creative teaching through play, play as diagnosis, and play therapy. Play theory, the third area needing an apportionment of more time, included the psychology of play, observations of play behavior, the importance of play, the philosophy of play and its integral relationship to development, and an understanding of how children play.

College teachers stated that play was very important and was thought to contribute highly to child development in all developmental areas. Yet they estimated only a limited willingness (M = 3.00, SD = 0.65) on the part of college administrations to support the suggested changes in their programs, even when these changes were limited or moderate.

The program data support this view. In reality, in a third of the courses there was no time allotment for teaching about play. In another third there was very little (10% or less) course time allotted to teaching about play. Only in the remaining one tenth of all courses on teaching methods in early childhood education was more than 30% of a course devoted to issues of play.

The relative importance attributed by college teachers to the various types of play is not reflected by the time allotted to play in programs on teaching methods in early childhood education. Although in the questionnaire, games with rules were found to be very important and necessitating active intervention by the teacher, only 7% of the time allotment to play was devoted to social play. Educational games received top priority in the program, and this fact matches the teachers' statements. Sociodramatic play received recognition as being in need of some intervention. This finding correlates with the allocation of 13% of the syllabus to sociodramatic play (refer to Figure 7.4).

DISCUSSION

The data analysis indicates that the state of play in early childhood teacher preparation in Israel is far from satisfactory. The data from the questionnaire responses do not fully validate or substantiate the picture reflected by the survey of the program syllabi. The content analysis of courses indicates that much work will be necessary if sociodramatic play is to become an accepted and integrated part of the curriculum. The data from the questionnaire responses offered only a slightly more positive picture.

There appear to be two inconsistencies when the data from the content analysis of the courses in early childhood education teaching methods are combined with those obtained from the instructors' questionnaire responses. One inconsistency is the gap between the importance that teachers attribute to play and the emphasis it is actually given in programs. The other inconsistency is the gap between principle and practice as expressed in the responses to the questionnaires. There is a significant discrepancy between teachers' actual readiness to make changes and the changes they stated should be made in their programs in response to the importance they attributed to play.

An explanation for this apparent inconsistency may be that in the last decades early childhood education programs have emphasized cognitive enhancement in their work with young children. Since play was not considered to be the most efficient vehicle to achieve this purpose (Smith, 1988), work and structured exercises have received priority status in early education programs. Play has been left to fill the void after "school work."

A double standard in teachers' attitudes has also appeared in the academic literature on play. The debate has arisen over whether play is actually a useful instrument for furthering school goals. Yet, even if the conclusion is that "play is not the only way of getting experience with objects and peers" and "that the word 'essential' be removed from hypotheses linking play and cognitive development" (Smith, 1988, p. 223), still, Smith argues,

> It would be wrong, and harmful, to conclude on this note. . . . Play, and especially fantasy and sociodramatic play, will remain enjoyable to children, fascinating to adults, fun to watch and to take part in. . . . The argument for play . . . should be decoupled from the . . . emphasis on its cognitive or educational benefits. (p. 223)

The academic literature has concluded that investigation or treatment should be of the child as a whole being, integrating cognitive, social, and emotional development, where no aspect of children's functioning comes at the expense of another (Case, 1988).

An explanation for the second gap, between principle and practice, is that it is also possible that in conscience and declaration teachers are aware of the importance of play to child development. They are willing to allot a fair proportion of program time to play. Yet when it comes to implementing their own statements into practice, they fail to do so because their regular habits in day-to-day teaching are stronger than their attitudes (Rogers, 1983). This inconsistency between belief and performance is a well-known phenomenon with teachers (Ashton, 1981; Brogden, 1983; A. Lamm, 1976; A. Lamm, 1973). According to Argyris and Schon's (1974) "theory in practice" approach and other change theories (Babad, 1985), exposing this contradiction can serve as a starting point in changing the teachers' practice and helping them to learn new ways of teaching that will be a closer match with their attitudes.

Teachers tend to mark their educational practice according to their inclinations and not according to their actual performances (Hook & Rosenshine, 1979; Marshall, 1981). According to Traub and Weiss (1982), teachers tend to rate their performance as better than it actually is. Nevertheless, their judgment has been shown to be relatively accurate.

RECOMMENDATIONS

There are some high points in the data that could serve as a starting point to enhance the subject of play in teacher preparation in the colleges. A few colleges were willing to allocate up to 50% of their teacher preparation program to play. The teachers' declared attitudes were clearly positive about play. These stances offer fertile ground for those interested in seeing play receive its due share of attention and emphasis. Exposing the gaps between their attitudes and practices can serve as a starting point for the learning of new ways to enhance play in the curriculum. Christie (1986) offers a useful summary of teacher interventions that enhance children's sociodramatic play. These interventions can be used as part of college teachers' new learning as well.

The following are some additional suggestions of ways that may be useful to help college professors implement their declared attitudes. These suggestions can help to raise both the quantity and quality of teaching about play in the college preparation of teachers of young children:

1. One-day conferences located in the university presenting the rationale for including play in the curriculum, as well as relevant research that has bearing on the importance of sociodramatic play.
2. One-day workshops in teachers' colleges that have experimental kindergartens, combining observations and practical workshops on sociodramatic play.
3. One-day workshops for kindergarten teachers and school principals, planned by professors and supervisors of student teachers and focused on ways to promote sociodramatic play.
4. Moral and financial support for action research by college professors, kindergarten teachers, school principals, and student teachers, on implementing sociodramatic play. This could be designed officially as part of the requirement for inservice studies during a teacher's sabbatical year.
5. Joint research on sociodramatic play by college professors, classroom teachers, supervisors, and university researchers.
6. "Think tanks" of college staff and academy professors, joined with governmental policy leaders in education, on the issues of children's play in early childhood education and the roles and responsibilities of colleges.
7. Encouragement for inservice courses to be taught by college staff for pre-

school and primary grade teachers and school principals on the topic of sociodramatic play.

8. Research participation in inservice courses for early childhood teachers and school principals that should be encouraged through financial support from governmental authorities. The courses should help to project ways to use research outcomes and knowledge in the field to enhance play as an important part of the daily routines of the kindergarten.

CONCLUSION

To sum up, the state of play in general, and that of sociodramatic play in particular, is less than satisfactory in early childhood education colleges in Israel and can be improved. The college instructors displayed positive attitudes toward play and thought play had an important contribution to make in all areas of child development. However, course content analysis indicated that in practice little time is actually allotted in teaching about play.

Despite college teachers' declared attitudes in regard to the importance of play, many educators did not indicate actual readiness for meaningful change. Educational games and games with rules were the types of play most appreciated rather than sociodramatic or other types of play. Even so, little or no time was allotted to games with rules. The only change seen to be feasible was teaching sociodramatic play as part of supervised field practice. In light of this circumstance, it is being recommended that the status of play in early childhood education colleges in Israel be changed by means of policy and rational, empirical persuasion.

APPENDIX
Questionnaire on Attitudes Toward Play in Early Education Programs

We approach you as an authority in the field of training student teachers in early education. We kindly request your help by providing us your stated opinion on the subject of play in early education programs of colleges. Please circle one of the numbers in the following items in response to each question.

PART I

	no				yes
1. Is it important to include play as a subject in early education programs?	1	2	3	4	5
2. Does play contribute to the enhancement of the child's academic ability (improving his intelligence and school achievement)?	1	2	3	4	5

3. Does play contribute to the child's social ability (communication, interpersonal relationships, cooperation)?

    1   2   3   4   5

4. Does play enhance the child's mental health and emotional state (personal relationships, cooperation)?

    1   2   3   4   5

5. Play also contributes to the child's _____

    1   2   3   4   5

(please specify)

The following items specify play categories. For each category please indicate your response to the two questions shown below.

Type of Play	a. *Is development important to this type of play?*		b. *Is active teacher intervention important to this type of play?*	
	yes no		yes no	
6. Functional play (run, jump, swing)	1 2 3 4 5		1 2 3 4 5	
7. Constructive play (sand, block)	1 2 3 4 5		1 2 3 4 5	
8. Sociodramatic play (father, mother, doc)	1 2 3 4 5		1 2 3 4 5	
9. Social games (football, tag, circle)	1 2 3 4 5		1 2 3 4 5	
10. Educational-table games (domino, lotto)	1 2 3 4 5		1 2 3 4 5	
11. Another type of play _____ (please specify)	1 2 3 4 5		1 2 3 4 5	

PART II

12. What percentage of time of all your early education programs (including pedagogy, methodology, curriculum studies, field practice, and skills development) do you actually allot to study and practice of the subject of play?

    100%   90   80   70   60   50   40   30   20   10   0%

13. What percentage of time of all your early education programs (including pedagogy, methodology, curriculum studies, field practice, and skills development) do you feel is important to allot to study and practice of the subject of play?

    100%   90   80   70   60   50   40   30   20   10   0%

Assuming that existing conditions in teacher training colleges are status quo, person-power cannot be added, and no additional budget is available, should effort be invested toward including sociodramatic play as part of the following aspects of the teacher education program?

	no				*yes*
14. Sociodramatic play in studies of theory and pedagogy	1	2	3	4	5
15. Sociodramatic play in studies of methodology	1	2	3	4	5
16. Sociodramatic play in field practice	1	2	3	4	5
17. Sociodramatic play in _____ (please specify)	1	2	3	4	5

In the following items please specify the extent to which you think these steps should be taken to enhance the study of the play in early education programs (especially sociodramatic play):

	no				*yes*
18. Change all time tables in early education programs (more hours for play)	1	2	3	4	5
19. Change contents of existing curricula (give more items to play in the relevant subjects)	1	2	3	4	5
20. Change the division of focus in practice in student training (more training in teacher roles as encouraging play)	1	2	3	4	5
21. In the play items of the existing program, devote more time to _____ (please specify type of play)	1	2	3	4	5

22. If it were possible to add more hours to your program in preparing teachers for early education, what subjects would you recommend adding?

    _____   _____   _____

23. If it were possible to add more hours but only for teaching play, what courses would you recommend?   _____   _____

    _____   _____

24. Do you think the college administration would agree to changes in the subject of play (as suggested above in items 18–21)?

    1   2   3   4   5

    no   *yes*

PART III:
Had you been asked to change your current program or your next year's program in the following ways, to what extent would you be willing to do so?

	no				yes
25. Divide the hours in the schedule so that more hours are devoted to study play	1	2	3	4	5
26. Give more time to study play in the theoretical part of the program	1	2	3	4	5
27. Give more time to study play in the methodological part of the program	1	2	3	4	5
28. Give more time in student training to practice the teacher roles in play	1	2	3	4	5
29. Give more time to study _____ (please specify play type)	1	2	3	4	5

30. If you have marked three or more items with "1" (not willing to change) or "2" (willing to change a little), kindly specify why: _____
_____
_____

Thank you very much for your cooperation.

REFERENCES

Argyris, C., & Schon, D. A. (1974). *Theory in practice: Increasing professional effectiveness*. San Francisco: Jossey-Bass.

Ashton, P. (1981). Primary teachers' aims, 1969–1977. In B. Simon & J. Willcocks (Eds.), *Research and practice in the primary classroom* (pp. 26–35). London: Routledge & Kegan Paul.

Babad, E. (1985). Psychological change processes, principles and strategies. In Z. Lamm (Ed.), *School and education* (pp. 37–45). Jerusalem: Magness, the Hebrew University, School of Education (Hebrew).

Borg, W. R., & Gall, M. D. (1971). *Educational research, an introduction* (2nd ed.). New York: McKay.

Brainerd, C. J. (1982). Effects of group and individualized dramatic play on cognitive development. In D. J. Pepler & K. H. Rubin (Eds.), *The play of children: Current theory and research* (pp. 114–129). Basel, Switzerland: Karger.

Brogden, M. (1983). Open plan primary schools: Rhetoric and reality. *School Organization, 3*(1), 27–41.

Case, R. (1988). The whole child: Toward an integrated view of young children's cognitive, social and emotional development. In A. D. Pellegrini (Ed.), *Psychological bases for early education.* (pp. 155–184). Chichester: John Wiley & Sons.

Christie, J. F. (1986, April). Play and theory comprehension: A critique of the recent training research. Paper presented at the annual meeting of the International Reading Association, Philadelphia, PA.

Hook, C. M., & Rosenshine, B. V. (1979). Accuracy of teacher reports of their classroom behavior. *Review of Educational Research, 49,* 1–12.

Hutt, C. (1979). Exploration and play. In B. Sutton-Smith (Ed.), *Play and learning* (pp. 175–194). New York: Gardner Press.

Johnson, E., & Ershler, J. (1981). Developmental trends in preschool play as a function of classroom program and child gender. *Child Development, 52*(3), 995–1004.

Johnson, J. E. (1988, July). *The role of play in cognitive development.* Paper presented at the United States–Israel Binational Science Foundation Summer Workshops: Implications of Children's Sociodramatic Play—Learning and National Policy, Wheelock College, Boston, MA.

Lamm, A. (1973). *Images of teaching, research of ideological opinions and perspectives of teachers and of prospective teachers.* Jerusalem: Ministry of Education (Hebrew).

Lamm, A. (1976). *Contradictory logics in teaching.* Tel-Aviv: Poalim Library (Hebrew).

Marshall, H. H. (1981). Open classrooms: Has the term outlived its usefulness? *Review of Educational Research, 51*(2), 181–192.

O'Connell, B., & Bretherton, I. (1984). Toddler's play, alone and with mothers: The role of maternal guidance. In I. Bretherton (Ed.), *Symbolic play, The development of social understanding* (pp. 337–368). Orlando, FL: Academic Press.

Peled, Ed. (1976). *Education in Israel in the eighties.* Jerusalem: Ministry of Education.

Piaget, J. (1962). *Play, dreams and imitation in childhood.* New York: Norton.

Proposition of outlines for a curriculum in theory and practice in methodology for first and second years of colleges for kindergarten and school teachers preparation. (1975). Jerusalem: Ministry of Education and Culture, Department of Teacher Preparation (Hebrew).

Rogers, C. (1983). *Freedom to learn in the 80's.* Columbus, OH: Bell & Howell.

Rubin, K. H., Fein, G. G., & Vandenberg, B. (1983). Play. In P. H. Mussen & E. M. Hetherton (Eds.), *Handbook of child psychology* (Vol. 4, pp. 694–774). New York: John Wiley & Sons.

Sax, G. (1979). *Foundations of Educational Research* (2nd ed.). New Jersey: Prentice-Hall.

Singer, J. L. (1973). Some practical implications of make-believe play. In J. L. Singer (Ed.), *The child's world of make-believe* (pp. 231–259). New York: Academic Press.

Smilansky, S. (1968). *The effects of sociodramatic play on disadvantaged preschool children.* New York: John Wiley & Sons.

Smith, P. K. (1988). Children's play and its role in early development: A re-evaluation of the 'play ethos.' In A. D. Pellegrini (Ed.), *Psychological bases for early education* (pp. 207–226). Chichester: John Wiley & Sons.

Smith, P. K., Takhvar, M., Gore, N., & Vollstedt, R. (1986). Play in young children:

Problems of definitions, categorization and measurement. In P. K. Smith (Ed.), *Children's play: Research developments and practical applications.* New York: Gordon & Breach, *Special Aspects of Education 6, 39–55.*

Traub, R., & Weiss, J. (1982). *The accuracy of teachers' self-reports: Evidence from an observational study of open education.* Paper presented at the sixty-sixth annual meeting of the American Educational Research Association. New York.

Part IV
IMPLICATIONS
OF SOCIODRAMATIC PLAY
FOR CHILDREN WITH
SPECIAL NEEDS

The focus of Part IV is the dramatic play of children from varied socio-economic and ethnic backgrounds and the dramatic play of children that occurs in hospital settings. As the authors point out, both of these groups of children have special needs.

Shefatya reviews the research into the differences between the play behavior of children coming from high and low socioeconomic groups and ethnically different settings. She points out the ways in which environmental factors impact the play behavior of children and cites the level of their parental education as the single most important cross-cultural variable relative to children's levels of make-believe play.

Shefatya draws a careful distinction between functional and constructive play and sociodramatic play. In the latter, role enactment is the major component. Through this medium children experience the complexities of their social world. Manipulation of materials is the main component of functional and constructive play, which does not necessarily have as its major focus imaginative role enactment and therefore does not allow children to experience aspects of their social world as readily. It is Shefatya's contention that without the direct fostering of make-believe skills, indirect influences in children's play will not be effective. She says, however, that once the essential skills of sociodramatic play have been acquired, indirect experience may then contribute to "the quality, diversity, and richness of the child's sociodramatic play repertoire."

Two aspects that require further study in relation to children's dramatic and sociodramatic play are the age at which socioeconomic status differences appear and the play elements that are found to be most salient. The chapter ends with specific recommendations both for adults working with children and for parents.

Kampe, while focusing on the child under stress, reviews, reports upon, and analyzes the role of play when a child is in a health care setting. She describes the stresses emanating from hospitalizations of either short term or long term. Ways of helping a child to cope with the anxiety and stress produced by hospitalization become the focus of the questions she raises. She asks to what degree play can prevent problems encountered in hospitalization. Kampe questions whether certain kinds of play materials can be more effective than others and what the role of the adult should be in the play experience. She further inquires whether adults working with children in health care settings require special training.

While discussing each of the issues through the rich use of illustrations from the field, the author interweaves the variety of out-of-home child health care settings, which range from hospitals to health maintenance organizations. In addition, she reviews the most recent research relative to play in the health care field. She returns to the fact that children have individual coping styles in dealing with anxiety and stress as they face health care situations. She also points out that sensitive and carefully trained adults are required to provide appropriate and supportive responses to each child's style of coping. Kampe finds that the content of child life training qualifies a person to undertake this task, for it provides, in addition to other aspects of training, a strong background in child development, knowledge of how to assess stress levels and coping capacities, and an in-depth understanding of the profound role of play in the complex process of health care.

Child life, as is true in other parts of the early childhood profession, suffers from a lack of commitment to play. Kampe points out that since play has not been quantified, "resources for the facilitation of play are not yet the right of every hospitalized child." She concludes that more empirical research is necessary in order to further validate the means by which play helps children cope with illness and with the demands of health care.

CHAPTER 8

Socioeconomic Status and Ethnic Differences in Sociodramatic Play: Theoretical and Practical Implications

Leah Shefatya

Socioeconomic status (SES) and ethnic differences in cognitive development and school achievement have been extensively studied during the last three decades in a variety of fields and in many cultures. These studies have contributed to a better understanding of cognitive development and functioning. They highlight the effect of environmental variables on mental development and have also laid the foundation for the designing of intervention studies for children of different age levels.

Similarly, the study of SES and ethnic differences in sociodramatic play has a considerable contribution to make to the understanding of the nature and dynamics of this unique behavior. The study of SES and ethnic differences can also provide the conceptual framework for the implementation of intervention projects that aim to improve play and enhance the cognitive, social, and emotional development of young children.

For the purpose of the following discussion, sociodramatic play is defined according to Smilansky's (1968) conceptual framework. When a child behaves "as if" he or she is somebody else, the child is involved in dramatic play. If the child interacts with at least one other child (or adult) in the framework of their pretend role, then the play is becoming sociodramatic.

WHAT DO WE KNOW ABOUT SES AND ETHNIC DIFFERENCES IN SOCIODRAMATIC PLAY?

At present, there is much evidence on between-group differences, but there is also much that we do not know. First, the existing evidence is presented; next, the implications of the findings are discussed; and, last, suggestions for the future are raised.

The first study on this subject was conducted in Israel by Smilansky (1968), as part of a comprehensive study of preschool children. The aim of the study was to identify areas of functioning that might explain the difficulties faced by children of North African and Middle Eastern origin in the schools.

In Israel, at the time of the study (the early 1960s), there was a strong overlap between parents' education, continent of origin, and economic status. Parents of European background had, on the average, more formal education and were better off vocationally. Most Middle Eastern and North African parents had either little or no formal education and were mainly nonskilled or blue-collar laborers. Among the parents with European backgrounds, those who had little formal education were often holocaust survivors who were deprived of formal education, but none were illiterate. On the basis of studies conducted with different groups since 1968 on sociodramatic play and other behaviors, there is good reason to state that parents' education, and not country of origin or ethnicity, accounts for the bulk of SES differences identified in Israel (Smilansky, Shefatya, & Frenkel, 1976).

The Smilansky study investigated two culturally different groups according to one or more criteria. Lacking evaluation tools at the time, the material gathered in that study on sociodramatic play was analyzed after the fact and summarized in an informal, descriptive way. Actually, the formal categories for evaluating sociodramatic play described by Smilansky (1968) had been derived from what was learned through these observations and the insights gained from analyzing the records. The descriptions are based on written material recorded by five field workers who observed children during free play in 36 kindergarten and nursery classes. The ages of the children ranged from three to six years. In 18 of these classes the children were of middle SES, while the other 28 classes were composed mainly of low SES children. For each of the two cultural groups, 20 observation sessions were recorded for each of five play settings: the block corner, the hospital corner, the kitchen and home corner, the doll corner, and playground free time. Detailed observations were recorded of the content of the play; the form and process of play; the number of children participating; the toys, tools, or other objects used; the length of time consumed; and the verbatim verbalizations of the children.

At the first stages of the observations, older preschoolers were observed, most of whom had made daily visits to some formal framework (nurseries or kindergartens) for at least two or three previous years. Thus, they had plenty of opportunity to experiment with toys and materials and had available to them toys that are suggestive of the popular make-believe roles. When large SES differences were found at ages five to six, younger age groups were included in the study as well.

The "between group" differences observed were dramatic indeed. They are summarized briefly in Table 8.1 (for a detailed description, see Smilansky, 1968).

From observations of the two groups, it appeared that for both, their style of play was established by the age of three; each group performed within its

Table 8.1   Summary of SES differences

Referent	Higher SES Group	Lower SES Group
Participation	Nearly all children	Very few of total group
Themes and roles	Primarily home and work themes; adult roles well elaborated	Same themes and roles; less elaboration
Toys	Not primary in importance; nonstructured materials, verbal substitution preferred	Of primary importance; replicas preferred
Verbalizations	For management, imitative speech and verbal make-believe	Mainly for management. Some imitation and almost no verbal make-believe
Leadership	Mostly shared; discipline by requirements of the medium	Authoritarian; discipline by status
Problems	Met by shared control, humor, criticism, focused on operations needed to fulfill theme, acceptance of deviance when based on reality. Rarely causing disruption of play	Met by leader control, personal criticism, and overt aggression against the deviant. Often caused termination of play

From The Effects of Sociodramatic Play on Disadvantaged Preschool Children (pp. 19-32) by S. Smilansky, 1968. New York: Wiley. Copyright 1976 by S. Smilansky. Adapted by permission.

characteristic cultural frame of reference by that age; almost no new elements seemed to appear that were not already present in at least germinal form at younger age levels.

QUANTITATIVE FINDINGS ON SES DIFFERENCES IN SOCIODRAMATIC PLAY

The differences found in the quality of play behavior between low SES (LSES) and high SES (HSES) children as identified through observation and analyses of play records led to the search for quantitative research data on the subject. There was no empirical evidence in the professional literature at that time, as pointed out by Freyberg (1973) several years later: "There is little information of a systematic nature regarding cultural or social class differences in make-believe play" (p. 129). Rather, it seemed to be taken for granted, on the basis of observations of middle-class European or American children, that this form of play is a universal aspect of early development. The major theories of play, whether the early instinct theory of Groos, the surplus energy approach of Schiller, the Piagetian developmental, or the psychoanalytic theories, all seem to make this assumption.

Still, in the United States there have been suggestions from several sources that the make-believe play of young lower class children is different (Murphy, 1956; Sigel & McBaine, 1966). It tends to be fragmented and lacking in imaginative or symbolic content when compared with the play of middle-class children. The fact that in spite of such awareness, even during the 1950s, there was a complete lack of systematic research on the subject can be explained by measurement problems. As Singer (1973) observes, "What we most seriously lack are large bodies of formal data, collected under conditions specified in sufficient detail that they can be replicated by others. In addition, we need a set of categories and formal tools for measurement of play behavior" (p. 26).

Quantitative Analysis of Speech During Play

The differences observed in the play of lower and higher SES children, and particularly the difference in the function of verbalization during sociodramatic play, were expected to be mirrored in several quantitative measures of speech.

The verbal material analyzed represents verbalization of LSES and HSES children during sociodramatic play that developed around the home and hospital corner and the block corner, plus verbal interaction in the drawing and painting corner. The inclusion of the last provided a larger sample of speech participators than would have been available in the LSES group by including only incidents of sociodramatic play.

LSES and HSES children were compared by use of the following speech criteria: amount of speech, length of sentence, analysis of parts of speech, range of vocabulary (categorized also by parts of speech). On all verbal criteria, considerable between-group differences were identified (Smilansky, 1968).

This study is regarded as preliminary in the field of verbalization during sociodramatic play. It seems that further studies in this field are needed. There are many possible directions for language assessment during play. One important distinction that should be made in such studies is the relevance of verbal utterances to the play itself. Another promising possibility would be the evaluation of speech (quantity and quality) according to its function in the framework of the play: imitative, substantive (make-believe), or managerial.

Differences in the Quality of Play

Even more important for the purpose of the investigations was the quantitative assessment of the play itself. On the grounds of the observational data previously gathered, the preliminary Smilansky scale was constructed using the following six categories of play behavior:

Imitative role play
Make-believe in regard to objects (substitution)
Make-believe in regard to actions and situations
Persistence
Interaction with at least one co-player
Verbal communication (in the framework of the play)

This scale was developed in order to assess the effectiveness of an experiment that explored ways to raise the level of play in LSES kindergarten groups. In that study (Smilansky, 1968), the scoring of each of the six play elements was in a dichotomous form—present or absent—throughout the observational sessions. Also the scores obtained were used in a global way, only to state whether the child demonstrated some form of sociodramatic play or behavior, or solitary dramatic play, or neither.

The pretest findings on the low and high SES control groups are presented in Table 8.2 (The pretest percentages of the LSES experimental groups are very similar to those of the LSES control group.)

Table 8.2 illustrates a striking between-group difference that was not repeated in this magnitude in later studies. It is probable that positive changes in the educational level of parents, as well as greater awareness among kindergarten teachers about the importance of this play behavior, has helped to nar-

Table 8.2   Proportion of Kindergarten Children Engaging in
            Dramatic and Sociodramatic Play, by SES

Groups	No make-believe play		Dramatic Play Only		Sociodramatic Play		Total	
	N	%	N	%	N	%	N	%
LSES	250	69	72	20	40	11.	362	100
HSES	13	3	81	19	333	78	427	100

From The Effects of Sociodramatic Play on Disadvantaged
Preschool Children (p. 122) by S. Smilansky, 1968.   New
York: Wiley. Copyright 1976 by S. Smilansky. Adapted by
permission.

row the gap. Also, later studies applied more flexible criteria (persistence was reduced from ten minutes to five minutes).

In a later Israeli study of the relationship between sociodramatic play and several dimensions of social adjustment in kindergarten, Taler (1976) compared the play of two socioeconomic groups (a total of 96 children) using the final version of the Smilansky scale for evaluation of their sociodramatic play. She found statistically significant differences ($p < .04$), with a mean score of 8.8 for the higher, and 6.4 for the lower socioeconomic groups. (Parents' education and occupation served as SES criteria.) Thus, a decade after the first study, differences by socioeconomic background did not disappear in Israeli kindergartens.

In the United States, using the same evaluation scale, an even larger socioeconomic difference was found by Griffing (1980). She compared the sociodramatic play of two SES groups of black kindergarten children (five to six years old), from nine Columbus and Franklin County schools in Ohio. (Parents' education and occupation served as SES criteria.)

The children were observed for one-half hour in groups of four, two boys and two girls each time, in a structured laboratory setting. One observer was assigned to each child and made a specimen record of verbal and nonverbal behavior. The records were evaluated by independent scorers with the final version of the Smilansky scale for evaluation of sociodramatic play. Table 8.3 presents play scores by SES and sex.

The mean scores presented clearly indicate strong SES differences in both sex groups on all of the six play categories, as well as on total play scores. These differences are highly significant as reflected in findings from analyses of variance (see Table 8.4). For the total scores, the F ratio for SES is very large. There is also a significant, but considerably smaller, F ratio for sex, while there is no interaction effect.

Table 8.3 Mean Play Scores by Categories and by SES and Sex

Play Variable	Low SES	High SES
Boys		
Imitative role play	6.19	10.24
Make-believe play with objects	5.93	8.12
Verbal make-believe with actions and situations	2.44	5.17
Persistence	5.16	9.17
Interaction within contexts	3.93	7.95
Verbal communication within context	3.40	6.76
Total play scores	4.51	7.99
N =	43	42
Girls		
Imitative role play	5.00	10.95
Make-believe play with objects	4.25	8.20
Verbal make-believe with actions and situations	1.20	6.37
Persistence	4.32	11.02
Interaction within contexts	2.59	9.70
Verbal communication within context	2.25	8.40
Total play scores	3.27	9.11
N =	44	42
Total N =	(87)	(84)
Imitative role play	5.59	10.59
Make-believe play with objects	5.08	8.16
Verbal make-believe with actions and situations	1.82	5.46
Persistence	4.74	10.35
Interaction within contexts	3.25	8.80
Verbal communication within context	2.82	7.56
Total play scores	3.88	8.54

Note. Mean subscores were derived from added scores, on six
five-minute observations (maximum 18).

From "The Relationship Between Sociometric Status and
Sociodramatic Play Among Black Kindergarten Children" by P.
Griffing, 1980, Genetic Psychology Monograph, 101, p. 17.
Copyright 1980 by Helen Dwight Reid Educational Foundation.
Reprinted with permission.

Table 8.4   Findings from Two-Way Analyses of Variance of
            Play Scores by SES and Sex

Source	Degrees of Freedom	F Ratios	Probability
SES	(6.160)	15.06	0.001
Sex	(6.160)	2.58	0.021
SES x Sex	(6.160)	1.64	0.140

From "The Relationship Between Sociometric Status and
Sociodramatic Play Among Black Kindergarten Children" by P.
Griffing, 1980, Genetic Psychology Monograph, 101, p. 21.
Copyright 1980 by Helen Dwight Reid Educational Foundation.
Reprinted with permission.

Highly significant findings are obtained also when the effect of SES and sex on each of the six play criteria is evaluated separately. This thorough study of Griffing, with a fairly large sample of American children, seems to imply that SES differences in the nature of sociodramatic play behavior of preschool children might be a cross-cultural phenomenon. Many other studies with different child populations that use a variety of evaluation procedures seem to support this statement. Some of them will be presented in chronological order.

Rosen (1974), who conducted an experimental study in a small southern community in the United States, found large SES differences. The subjects for Rosen's study were 58 children from four kindergarten classes of black low SES children and from one white middle-class kindergarten group. Demographic data pertaining to individual children revealed, however, that one of the black groups was middle class or middle-class oriented in the sense that both parents worked and the family was characterized by stable job incomes. More than half of the lower class children, on the other hand, came from welfare families. Observations of free play in school, using an adaptation of the Smilansky scale for evaluation of sociodramatic play, showed a highly significant difference between the middle-class white group and the three lower class black groups. All of the white middle-class children were observed to engage in dramatic or sociodramatic play, whereas few of the lower class black children did. Most important, the "middle-class-oriented" black group displayed significantly more sociodramatic play than the lower class black groups.

In Great Britain, Tizard, Philps, & Plewis (1976) studied 109 three- to four-year-old children in three types of preschool centers: traditional English nursery schools, staffed by trained teachers; similar nursery schools but with special emphasis on language programs; and nursery schools with untrained teachers intended to provide care for the children of working mothers. They report large social class differences in the amount of symbolic play of any kind. Another important finding reported is that SES differences were similar in an additional sample of 23 low SES children who were integrated in predominantly middle-class nurseries. The Tizard et al. study dealt, however, with symbolic play as a general category and did not relate to sociodramatic play or to the elements of make-believe.

Another study of Great Britain was more specifically focused on fantasy play criteria. Smith and Dodsworth (1978) observed 64 children aged three and four, equally divided by age, gender, and social class. Each child's behavior was sampled during free-play conditions three times, on separate occasions, each for a five-minute period. Social class differences were significant on all fantasy play criteria applied (except on mean duration of play episode): time spent in fantasy play per child, mean number of participants, elaboration beyond properties of an object, and replica use of objects (low SES subjects scored higher than higher SES children on this last criterion).

These researchers continue to challenge the contention that SES makes a significant difference in children's sociodramatic play and state that a majority of lower class children exhibited some fantasy play. It is possible that there are substantial differences between the Israeli lower SES sample and the English working-class sample observed by Smith and Dodsworth (1978). But surely there is also a considerable difference in the criteria applied, as pointed out by the authors. If fantasy play is defined as any imitative action or sound or any imitative use of a toy replica, SES differences are considerably smaller than with the Smilansky criteria. Differences in criteria also explain the contradictory findings cited by Fein (1981) and Eiferman (1971). True symbolic play goes much beyond this definition. Manipulating replica toys in rote imitation, or running around and making the sounds of vehicles, even while declaring "I am . . . ," is not the type of play that holds the best promise for enrichment and personal growth. It means not much more than functional play and probably less than constructive play.

In the United States, Christman (1979) observed 48 Mexican-American children, aged three and four, in a structured but familiar play setting during six five-minute sessions. Using the Smilansky Scale, she reports low-level play at both age levels and for both genders.

Among 36 black and white low SES five-year-olds observed in the usual setting of a preschool center, Dansky (1980) found only six children who engaged in sociodramatic play at six five-minute observation sessions during a two-week period.

In a more recent study conducted in Israel and South Africa by Udwin and Shmukler (1981) with a sample of 15 SES and 15 middle-class preschool children in each of the two countries, the effect of socioeconomic level on the occurrence of imaginative play was highly significant. The effect of culture

(Israeli or South African) was nonsignificant when a two-way analysis of variance was applied. For the middle class alone, however, a significant cultural difference was obtained with a test. Analyses were based on two ten-minute observations during indoor and outdoor free play. The use of imagination in play was evaluated on a 5-point scale developed by Singer (1973). Since the reported findings relate to imaginative play, solitary or social, there was also a significant SES and cultural effect on the criterion of interaction with peers. Middle-class children scored higher than lower class children, and Israeli children scored higher on those categories than South African children. Findings were interpreted by the authors in terms of environmental stimulation and parental practices, as well as the opportunity for peer contact.

Table 8.5 summarizes the major details of the previously cited studies.

In view of the empirical evidence presented here from various sources, and in the absence of any contrary findings, we can conclude with confidence that environmental factors have an impact on the child's play behavior. It seems that across various cultures, the level of parental education is the single major background variable that relates to the level of children's make-believe play. Children whose parents have little formal education do not tend to develop the type of imaginative play that their peers, whose parents have more extended formal education, enjoy so much.

THEORETICAL IMPLICATIONS

Findings on cultural and SES differences in dramatic play raise important questions, not only about environmental influences on play, but also about the nature and function of this type of play. Three major issues are raised;

1. Why is the child playing make-believe at all? What developmental needs is the child attempting to satisfy?
2. What are the elements of the play that enable the fulfillment of these needs and the realization of the child's goals and intentions within the framework of make-believe play?
3. Are the motives for playing make-believe universal? If so, why do we find groups of children who do not actualize their needs for make-believe?

Need for Make-Believe Play

In making reference to the child's need or motive for make-believe play, our concern is from the point of view of the overall experiential needs of the growing child and the need for actualization of the child's developing mental,

Table 8.5   Studies on Cultural and SES Differences in
Dramatic and Sociodramatic Play

Investigators	Subjects	Criteria
Smilansky (1968)	4-6.6 Israeli	Preliminary Smilansky scale
Rosen (1974)	5-6, American black low & middle, & white middle	Adaptation of Smilansky scale
Tizard et al. (1976)	3-4, British	Amount of symbolic play
Taler (1976)	5-6, Israeli	Smilansky scale
Smith & Dodsworth (1978)	3-4, British	Fantasy play (time spent, number of participants, elaboration, etc.)
Griffing (1980)	5-6, American black	Smilansky scale
Christman (1979)	3-4, Mexican-American	Smilansky scale
Dansky (1980)	5, low black & white	Amount of sociodramatic play, 5 behavioral categories
Udwin & Shmukler (1981)	4-6, South African	Imaginativeness
Singer (1973)	Israeli, low & middle	Imaginativeness

emotional, and social capacities in relation to the environment. What do we know about this aspect of development? Much of the research on the early stages of symbolic play that was conducted within the framework of developmental psychology and Piagetian theory addressed itself mainly to the cognitive elements underlying the symbolic performance at various age levels. It was from the point of view of the cognitive developmental psychologist. This is exemplified by the terminology used (symbolism, representation, attribution, substitution, sequencing, etc.). Although this body of research contributed a great deal to the understanding of cognitive processes in play, it did not highlight the motivational elements. In order to understand this aspect, we have to look at symbolic play from its earliest formative stages from the point of view of the playing child and to infer underlying motives from the child's actions and verbalizations.

The thesis suggested here is that make-believe play is motivated by the universal need of the child to experience and understand the social environment. Children who make-believe tend to detach themselves from the material properties of the surroundings and instead center on social roles. This property of dramatic play is its principal characteristic and the major distinction between this form of play and all the others. This play is not object centered and is not even activity centered. It is role and theme centered. Without being aware of this distinction, one cannot understand the child's behavior. Play objects might be triggers, raise suggestions for roles, or add some temporary fascination to the play, but they are not the center of the interest. Play objects can be, and frequently are, substituted. This is in sharp contrast to other types of play that coexist with dramatic play at the same age levels. Such contrasting types of play include functional play and goal-oriented constructive play, which may contain make-believe elements. In both of these, the properties of the materials and the nature of the activity itself are the center of the child's interest and satisfaction. In functional and constructive play the child is experiencing and learning about the material world. In dramatic and sociodramatic play the child experiences and learns about the social world.

El'Konin (1971) provides an enlightening example of this distinction. He cites an experiment by Slavina in which children who manipulated play objects according to their material properties were asked what they were playing with. The answers were straightforward: "With blocks, with pebbles." Later, when play things directly suggestive of roles were introduced, the blocks and pebbles received an entirely new meaning. As cited, "The immediate relationship of the child to the objects, which had been determined by their physical qualities, was changed into a relationship mediated by the role adopted by the child" (p. 229). The manipulation was changed into "preparation of dinner," the blocks or pebbles into diverse "food," the frying pans into a plate, and the child himself into a "cook" or a "mama."

These examples highlight the fact that actions and verbalizations during play can be fully understood only from the point of view of the roles assumed by the children involved in the play. This is also the key to answering our first question: Why does the child play make-believe? In the simplest terms, it is the child's way to experience, explore, and learn about roles in the social milieu. It is not by accident that at the earliest stages the prevailing roles are mommies and daddies. The strong identification of the child with the parents is the emotional basis for the child's attempts to be like mommy and daddy, to find out how it feels to do what they do, to behave as they behave. Later this will transfer to using play to experience other roles and other kinds of relationships. Even a well-adjusted child may want to experience in a safe setting how it feels to be an aggressive child (Marshall, 1961) or a baby, a dog, an older child, or the whole range of adults observed in varied roles, professions, and activities.

The aforementioned does not exclude the affective component of play. Make-believe play offers the opportunities for many-faceted expressions of thoughts and feeling, including emotional pressures. But most children usually engage in make-believe just for the fun of the experience. The gay atmosphere that characterizes dramatic and sociodramatic play is easily perceived by the observer.

It is our contention that children's role enactment allows for the experiencing of the complexities of the social world in a manner analogous to the ways in which sensory-motor functioning and constructive activity support experiencing of the properties and potential of the material world.

The gradual transition from solitary to social make-believe mirrors not only the need of the child for the company of peers but also the child's growing awareness of the nature of social relationships. Fuller experiencing of these by means of make-believe invites interaction with partners, joint elaboration of themes, and sharing of ideas and reciprocity.

Necessary Elements of Play

We turn now to our second question: what elements of the play facilitate the satisfaction of the child's experiential needs? We have already pointed out that toy replicas and other materials are not the central elements of need satisfaction. If the hypothesis is accepted that role enactment is at the core of dramatic play, then it seems that imitative behavior is of central significance—acting and speaking like the role model as that model is understood by the child. Indeed, by definition, this is the most obvious element of make-believe play. However, imitation has its limitations. Rote, copy-like imitation, does not satisfy the experimentation need of the child. Analogous to the child's need to experiment with materials and actual things by taking them apart or using them in various ways to see what happens is the child's motivation to experiment with roles, to see how it feels to behave in a variety of ways (be affectionate to the baby doll, to scold it, etc.). As the child's understanding of social relationships grows, imitative acts will be less likely to satisfy experiential needs. The child will want to be like the role model, not merely copy what the role model does. This is where substitutive behavior is needed. It is meant to overcome material constraints to the realization of the child's ideas about the role and the theme. If the child is lacking the appropriate toys, any substitution, even a gesture, will do instead. If the child's fluency of ideas demand a change of scene or a lapse in time, events that cannot be enacted because of circumstantial limitations, verbal substitution will perform the change (make-believe with actions and situations, often designated metacommunications). Verbal elaboration of the theme is the most powerful element of sociodramatic play.

Differences in Development of Play

The third question emerges. Why are there groups of children who do not develop this form of play? This question cannot be answered without reliable cross-cultural data on the early developmental progression of dramatic and sociodramatic play.

Whereas almost all of the basic research on symbolic play has been at the early formative levels, most of the studies on SES and cultural differences in play behavior were concerned with older children. All the work cited above was with three- to six-year-olds. In the work of Piaget, who stressed the primacy of biological disposition and direct, nonmediated experience on early development, this issue was not addressed. His work was done with middle-class infants. This does not mean that Piaget was not aware of the possible impact of the social milieu. In one of his later articles he expressed the hope that cross-cultural research might contribute to better understanding of the influences of culture and the social milieu on developmental progression (Piaget, 1966). Piaget cited research that demonstrates the same sequences in operational tasks in various cultures, although, owing to environmental conditions, in some cultures they will occur considerably later. But Piaget expressed his belief that, "in the area of figurative thinking, one could possibly find everywhere the same age for the appearance of the semiotic function (e.g. symbolic play, mental images, and the development of language), which develops in our culture between one and two years of age" (p. 305). Indeed, there seems to be considerable consistency in the appearance of early imitative acts during the second year. This appears to be the case based on nonformal and somewhat limited observations.

Fein (1981) reports percentages of pretend acts of Guatemalan babies (11–15 months old) from impoverished villages as being similar to those of middle-class American babies (Fenson, Kagan, Kearsley, & Zelazo, 1976; Kagan, Kearsley, & Zelazo, 1978). This study seems to indicate that the disposition toward imitative activity and the basic need for it are universal. In this case, we can assume that it is a typical expression of the infant's growing interest in the social surroundings and the infant's need to assimilate experiences by means of imitation. Lacking additional cross-cultural data, it seems at this time to be too early to make this generalization. It is quite possible, however, that children's imitative acts at early ages will be found in all intact environments. If so, why does not this imitative tendency develop in all cultures as it does in the sociodramatic play observed in middle-class Western cultures?

The hypothesis is offered that the transition from imitative acts toward substitutive behavior, especially verbally expressed substitutions for actions and situations, is dependent on environmental stimulation. Without it the imitative tendency will be extinguished or will remain at the concrete level, though there is very little evidence to support this hypothesis. Whereas object substitution has been frequently studied, make-believe play with actions and situations has not earned attention in Piaget-oriented research, which has tended to concentrate on object use activities and to neglect verbalizations during play. Also, as already noted, no attention has been paid to adult influences on play development.

It is not surprising that Soviet psychologists, who tend to regard cultural factors as central for development (Vygotsky, 1934; Luria & Yudovich, 1959), have addressed themselves to the study of environmental influences on symbolic play. El'Konin (1971) describes a progression in object use at the early stages of play development as a function of adult suggestions and demonstrations. He cites Soviet experiments on object substitution that show that the child will "feed" only those "animals" that were "fed" by the adult, using only those objects that the adult has used. There is no transfer in object substitution up to about age two. Later, following many adult demonstrations, the child will generalize the principle of substitutive behavior. Although the Soviet research reported by El'Konin deals with object substitution and not with verbal make-believe for actions and situations, it does suggest that the substitutive element in sociodramatic play might be a learned one.

According to observational data (Smilansky, 1968), high SES children enjoy an environment that is conducive to make-believe, in the sense of relevant parental influences, both direct and indirect.

High SES parents tend to provide some sort of tutoring in make-believe play skills because it keeps the child satisfied and conveniently busy and because they probably enjoyed sociodramatic play as children. This tutoring can take the form of suggestions ("Why don't you take your baby for a walk?" "Maybe you two can take your children to the seashore." "Don't forget to prepare food!"), or even participation ("All right, let's pretend I am the father, but I am busy at work, so you cannot disturb me too much."). In general, there is very little real investment in these forms of play tutoring, but there is a gain of peaceful time for housework. But even rare remarks convey the message of substitutive behavior.

Low SES parents were not observed to encourage make-believe, even though there were dolls and imitative replicas in the homes. Excessive doll play was regarded by some mothers with hesitancy, perhaps because of a fear of too much "imagining" (Smilansky, 1968). Recent observations point to greater acceptance of make-believe play but not to changes in amount of parental encouragement.

Smilansky's observational data show that high SES parents tend to make social relationships and experiences better understood and thus provide the child with a wealth of content areas to be expressed within the framework of themes and roles.

The importance of mediated experiences for make-believe play is demonstrated in Marshall's study (1961), based on structured home observations and interviews. A comparison of parental behavior (all high SES) of "good" players as opposed to "poor" players showed that they provided wider informational experiences for their children about dramatic play topics.

The Marshall study pointed also to the effect of the emotional climate of the home. There may be additional environmental factors related to sociodramatic play, such as encouragement of peer contacts at home and availability of materials.

It is our contention that without direct fostering of make-believe skills, indirect influences will not be effective. But if the child has acquired the skills essential for sociodramatic play, mainly the use of substitutive behavior, indirect experiences may contribute to the quality, diversity, and richness of the child's sociodramatic play repertoire.

In concluding the discussion on SES and sociodramatic play, it seems justified to state that there is well-founded evidence about the existence of differences but much remains unknown. The main questions remain about the age at which SES differences appear and in which play elements the differences are most salient.

PRACTICAL IMPLICATIONS OF THE FINDINGS

If we take present knowledge about SES and cultural differences into consideration, what course of action would be most advisable? It seems clear that some kind of early intervention is implied in order to help all children to benefit from the experiences that pretend play can offer. On the assumption that the need, motivation, and capacity for make-believe are universal, the next step is to facilitate its actualization starting at the earliest stages. The following recommendations seem warranted in view of the current level of knowledge.

1. Sympathetic adults can take on the role of play facilitators instead of the parents. It can be done in nurseries, day care centers, mother-child clinics, home-based infant programs with paraprofessionals, in fact, in any framework that has direct access to infants and young children. Numerous studies have documented the feasibility and effectiveness of even short-term intervention.
2. Parents for whom this type of play seems remote or not proper should not

be taught or pressed to change their behavior in order to promote make-believe play. They can, of course, be sensitized to the need of the child for this type of experience and to the benefits it contains for the child's growth. But the direct intervention in this field should remain in the hand of the caretakers outside the family.

3. Infant caretakers and nursery and kindergarten educators should receive systematic training and inservice guidance in the theoretical issues related to symbolic play and in possible methods of promoting and enriching the child's efforts to enact roles and themes.

4. Intervention should be skill oriented and not content oriented; that is, the purpose is to provide children with tools to express and actualize their needs, to experience the roles that fascinate them to their fullest and, accordingly, to enact and develop themes with content that interests them.

   It seems that the basic skills that should be emphasized at early age levels are the ones that characterize well-developed play of older children: role declaration; make-believe with objects, actions, and situations (substitution); cooperation; and elaboration of themes according to role. All of these should be supported, of course, with sensitivity to the child's level of play development and in congruence with the content the child is trying to express.

5. Since there is experience only in fostering sociodramatic play of older preschoolers, it is important that intervention at early age levels should be open, creative, and diverse so that we can learn what methods are more successful and which do not affect play in the desired direction.

6. Intervention at all age levels should be based on diagnosis of the child's play level. While the Smilansky scale for evaluation of sociodramatic play proved to be effective for the three to six age level, there is no experience with it for younger age groups. Evaluation tools for the one to three age level have yet to be constructed. There are promising beginnings derived from Piagetian theory (McCune-Nicolich, 1977), but further work on assessment of symbolic play and verbalization during play seems important for educational intervention and for research purposes.

In concluding the implications of findings about SES differences in sociodramatic play and advocating intervention to help children realize their need and potential for this important form of experience, support can be found in Dewey's (1902) warnings against misinterpretation of the child study movement delivered at the beginning of this century:

> It is the danger of the new education that it regards the child's present powers and interests as something finally significant in themselves. . . . Its genuine meaning is in the propulsion it affords toward a higher level. . . . Con-

tinuous initiation, continuous starting of activities that do not arrive is, for all practical purposes, as bad as the continued repression of initiative. . . . It is as if the child were forever tasting and never eating. (pp. 14–15)

This last sentence describes with great accuracy the behavior of children for whom adult intervention should not be denied.

REFERENCES

Christman, M. L. (1979). A look at sociodramatic play among Mexican-American children. *Childhood Education, 56,* 106–109.

Dansky, J. L. (1980). Cognitive consequences of sociodramatic play and exploration training for economically disadvantaged preschoolers. *Journal of Child Psychology and Psychiatry, 21,* 47–58.

Dewey, J. (1902). *The child and the curriculum.* Chicago: The University of Chicago Press.

Eiferman, R. (1971). Social play in childhood. In R. E. Herron & B. Sutton-Smith (Eds.), *Child's play* (pp. 270–297). New York: John Wiley & Sons.

El'Konin, D. (1971). Symbolics and its functions in the play of children. In R. E. Herron & B. Sutton-Smith (Eds.), *Child's play* (pp. 221–230). New York: John Wiley & Sons.

Fein, G. G. (1981). Pretend play in childhood: An interpretive review. *Child Development, 52,* 1095–1118.

Fenson, L., Kagan, J., Kearsley, R. B., & Zelazo, P. R. (1976). The developmental progression of manipulative play in the first two years. *Child Development, 47,* 232–235.

Freyberg, J. T. (1973). Increasing the imaginative play of urban disadvantaged kindergarten children through systematic training. In J. L. Singer (Ed.), *The child's world of make-believe* (pp. 129–154). New York: Academic Press.

Griffing, P. (1974). *The relationship between socioeconomic status and sociodramatic play among black kindergarten children.* Unpublished doctoral dissertation, Ohio State University, Columbus).

Griffing, P. (1980). The relationship between sociometric status and sociodramatic play among black kindergarten children. *Genetic Psychology Monograph, 101,* 3–34.

Kagan, J., Kearsley, R. B. & Zelazo, P. R. (1978). *Infancy: Its place in human development.* Cambridge, MA: Harvard University Press.

Klein, P. (1986). Mediated learning experience. In D. Tamir, T. Brazelton, & A. Russell (Eds.), *Stimulation and intervention in infant development* (pp. 59–75). London: Freund.

Luria, A. R., & Yudovich, F. I. (1959). *Speech and the development of mental processes in the child.* London: Staples.

Marshall, H. R. (1961). Relations between home experiences and children's use of language in play interaction with peers. *Psychological Monographs, 75*(5), 509.

McCune-Nicolich, L. (1977). Beyond sensorimotor intelligence: Assessment of symbolic maturity through analysis of pretend play. *Merrill-Palmer Quarterly, 23,* 2.

Murphy, L. (1956). *Methods for the study of personality in young children.* New York: Basic Books.

Piaget, J. (1966). Need and significance of cross-cultural studies in genetic psychology. *International Journal of Psychology, 1,* 3–13.

Rosen, C. E. (1974). The effects of sociodramatic play on problem solving behavior among culturally disadvantaged children. *Child Development, 45,* 920–927.

Sigel, I., & McBaine, B. (1966). *Cognitive competence and level of symbolism among five year old children.* Paper read at the American Psychological Association, New York, September 1966.

Singer, J. L. (1973). *The child's world of make-believe.* New York: Academic Press.

Smilansky, S. (1968). *The effect of sociodramatic play on disadvantaged preschool children.* New York: Wiley.

Smilansky, S., Shefatya, L., & Frenkel, E. (1976). *Mental development of infants from two ethnic groups.* Jerusalem: The Henrietta Szold Institute for Research in the Behavioral Sciences.

Smith, P. K., & Dodsworth, C. (1978). Social class differences in the fantasy play of preschool children. *Journal of Genetic Psychology,* Tel Aviv University, Israel.

Taler, E. (1976). *Social status of kindergarten children and their level of sociodramatic play.* Unpublished master's thesis, Tel Aviv University, Department of Psychology.

Tizard, B., Philps, J., & Plewis, I. (1976). Play in preschool centers: Effects on play of the child's social class and of the educational orientation of the center. *Journal of Child Psychology and Psychiatry, 17,* 265–274.

Udwin, O., & Shmukler, D. (1981). The influence of socio-cultural economic and home background on children's ability to engage in imaginative play. *Developmental Psychology, 17,* 66–72.

Vygotsky, L. S. (1934). *Thought and language.* New York: M.I.T. & Wiley.

CHAPTER 9

Children in Health Care: When the Prescription is Play

Elizabeth Kampe

The playful nature of children is legendary in our culture. Recent writings point out that in actuality this perception may indeed be mostly legend as the stress inherent in adult life increasingly encroaches on the magic world of childhood. Commercially, we still adhere to that legend and use the toy industry to support that faith (Sutton-Smith, 1986). It is the general belief that children can play anywhere and at anytime. Observation of children in health care settings is providing a test of that hypothesis.

It is noted that children need space, time, and materials in order to play (Johnson & Ershler, 1981). A supportive adult and freedom from distractions and bodily needs also facilitate play. Are these conditions met for children in health care settings? Not all children play as easily as others, yet play has been demonstrated to help children deal with the stress of hospitalization, with medical procedures, and with separation, and it also brings about an increase in their levels of understanding. Play is often thought to be something that happens when "work" is over, or as a means to avoid the more serious "for real" aspects of human endeavor, as exemplified by the phrase "quit playing around and get down to business." This chapter will draw on research and experience that demonstrate the functions of play in the effective coping by children with the stresses associated with their health care experiences. These experiences associated with treatment occur in hospitals, clinic waiting rooms, emergency rooms, physician's offices in private or group practices, and center-based health maintenance organizations (HMOs). Most of the information available comes, however, from the study of children's reactions to short-term medical/surgical hospital inpatient admissions.

HOSPITALIZATION AND HEALTH CARE EXPERIENCES
AS A SOURCE OF STRESS

The principal factors making hospitalization stressful for children can be listed as follows: the unfamiliar environment, separation from family, physical pain and discomfort, a heightened sense of vulnerability, and changes in parent-child relationships that result from the interaction of other conditions on both child and family. In addition to these external sources of stress are those related to developmental issues (Poster & Betz, 1983).

Children between the ages of two and seven are particularly vulnerable to the effects of hospitalization because this age group is characterized by developmental concerns about autonomy and control of one's bodily functions. Fear of abandonment and mutilation (Oremland & Oremland, 1973; Petrillo & Sanger, 1980) are both developmentally based and prevalent. This is also the stage of cognitive development when causality is understood within a framework of concrete operational thought (Bibace & Walsh, 1980; Piaget, 1962).

Stress may be generated by the effects of a large, complex organization, such as a hospital, on both the individual and the family. The organizational structure is oriented toward groups rather than individuals. The organization's procedures, customs, and routines are often interpreted by the individual patient as depersonalizing. Choices are limited, if available at all, and privacy can be perceived as compromised even during the best of psychosocially oriented care. Dependence on strangers for basic needs is unsettling, and the necessary restriction in activity caused by interventions, equipment, and illness itself contributes to a sense of powerlessness.

Starting in the 1940s the effects of hospitalization on children have been noted in the literature. Most of the studies have relied on parental reports and there was not much variety among the conditions experienced by the children. Prugh, Staub, Sands, Kirschbaum, & Lenihan (1953) found that 58 percent of the control group and 44 percent of the experimental group (those permitting parental visiting and opportunities for play) were reported by parents to exhibit at least a moderate degree of disturbance. Burned children have been reported to continue to be severely upset at a rate of 81 percent even two to five years after their hospitalizations (Woodward, 1959). Research results usually present a picture of temporary upset for ten days to two weeks postdischarge and improvement in psychological status by two months after the children leave the hospital. Some retrospective studies suggest that extended or repeated hospitalizations prior to age five or major medical/surgical interventions affect self-esteem, anxiety level, and level of dependence in later years. Douglas (1975) found adjustment problems in 22% of the adolescents who had experienced hospitalization of more than one week before age five and problems in 38% of those who had experienced repeated hospitalization. Quinton and Rutter (1976), in replicating Douglas's study, found that repeated hospitalizations, rather than a single hospital experience, before or after the age of five were associated with emotional disturbance at age ten.

Given the numbers of children involved in hospitalization (4.5 million per year, according to the Association for the Care of Children's Health [ACCH], 1989), and those seen in offices for their first visit each year (13.8 children per 1,000 of the population under 15 years of age, according to the National Center for Health Statistics, 1985), the role of play is an important consideration in the overall well-being of this group. Information on the potential of play as a stress reliever, understanding of the conditions necessary for the production of play, and discrimination about what kinds of play would be most beneficial in a given case merit consideration.

Since the 1940s concerned people have been involved in facilitating play for children in hospitals. Now in the 1990s health care is occurring in a variety of settings: the playrooms of inpatient units, play areas in clinics, HMOs, emergency rooms, and in such diverse settings as the toy box in the private physician's office or amid the high-tech equipment of a pediatric intensive care unit. Following are glimpses of children at play in these various settings. The questions to be asked about these pictures of play are

1. To what degree can play prevent problems?
2. Can certain kinds of play materials be more effective than other kinds in enhancing children's play?
3. What should the role of the adult be and should that person receive special training?

How Do Children Play in Health Care Settings?

In the inpatient playroom of a medical/surgical unit, Harry, age five, is climbing on the floor pillow. Harry had been operated on for a brain tumor and has had several subsequent surgical procedures. He comes to the playroom attached to a portable oxygen tank with a long hose. He is nonverbal and unable to walk or stand without support. Although he is extremely small and fragile, play makes him feel big. Perched on top of a huge floor pillow, he is "king of the mountain," and cautiously approaching adults fall backward in response to his pushes. He relishes the opportunity to throw dozens of tennis balls in all directions and observe the adult trying to catch them all at once, clearly caught in his great power.

Steven, age six, is imaginatively reenacting his experience of having been in a coma. He lies on a floor mat, hauls himself into a sitting position, and says, "I'm alive!" Steven now puts the adult in the role of his mother and then runs away by scooting across the floor and refusing to come home. Sometimes he says, "Mother, can I go outside?" The pretend mother says, "No, it's too cold, you must wear your boots." Steven starts to protest and disobey the play rules! The accident that had resulted in his hospitalization occurred when he played near a dumpster, against his mother's orders.

Kathy, at eight, is locked in by a temporary loss of motor function. She has a weak grasp and a three-inch swipe of one hand available as movement for the creation of play. A pile of foam blocks and a long foam rubber tube enable her to wreak havoc on a peaceful neighborhood with towers that would never fall down. Amid gales of laughter, the peace ends as disaster strikes. Kathy had been traumatically injured by an automobile as she was riding her bike on the streets of her peaceful suburban neighborhood.

Playdough is out on the table and a child who received a skin graft uses it to make "skin." Another child cuts, cuts, and cuts the dough until his share is in little bits and crumbles. Nearby, a child in a spica cast from upper chest to below the knee is drawing a picture of a hamster in a cage. At the water table a toddler splashes with glee and a serious-faced seven-year-old squirts water from a syringe into a long tube. He is waiting for surgery to repair the dislocation of the opening of his urethra (Oremland, 1980).

There is a corner of the playroom with a sofa for parents. It has a low table and books that seem to invite a quiet retreat from the usual level of activity. Here, a mother reads aloud from a picture book while the child, thumb in mouth, drapes herself over one of the mother's knees and stares into space. A preteen youngster idly moves around the room, expressionless, pushing the intravenous (IV) pole attached to fine tubing that ends up in the bandaged and taped area at the back of his left hand. He watches the other children, sighs, and stares out the window. The child life specialist, with training and knowledge of the interface between child development and health care stress, draws his attention to a computer game. Soon he is actively engaged in electronically destroying and constructing, using his free hand. Gradually his affect returns, and his eyes sparkle as he grimaces at the screen.

Down the hall, in a two-bed room, a four-year-old repeatedly shuts the play cow in the barn and then opens the door. Her mom, in a nearby chair, watches and responds, "Where is the cow? Oh, you found him!" Farther down the hall, a child is representing the steps in getting an IV started using a stuffed bear and real medical equipment. The nurse is about to show the child photographs of other patients attached to IVs who are involved in various activities In the teen lounge four adolescents are arguing over a script for the closed-circuit TV station. They are planning the presentation of a program about living with diabetes.

A tour that includes six youngsters and their parents has just returned from visiting the day surgery suite and has seen the beds where the children, attended by their parents, will be when the anesthesia wears off. Hospital-related equipment is laid out for the children to explore and play with, while a child life specialist answers questions.

In the pediatric waiting area of a health maintenance organization, a child life specialist has helped two preteens, strangers until ten minutes ago, laugh and talk to each other during a game of "Pictionary." A three-year-old and her mother are exploring the contents of a play medical kit. The child life specialist leaves the teens to introduce herself to the mother and is soon listening to a developmental concern and reports of observations of the child's behavior during routine medical visits. It is often a battle to get through a simple routine physical examination. The specialist begins to discuss ways in which the parent might help her child to prepare for, and cope with, this visit. The child life specialist begins to play doctor with the toddler, incorporating a process of desensitization.

These are all examples of some of the many ways in which play can be used by children in health care settings. There are a number of interesting contrasts to be observed. First, there are children who play at more elaborate levels than others do. Different forms of play are represented, including sensory motor (splashing in water), exploratory (manipulating a stethoscope), functional use of symbolic toys (medical kit), sociodramatic (the scenes of mothers and naughty children, the teenagers writing a joint script), expressive (making playdough skin, drawing the hamster, water shot through hoses), and games with rules (Pictionary, video games). Analysis of the content of the symbolic play shows that play has been used as a way in which to express fear (cutting the dough), understand an experience (the symbolic enactment of rule breaking), or reverse an outcome (being king of the mountain). Although these interpretations of the content might be viewed differently, in each case the play contributes significantly to the child's creation of meaning from experience. When the act is symbolized, it helps the player gain some control over the event and allows greater understanding of life experiences.

Included among the examples was one child who was not playing and seemed withdrawn and disengaged. Other children like this can be in found in any cross-sectional view of hospitalized children. Not all children play, and children do not all use play in the same way. Why this is so will be discussed presently.

Can Play Help Children in Hospitals?

In approaching the available literature relative to this question, one is struck by what Thompson (1985, 1988) has pointed out in his research reviews. Two apparently opposite pictures emerge, each with a different theoretical basis and each with some supporting evidence. One position is that play is used by children to reduce anxiety caused by stress (Erickson, 1963; Piaget, 1962). The other position is that play behavior actually declines in certain stressful conditions or when arousal is too great (Burstein & Meichenbaum, 1979; Tisza, Hurvitz, & Angoff, 1970). One can think of the hospitalized child shrieking in protest or withdrawn and vigilant. There is no play; the energies of the individual are being used in defense against perceived attack or in a quiet withdrawal and sense of hopelessness. The examples cited above serve to illustrate both of these processes. Why do some children play and others do not? What are the predetermining conditions? Is play more effective than other means of reducing stress?

Studies of hospitalized children have shown that although some disruption occurs, play opportunities do help with adjustment to the hospital (Burstein & Meichenbaum, 1979; Cataldo, Bessman, Packer, Pearson, & Rogers, 1979; Pearson, Cataldo, Tureman, Bessman, & Rogers, 1980; Tisza et al., 1970). Play provides opportunities to establish supportive relationships with adults and other children and promotes a sense of mastery, as well as a sense of continuity, with the child's life outside health care. Children in intensive care units are reported to profit from having adults play with them even though they exhibit little spontaneous play behavior when left alone (Cataldo et al., 1979; Pearson et al., 1980). This observation of the dramatic change in ability to use play when it is facilitated by an adult raises questions about whether the power of the relationship may be just as effective as the play activity itself.

Evidence for a relationship between level of anxiety and play behavior is presented by Gilmore (1966) who found an increased tendency for hospitalized children to select material for play that was particularly relevant to their condition. However, Burstein and Meichenbaum (1979) found that the children they studied who were the least defensive before surgery had spent significantly more time playing with medically related toys before surgery and also had less postoperative anxiety. The researchers called this "doing the work of worry" and saw in the play an opportunity for cognitive anticipation and rehearsal. In this same study, it is reported that highly defensive children avoided presurgical play with hospital-related toys and reported higher levels of anxiety following hospitalization. This finding points to an optimal level of arousal for play and also underlines another important variable, the defensiveness of individual children. This characteristic interacted with the level of anxiety to produce a coping response that allowed or precluded play as helpful. The nature of a child's play and, indeed, whether the child plays at all reflect, among other things, the individual's style of coping. The authors conclude that moderate amounts of anxiety bring about or enhance the "work of worry."

Clatsworthy (1981) used 30-minute play sessions conducted by a nurse therapist. The control group showed a level of anxiety higher than that shown on admission, while the play intervention group maintained their initial level of anxiety. Schwartz, Albino, and Tedesco (1983) found play that was unrelated to hospital themes to be equally effective in control of anxiety level as play with related materials. Their experimental group, using the related materials, was less anxious at the time of anesthesia induction. These studies did not have groups to control for the effect of adult attention or to compare the results with child-controlled play. Therefore, the role of play per se in altering children's emotional distress remains unclear. Lockwood (1970) proposed that situational doll play sessions on the day of admission lessened children's defensive behavior and helped to focus their fears and anxieties on a more clearly perceived reality, that of the doctors and/or medical procedures. This seems to support the idea that play can not only reflect a child's willingness to confront issues but also in structured settings may facilitate children's spontaneous play by reducing initial anxiety through adult guidance.

The question of play's efficacy in helping children deal with the experiences of health care is then answered from the perspectives of both observations and research. The answer seems to be in the affirmative under certain conditions and for certain children. What then are these conditions? Is one of the conditions an interested, involved, and supportive adult? Are other important conditions the level of play ability of the individual child, the individual coping style, and/or the kinds of toys that are available to that child in the light of the condition?

Toys Appropriate for Enhancing Play in Health Care Settings

Most studies compare issue-related toys to unrelated activities. From observation it is known, however, that children use many forms of play and many kinds of toys. Miniature hospital figures and furniture and anatomic dolls with abdomens that unsnap and miniature organs attached with velcro are examples of issue-specific materials. Hospital storerooms offer interesting discards of clean tubing, cups, syringes, bandages, etc. (McCue, 1988) that can be used by children in more personal ways. Toys that are just like those at home or school offer the comfort of continuity and give the child a sense of competence and predictability. A favorite toy from home is usually a strong source of emotional support. Electronic toys and video games offer play that requires a minimum of physical energy (Wilson, 1988) and can be adapted to the needs of children with physical disabilities so that they can be operated with switches responsive to light movement.

Child life specialists view toys as tools for the development of relationships with peers and staff, a means of creative expression, a catalyst for the mastery of a new environment, and an important link to home when a child brings a most favored play object to the hospital.

What Are the Special Characteristics of Children Who Play Under Stress?

The concept of locus of control has been applied to thinking about children in the hospital. Children with an internal orientation or locus of control perceive that there is a relationship between their own acts and the outcomes of those acts (Werner, 1984). People of any age with an internal locus of control are less anxious, less influenced by others, more flexible, and more inquisitive. These characteristics facilitate coping in health care settings. The adults' role, according to Bolig, Fernie, and Klein (1986) is "to respond to and elaborate upon children's action, ideas and roles" (p. 101). In order for the child to benefit from play, the actions of the adult must be aimed at insuring that the control of the activity remains with the child.

Besides a characteristic internal locus of control, resilient children also have the ability to fantasize and to control their impulses. These are children who use play and relationships with ease to assist in coping with their stress. Bolig and Weedle (1988) caution that children with these characteristics can have their natural resiliency weakened by too many adult interventions focused on information-giving and compliance with the adult structure. These two conditions are often characteristic of situations in which adults have planned preparation programs or activities for children who anticipate health care encounters.

Can Play Be Used in Preparation for Hospitalization and Medical Procedures?

Play can be used by adults as the context within which information about hospitalization and health care procedures can be imparted, as well as a means of observing and clarifying children's misconceptions. It requires a knowledgeable adult who is able to distinguish between the distortion of reality in the service of feeling expression and the distortion of reality due to a lack of information or the inability to understand the information. The imparting of information is called "preparation" or "emotional preparation" by child life specialists or "patient education" by nursing personnel. In an inpatient setting, nursing personnel, childlife workers, or both will prepare children. In an HMO setting the child life specialist might prepare a child and family individually for a specific procedure or referral. This occurs most regularly as a prehospital visit, a tour, and/or a puppet show that introduces the child and family to the setting. Research by Bates and Browne (1986) indicates that the provision of information, encouragement for expression of feelings, and the establishment of a relationship with hospital staff are the three major objectives of these kinds of preparation programs. The use of tours is the most common method.

This continues to be the case despite study findings that information and modeling are the most effective methods of reducing anxiety. Studies of puppet play and the uses of puppets are less clear in their outcomes. Frequently the hospital preadmission tour is accompanied by a puppet show. Other variables that contribute to the effectiveness of preparation intervention are the age of the child, the child's developmental stage, the timing of the preparation, the child's previous experiences, the level of parental anxiety, and the type of nursing care that will be available.

A recent study at Phoenix Children's Hospital (Wolfer, Gaynard, Goldberger, Laidley, & Thompson, 1988) found that those children between the ages of 3 and 13 who were admitted for acute conditions and received experimental child life care were significantly better at coping effectively during procedures and had a better posthospital adjustment and physical recovery. The program highlighted the use of preparation as part of an ongoing interactional process between the child life specialist and the child's family. Child life specialists formed relationships with the child and with the family within half an hour of admission and utilized a personified cloth doll as a teaching tool. Children were prepared for procedures and participated in developmentally appropriate play in play rooms, as well as in guided medical play timed to occur after their procedures. The authors state at the end of their study that the question of timing, information, or support as the crucial element in the effectiveness of their interventions remains unanswered. The role of play itself was not directly addressed. The central role of the adult in enabling the child and family to cope, rather than focus on the uses of spontaneous play, leads to a further discussion of the role of the adult in the play of children.

IS ADULT INTERVENTION IN PLAY
USEFUL OR NECESSARY?

The examples of children using play in health care settings illuminate the role of the child life specialist. This is the title of a person with special training and knowledge about the interface between child development and the stress of health care. Knowledge about the impact of family, culture, and systems interactions, as well as the ability to assess sources of stress and coping responses, are part of the expertise of a person trained in child life. So, too, is a thorough understanding of the role of play and other expressive activities and their uses in alleviating stress and supporting healthy development.

The profession of child life has been developed on the premise that adult intervention with children under the stress of hospitalization and/or health care procedures can help prevent and/or ameliorate both the immediate and the long-term negative effects of the experience of children's development and behavior. The focus of adult intervention in this profession has shifted dramatically during the last 25 years. It has gone from an emphasis on the facilitation of spontaneous play as a means of expression, to more adult-directed forms of intervention such as preparation and stress management techniques in which play materials are used. This is a reversal of the previous passively endured experiences into current active representations and other psychodynamically based rationales.

Often the adult's goal is to impart information in a playful way. To some degree the moving forces behind this shift are the increased acuity of children admitted to hospitals, the shortened stay for some, the extensive stays of technology-dependent children, and the increased use of ambulatory pediatric services. In the United States, the financing system for health services is also a factor. Consequently child life specialists are now required to classify patients according to need for services and their competency in coping as a way to set priorities for the allocation of their services. Resources for the facilitation of play are not yet the right of every hospitalized child, and evidence must still be presented to show the efficacy of adult time spent in specific interventions. Play has never been easy to quantify, nor is it often perceived as a valuable activity in which adults should engage. Given the evidence presented thus far about the positive effects of play on children's behavior, and recognizing the limits of time, anxiety levels, lack of play skills, or a conducive context that may confront children in health care settings, adult intervention seems a necessary corollary of emotional care contributing, as it does, to the efficacy of the physical care.

The adult is needed to provide a context within which the play of the child can be supported and used. As seen in the examples presented earlier, how play works to reduce anxiety and what form it takes will vary from child to child and situation to situation. It can be expressive, allow mastery of skills or experiences, provide the context for a supportive friendship, provide information, or divert the mind and relax the body.

Research on Adult Intervention

In a study by Milos and Reiss (1982) an attempt was made to demonstrate why play helps to reduce anxiety. In their conclusion the researchers note that the form of the play did not matter but quality did. Their findings support the need for adult intervention. They explored two hypotheses: (1) that play provides a less threatening situation within which the child can experiment with problem solving and (2) that play reduces anxiety through a process of desensitization and repetition of play themes (Erickson, 1963; Piaget, 1962) or by a sense of mastery over a fragmented problem that increases feelings of self-efficacy (Bandura, 1977). The clinical situation studied was separation anxiety.

Sixty-four children between the ages of two and a half and five and a half years were assigned to one of three play conditions, each one using a doll house and figures representing a school/home situation and control condition of nonthematic toys (puzzles, blocks, and crayons). The following play conditions relative to the adult's role were set up.

- Free play that permitted separation-relevant play according to the child's wishes.
- Directed play in which instruction focused the child's attention on separation play.
- A modeling condition wherein the child watched the adult play out a separation theme.

The children in the three play conditions did not differ significantly among groups in regard to their pretest and post-test anxiety levels. Separation-relevant play was, however, associated with lower post-test separation anxiety when compared with the control condition. The form of the separation play was relatively unimportant. The higher the quality of play, the lower the degree of separation anxiety. Quality was measured by the extent to which the child expressed emotional involvement, and an effort was made to master the issue and work out a resolution. In this case, a relationship, a clinical interpretation, and a direction for how to play were not essential for the play to be effective. Even if the child only watched someone else playing, anxiety was reduced. Adult intervention can take a variety of forms provided it allows the opportunity for the child to experience emotional involvement in the play and to facilitate the observation or creation of a resolution to the issues at hand. Whether the nurse uses a teddy bear to demonstrate the site of a postoperative drainage tube or a child undergoing the experience of the IV treatment (kelation therapy) for lead poisoning shoots water from a syringe, the ability to create meaning through the use of emotions and imagination (the capacity to conceptualize "as if") determines the potential for the activity to be helpful to the child in stress.

Oremland (1988) emphasizes that it is essential to observe a child's play response in the light of that child's experience with medical procedures, either to discover meaning or to offer support. In order to keep the child as an active participant, spontaneity must be allowed for, even in adult-structured activity such as "preparation." The preparation play itself induces a degree of stress and, optimally, an experience that is manageable. Supportive relationships can enhance the expression of meaning. Oremland cautions against interpreting content of which the child may not be aware since it may be expressed in play and suggests verbal comments within the framework of the activity.

McCue (1988), in discussing the adult role in medical play, states that the role taken by an adult should always be the result of a thoughtful and conscious decision. The benefits, in contrast to those resulting from spontaneous, child-directed play, should always be carefully evaluated.

Who Should Play with Children?

From this discussion it can be concluded that thorough training is needed to achieve adult involvement that can effectively assist the child in overcoming the various barriers to play that are indigenous to health care settings.

Gibbons and Boren (1985) state that nurses often cite both lack of time and lack of know-how about ways to incorporate play into the routine care of children. The researchers recommend that through playing with children, nurses can gain added information for their assessments of developmental and stress levels. Wilson (1988) sees in the future a shared responsibility between nurses and child life specialists for play, especially in ambulatory, intensive care, and infant units. If care-by-parent units develop more, parents will have additional opportunities to play with their children. If technicians handle the increasing mechanically complex aspects of monitoring and treatment equipment, nurses will develop into coordinators of care with more time to devote to assistance with coping and to development of meaningful relationships.

Parents can be supportive of play for children in health care. Child life specialists include as part of their role encouraging and assisting parents to play with their children. A study by Gutstein (1980) looked at parent involvement in the preparation for tonsillectomies of 34 children aged four to five. Parents who focused children's activities and pointed out relevant aspects of the environment while the children played with hospital and surgical equipment and who also based their behavior on the children's behavior found their children to be more actively involved in play and to show more information-seeking and rehearsal behavior. Not all parents are equally capable of providing this kind of support for their children. The hospital setting is sometimes not an optimal one in which to learn new skills. If parents have enough support, however, they can be the best persons to support their own children both in play and in other coping behaviors.

WHAT DO WE STILL NEED TO KNOW?

Research on play in health care settings that is experimental in design is limited to the study of children's emotional states. It would be interesting in the future, suggests Thompson (1988), to look at the capacity of play to contribute to the maintenance of development, increase sociability, provide knowledge, and enhance self-esteem. In the future of health care, play will occur in more difficult circumstances (Wilson, 1988). Children in hospitals will be more acutely ill and more in need of facilitation in order to be able to play. Nurses and parents will become increasingly involved. Child life specialists, with their training in child development, assessing stress levels and coping capacities, and understanding of the special role of play, will be increasingly challenged.

There is still the unanswered question of exactly what are the means by which the activity of play helps children. Although there is much common wisdom about the effectiveness of play therapy in hospital settings (Phillips, 1988), the empirical research remains sparse. In fact, Phillips suggests that this common wisdom may actually get in the way of the pursuit of research. He also points to the current lack of research with children who are chronically ill or who have repeated hospitalizations.

What makes it so difficult to use empirical evidence to guide the clinical uses of play? Phillips (1985) offers the following:

1. There is no conceptual model of how children are helped or changed by play therapy.
2. The strength of the common wisdom that play works may have functioned to prevent the needed research.
3. It is difficult in a clinical setting to withhold a possible "cure."

Empirical research that would clarify the workings of play as a contributor to the health care of children would assist adults in meeting the increased challenge of more seriously ill and chronically ill children, and the shorter time of most hospitalizations.

In summary, the context of play is useful to children under the stress generated by out-of-home health care. Play provides a context for understanding and creating meaning, for regaining a sense of self-control in a strange environment, for building relationships, for learning new information, and for making pain and discomfort more bearable or waiting more tolerable. The context of play can promote relationships and create optimism and the potential for releasing humor. Wherever adults really help children with coping, the context of play will be created, nurtured, and valued.

REFERENCES

ACCH (1989). *Children-hospitals week planning guide.* Washington, DC: Association for the Care of Children's Health.

Bandura, A. (1977). *Social learning theory.* Englewood Cliffs, NJ: Prentice-Hall.

Bates, T. A., & Browne, M. (1986). Preparation of children for hospitalization and surgery: A review of the literature. *Journal of Pediatric Nursing, 14,* 230–239.

Bibace, R., & Walsh, M. E. (1980). Development of children's concepts of illness. *Pediatrics, 66*, 912–917.

Bolig, R., Fernie, D. E., & Klein, E. I. (1986). Unstructured play in hospital settings: An internal locus of control rationale. *Children's Health Care, 15*, 101–107.

Bolig, R., & Weedle, K. (1988). Resiliency and hospitalization of children. *Children's Health Care, 16*(4), 255–260.

Burstein, S., & Meichenbaum, D. (1979). The work of worry in children undergoing surgery. *Journal of Abnormal Child Psychology, 7*, 121–132.

Cataldo, M. F., Bessman, C. A., Packer, L. H., Pearson, J. E. R., & Rogers, M. C. (1979). Behavioral assessment for pediatric intensive care units. *Journal of Applied Behavioral Analysis, 12*, 83–97.

Clatsworthy, S. M. (1981). Therapeutic play: Effects on hospitalized children. *Children's Health Care, 9*, 108–113.

Douglas, J. W. B. (1975). Early hospital admission and later disturbances of behavior and learning. *Developmental Medicine and Child Neurology, 17*, 456–480.

Erikson, E. H. (1963). *Childhood and society*. New York: W. W. Norton.

Gilmore, J. B. (1966). The role of anxiety and cognitive factors in children's play behavior. *Child Development, 37*, 397–416.

Gibbons, M., & Boren, H. (1985). Stress reduction: A spectrum of strategies in pediatric oncology nursing. *Nursing Clinics of North America, 20*(1), 83–103.

Gutstein, S. E. (1980). Parental facilitation of children's involvement in preparation for elective surgery. *Dissertation Abstracts International, 41*, 2761-B.

Johnson, E., & Ershler, J. (1981). Developmental trends in preschool play as a function of classroom program and child gender. *Child Development, 52*(3), 995–1004.

Lockwood, N. L. (1970). The effects of situational doll play upon the preoperative stress reactions of hospitalized children. *ANA Clinical Sessions, Miami*. NY: Appleton-Century-Crofts, pp. 113–120.

McCue, K. (1988). Medical play: An expanded perspective. *Children's Health Care, 16*(3), 157–161.

Milos, M., & Reiss, S. (1982). Effects of three play conditions on separation anxiety in young children. *Journal of Consulting and Clinical Psychology, 50*, 389–395.

National Center for Health Statistics. (1985). Health United States, 1985. DHHS Pub. No. (PHS) 861232. Washington, DC: Public Health Service, U.S. Government Printing Office.

Oremland, E. (1980). Presentation at the Association for the Care of Children's Health National Conference. Dallas, TX.

Oremland, E. (1988). Mastering developmental and critical experiences through play and other expressive behaviors in childhood. *Children's Health Care, 16*(3), 150–155.

Oremland, E., & Oremland, J. (Eds.) (1973). *The effects of hospitalization on children*. Springfield, IL: Charles C Thomas.

Pearson, J. E. R., Cataldo, M., Tureman, A., Bessman, C., & Rogers, M. C. (1980). Pediatric intensive care unit patients: Effects of play intervention on behavior. *Critical Care Medicine, 8*, 64–67.

Petrillo, M., & Singer, S. (1980). *Emotional care of hospitalized children*. Philadelphia: J. B. Lippincott.

Piaget, J. (1962). *Play, dreams and imitation in childhood.* New York: W. W. Norton.

Phillips, R. D. (1985). Whistling in the dark? A review of play therapy research. *Psychotherapy, 22,* 752–760.

Phillips, R. D. (1988). Play therapy in health care settings; promises never kept? *Children's Health Care, 16*(3), 182–187.

Poster, E. C., & Betz, C. L. (1983). Allaying the anxiety of hospitalized children using stress immunization techniques. *Issues in Comprehensive Nursing, 6,* 227–233.

Prugh, D. G., Staub, E., Sands, H. H., Kirschbaum, R. M., & Lenihan, E. A. (1953). A study of the emotional reactions of children and families to hospitalization and illness. *American Journal of Orthopsychiatry, 23,* 70–106.

Quinton, D., & Rutter, M. (1976). Early hospital admission and later disturbances of behavior: An attempted replication of Douglas's findings. *Developmental Medicine and Child Neurology, 18,* 447–459.

Schwartz, B. H., Albino, J. E., & Tedesco, L. A. (1983). Effects of psychological preparation on children hospitalized for dental operations. *Journal of Pediatrics, 102,* 634–638.

Sutton-Smith, B. (1986). *Toys as culture.* New York: Gardner Press.

Thompson, R. H. (1985). *Psychological research on pediatric hospitalization and health care.* Springfield, IL: Charles C Thomas.

Thompson, R. H. (1988). From questions to answers: Approaches to studying play in health care settings. *Children's Health Care, 16*(3), 188–194.

Tisza, V. B., Hurvizt, I., & Angoff, K. (1970). The use of a play program by hospitalized children. *Journal of the American Academy of Child Psychology, 9,* 515–531.

Werner, E. E. (1984). Resilient children. *Young Children, 40,* 68–72.

Wilson, J. M. (1988). Future of play in health care settings. *Children's Health Care, 16*(3), 231–237.

Wolfer, J., Gaynard, L., Goldberger, J., Laidley, L. N., & Thompson, R. (1988). An experimental evaluation of a model child life program. *Children's Health Care, 16*(4), 244–260.

Woodward, J. (1959). Emotional disturbances of burned children. *British Medical Journal, 1,* 1009–1013.

Part V
POLICY AND THE
ADMINISTRATIVE
PERSPECTIVE OF PLAY

The two authors of Part V address the complexities of working toward play as a focus of policy development. Kagan deals with attitudinal, structural, and functional barriers that prevent support for play, and Klugman specifically addresses the role of the principals in supporting play in schools.

Kagan sets the stage by briefly reviewing the rich literature extant that attributes to play a prominent role in the early childhood curriculum. She cites the many contributions to child development provided through play, from concept development and problem solving to supporting the child's emotional and social development. Kagan identifies three barriers that seem to block the ready inclusion of play in the curriculum. She discusses the attitudes toward play among adults in general and parents in particular. She points to the teachers' own attitude toward play as being frequently affected by the attitudes prevalent in the society. Teachers, she says, are also affected by the classroom "materials, publishers, and 'teacher-proof' curricula" that dictate their lives.

Among the structural barriers Kagan identifies are curricula, space, materials, and time. Time is identified as one of the greatest structural inhibitors: time for children in programs; and for teachers to observe and share with others. Kagan discusses the functional barriers, in which are included the incredible teacher turnover rate that exists simultaneously with a great expansion of the field and the reality that fewer teachers are entering it. Her chapter concludes with some suggested strategies for addressing the issues: a stronger collective commitment from professional organizations; a public information effort by play advocates and the toy industry; structural issues; and greater emphasis in the preservice education of future early childhood teachers on developing an understanding of the comprehensive nature of play in the lives of children.

Klugman describes the social energy for positive early childhood legislation that now has been generated on local, state, and national levels in support of appropriate early childhood programs. He cites reports, journal articles, and current legislative efforts as the backdrop for this energy. Klugman focuses on public school leadership, which is currently assuming the responsibility for many of these programs. He reports on research into the perceptions and attitudes toward early childhood of elementary principals in the public schools. His research findings indicate three areas to be addressed: preparing elementary school principals, finding ways to more widely disseminate and act upon the new definition of early childhood education, and working toward reconceptualization of the organizational structure of the elementary school to more nearly adequately address the needs of early childhood.

The professional preparation of principals, he states, should be designed to include, in addition to the commonly accepted prerequisites, a focus on early childhood education, study of young children, study of child development, study of curriculum and play, and background and experience in work with young children. In terms of the definition of early childhood education, Klugman states that the currently accepted definition of early childhood as encompassing all of the developmental stages from birth through age eight has not yet been fully understood or widely accepted. He recommends a major public information effort. The reconceptualization of the organizational structure of the school in order to encompass as its focus the child from birth through age eight would begin the process of recognition of the developmental and pedagogical differences between the elementary school culture and that of early childhood education. Only then, he states, can the current wide differences begin to be addressed and reconciled.

CHAPTER 10

Children's Play: The Journey from Theory to Practice

Sharon L. Kagan

By ordinary standards, implementing children's play in today's early education programs should be easy. A growing research body establishes the importance of play in children's development. Basic tenets of childhood pedagogy—interaction, active learning, initiation, and choice—all are embraced in the act of play. Early childhood personnel gain exposure to play as a cornerstone of curriculum through books, inservice workshops, and preservice curricula. The stage has been set for play to commence. But in reality, it is not that simple. Play, like the pot of gold at the end of the rainbow, remains a vision, pictorially clear but illusive.

The purpose of this chapter is to examine the dichotomy between conceptions of what play can and should be and what play is. The chapter explores the field's fascination with establishing a rationale for play—for justifying its utility in the developmental process—and documents the barriers to implementing play. It suggests that the journey from theory to practice is a long one, festooned with detours and barriers. Examining strategies to overcome the obstacles is the main focus.

In terms of the history of the civilization, the fascination with play is fairly recent. While there were hints about children's play in the Bible and in various writings from ancient civilizations, Singer (1973) points out that until the European Renaissance these descriptions were sketchy and of little importance, preventing empirical conclusions about the nature and quality of play. It is known that pre-Renaissance children tended to follow the patterns set by the adults in their presence: boys were involved in their fathers' trade and girls in housekeeping duties. In noble families, children were socialized to courtly routines and skills needed at the time. Although children's play was represented intermittently in various art forms (Shakespeare was sensitive to childhood fantasy in his writings; Brueghel's painting *Children's Play* depicts the vigorous play of village children), it was nineteenth-century romantics who helped seed interest. In Germany, Goethe and Schiller explored the imaginative component in children's play. In England, Coleridge and Wordsworth were fascinated by children's imagination. In poetry, Robert Louis Stevenson, and in fiction, Mark Twain, sanctioned children's rights to imagine and fantasize. And, of course, educational pioneers Froebel and Pestalozzi advocated the use of play in childrearing and education.

THEORIES OF PLAY

Since that time, the issue of children's play has risen from dormancy with scholars advancing various theories of play. The surplus energy theory argues that children, not having to attend to daily survival activities, let out their excess energies in play behavior, rather than work. Groos' (1901) instinctual theory explains children's play as a way of developing behaviors that are essential for later survival. In this view, play is seen as a necessary rehearsal—a preamble to adult life. Hall's (1906) recapitulation theory suggested that the individual's development cycle recapitulates the evolutionary history of the race: play, rooted in savage behavior, had to be worked through before one could go on to the realities of adult life. Psychoanalytic theory offered a different interpretation: much of play is an attempt to satisfy drives, to resolve conflicts, and to cope, by repetition, with anxiety-provoking situations. For Piaget and cognitive theorists, play is viewed in a broader context. More than adaptive or conflict-resolving behavior, play is the mode by which children understand their experience and development. For Piaget, accommodation—the attempt to initiate, modify, and interact with the environment—is mastery play or "work" in Elkind's (1988) words. Assimilation—the incorporation of the world to match our concepts—is associated with symbolic play, or "play" in Elkind's words.

Piagetian theory marked a turning point for early education. Sanctioning the adaptiveness of behavior, Piagetian theory fostered a role for adults as those who could enhance children's imaginative behavior. Piaget's theory could be translated into concrete classroom practice. Further, cognitive theory could be related to social learning and developmental theory. With Piagetian theory as a springboard, additional concepts of child's play emerged. Far too plentiful to recount here, such theories have explored play with respect to the affective domain, Curry (1972) suggesting that play affords children a means of clarification and relief from emotional distress. The relationship of play to creativity, convergent and divergent thinking, has received much attention (Guilford, 1967), as has the relationship of play to personality structure (Berlyne, 1969). Clearly, there is no lack of theoretical or conceptual models of children's play.

As research increasingly demonstrates the importance of play in children's development, the commitment to encouraging the practice of play grows. Isaacs (1933) pointed out that early childhood educators have long cherished the belief that play can nourish children's intellectual and social development. In terms of enhancing children's cognitive potential, play has been acknowledged as a primary vehicle for concept development and problem solving. Play brings children into contact with multiple stimuli that induce the development of categorization, generalization, and conceptual acquisition skills. For example, in the house corner, children categorize things to eat, things to cook with; at the water table, they learn which things sink and which float; they generalize from present objects to objects not immediately available. In the science area, they learn concepts of time—a seed planted today is a vine tomorrow. Natural play situations also provide countless opportunities for problem solving. Smith and Simon (1984) found in their review of 11 studies of play and problem solving that compared with children in nonplay situations (e.g., direct instruction, observation), youngsters in play situations are just as likely to solve problems successfully. They found that children in play conditions generate more responses than nonplay or control youngsters, suggesting that play enhances innovative and creative problem-solving behavior. Athey (1988), in summarizing the relationship between play and cognitive development, suggests that play contributes to a vast range of specific cognitive processes (association, hypothesis testing) and to generic functioning (information discrimination, generation, and abstraction).

Repeated work validates the relationship between play and children's social and emotional development. The psychoanalytic view suggests that play is the projection of the individual's inner or emotional life; hence, play, particularly sociodramatic play, has intrigued theorists and clinicians. Erikson (1950) supports the role of play in ego development. Play acts are "a function of the ego, an attempt to bring into synchronization the bodily and social processes of which one is a part even while one is a self" (1950, p.184). In symbolic role taking (Fein, 1984), children demonstrate their perceptions of themselves and others. They struggle to come to terms with their senses of goodness and badness that are played out in fantasy play. They identify their own feelings and those of others (Hartley, Frank, & Goldenson, 1952). Through repeated contacts with playmates, children develop cooperative reciprocal relationships and gain mutual understanding and trust. Prosocial behaviors can develop through play opportunities. Further, dramatic play provides children with opportunities to develop confidence, to master reality, and to structure their own reality.

In addition, play accelerates communication in verbal and nonverbal youngsters. For young nonverbal children, play is the means through which impulses, feelings, and fantasies are translated into actions: play offers a means of dealing with challenges. As a vehicle to stimulate language, play is ideal because it fosters the three basic functions of language: communication, expression, and reasoning. Bruner (1982) and others suggest that conversations are most likely to occur when children are in small groups, with or without an adult present. Clearly, acquisition is enhanced when children are engaged in conversation rather than when they are simply passively exposed to language (Wells, 1983).

Armed with theories of play and convincing arguments extolling the benefits of play, early childhood educators are steeped in *why* play should be an essential part of classroom practice—in its rationale. To varying degrees, early childhood professionals are also trained in the *"how tos"*—the components— of play. Some preparatory institutions strongly recommend courses on play or include them as requirements. Through teacher practice, young professionals may be exposed to play in actual preschool classrooms.

Beyond learning the general contributions of play to child development, teachers must understand the characteristics associated with various forms of play. *Imaginary play*, for example, is considered a common occurrence and is thought to provide a mental rehearsal for social development by offering a forum for experimentation with new roles and solutions (Breger, 1974). Imaginary playmates appear most often in children between three and six years of age; their arrival may be triggered by negative circumstances or by a story or picture. Frequently, imaginary playmates appear in a recurring play theme involving parental discipline.

Children who develop imaginary playmates differ on a number of dimensions from those who do not. Those children with imaginary playmates generally have less sibling contact and have parents who believe fantasy to be valuable (Partington & Grant, 1984). They have a slight edge in verbal-literary skills, and according to parents' reports, are better able to interact with adults and exhibit more "self-initiated" play (Manosevitz, Prentice, & Wilson, 1973).

Prospective teachers may learn about *dramatic* or *sociodramatic* play and may come to realize that it tends to center around three themes: the need for protection, the need for power over things and people, and the need to attack and destroy. Teachers realize that dramatic play changes with age and that children are likely to adopt a variety of roles in their play. Most important, teachers come to realize that by observing dramatic play, they gain insight into the child's inner world.

Adding to the repertoire of play behaviors, teachers learn that *rough-and-tumble play* is common and exists along a continuum commensurate with children's developmental ages. Although motor patterns may be similar (Neill,

1976), teachers, it is hoped, learn to distinguish between rough-and-tumble and aggressive play. *Water play* helps children develop sensations and feelings and allows for intellectual experimentation and exploration. Because of its unique properties, water play can simultaneously stimulate inhibited children and soothe explosive youngsters.

Teachers are exposed to the properties and values of paint, clay, and blocks as play instruments. Children are likely to begin by exploring and experimenting with objects—characteristic of Piaget's sensorimotor period. After focusing on the materials themselves, children begin to realize that materials have unique characteristics and that they can be manipulated. Later, children realize these items are raw materials, a means of making something else. *Paint* allows the opportunity for emotional release, permitting controlled messing. Finger painting—involving visual, tactile, and kinesthetic sensations—allows messing, tactile pleasure, and the visual stimulation of color transformation. *Blocks,* the most frequently used play material, provide a means for children to integrate their observations and activities. Simultaneously, they are obstacles to master, play symbols, and the means of creating environments. *Clay,* the most tactile of the media, is a wonderful outlet for aggressive impulses and a valuable tool for "creating" conceptions of reality. All totaled, the media present a rich array of "assists" to hasten the infusion of play into classrooms and programs (Hartley et al., 1952).

In addition to theories that fortify the rationale for play, research that documents its impact, and pedagogy that helps translate theory to practice, new curriculum and professional guidelines also emphasize the importance of play. Volumes on the theory and practice of play are emerging, particularly to fend off the "back to basics" phenomenon sweeping preschool and early education programs. Buffering the importance of play, the National Association for the Education of Young Children (NAEYC) has taken a strong stand on what constitutes appropriate practice for young children. Through its work, *Developmentally Appropriate Practice* (Bredekamp, 1986), play emerges as a hallmark of appropriate early education environments, be it for infants, toddlers, preschoolers, or elementary schoolers. Verifying the commitment to play, performance standards or program guidelines of many early education efforts (Head Start, Project Giant Step) encourage the provision of opportunities for children to play, to initiate their own activities, and to participate in small group activities.

THE REALITY OF PLAY

Given all of this emphasis on play, one would expect to see classrooms in schools, child care centers, and Head Start programs alive with play. One would expect to see well-defined and richly endowed play areas, robust with elaborate sociodramatic and block play. One would expect to see extended periods of time set aside for self-selection, and self-initiated play. One would even expect to see teachers and teacher assistants encouraging richly elaborated play.

But the reality of today's early childhood classrooms is quite different from the picture and principles detailed above. Classrooms for preschoolers are often marked by rigid schedules (which are not only posted but monitored). Short sessions of two and a half or three hours are interrupted by teacher breaks, or nonclassroom tasks such as the completion of attendance, reimbursement, or procurement forms. In some programs, meal time, though an essential part of the curriculum, cuts into play time. Teachers complain that play is inhibited because materials are inadequate or because parental or organizational pressures discourage play. Classes that should be buzzing with the active voices of children engrossed in play are frequently characterized by the buzz of bells calling children and staff to the next activity, the next event. Spontaneity, so essential in settings for young children has been subjugated to schedules, lego traded for logo, and workbenches for workbooks. The hallowed theories of play have been relegated to a harassed, uncomfortable reality.

Certainly, this is not the case in all early childhood programs, but it is the case in many and, more important, represents a trajectory for early education. A recent California study (Smith, 1987) indicated that in more than 400 kindergartens, workbooks and worksheets were used more frequently than any other activity. Interestingly, teachers indicated they would continue these practices even though 62 percent of them were concerned about too much academic pressure! In another soon-to-be-reported study on preschool programs, the findings were more problematic. Even when children were given opportunities to self-select activities and to play, teacher input into choice and teacher monitoring/directing of the play was frequent.

What does this mean? Why, given all the knowledge about child development and the importance of play, has treasured pedagogy been converted into poor practice? And why, when rich play environments exist, is it so difficult to sustain them? Three groups of barriers seem to prevent elaborated play in many early childhood settings: (1) attitudinal, (2) structural, and (3) functional.

Attitudinal Barriers

At once, the most overt and covert attitudinal barriers that mitigate against play as a valuable activity permeate American culture. At the broadest level, the American ethos does not value play. The Horatio Alger mystique, in fact, the American path to success, is rooted in hard, sustained work. People's sociocultural perceptions separate work and play in hundreds of ways. There are special days for work—the weekdays—and special days for play—the weekend, after work ends. People bifurcate their lives: they "work" with colleagues in offices or factories; they "play" with friends at home. In essence, work and play are separate and distinct. Furthermore, play occurs only when work is finished.

It is interesting that when children "play" they imitate, not the play of adults, but the work of adults. For decades, children have played "house" or "school." Now, given the prevalence of women in the labor force, it is not at all uncommon for children to play "office." Little boys and girls fabricate "brief cases" and replicate the office hierarchy. "I will be the boss and you send a letter," said one four-year-old, phone in hand, pencil in the other.

Given the prevalent societal orientation toward separating the world of work and the world of play, and given the lower status generally accorded play, it is not at all surprising that most adults do not value play in their own lives or in their children's lives. Caldwell (1985) points out that even when adults "play," their games lack spontaneity, are deadly serious, and focus on doing it correctly and well—characteristics of the work world. Adults view play as a means to an end, while children focus on play as the end itself (Fagan, 1984). Parents often impose this work standard on their children. Given the advent of fewer, more "gourmet" babies, parents seek out alternatives that prepare children for their futures. Play is accorded value to the extent that it can be linked to advancing cognitive functioning. Teachers frequently report being inhibited in fostering classroom play because parents (regardless of socioeconomic class) are interested in having children "ready" for the next phase of their out-of-home education. When parents are convinced that play is "children's work" or that play is beneficial to development, it is accepted, sometimes still quite skeptically.

Pushing children, assessing readiness, and screening youngsters early also relegates play to a secondary status within the early childhood classroom. To ready children for tests that may determine placement or school entry is a threatening challenge—one that teachers often meet by increasing classroom pressure. Recently, professional groups including the National Association for the Education of Young Children (NAEYC) (1988), the National Association of Early Childhood Specialists in State Departments of Education (1987), and the California School Readiness Task Force (1988) have all taken strong positions on the appropriateness of testing and developmental screening. That they have had to do so indicates the degree to which testing mania and a testing readiness industry have taken root in our nation. We cannot underestimate the pervasiveness of testing in the early years and its negative impact on classroom practice. Presently, the pressure to prepare children for tests is one of the strongest obstacles to play implementation.

While accelerated by testing mania, resistance to play is deeply rooted in the educational profession. Two divergent theories suggest that teachers, in spite of their training, are inhibited in their attitudes toward play. One suggests that teachers do not see themselves as "intellectual workers." Infantilized by a system that segregates them into isolated cubicles (classrooms), teachers abdicate responsibility and initiative. Feeling undervalued by a system that relegates them to managerial functions, teachers allow materials, publishers, and "teacher-proof" curricula to dictate their lives.

Refuting the impotence theory, an alternate conception of why teachers have difficulty fostering play is rooted in inherent contradictions of teachers' roles. As Monighan-Nourot, Scales, Van Horn, and Almy (1987) point out, the need for teachers to supervise, schedule, and allocate materials conflicts with the preschool teacher's need to guide and facilitate. Trained to be classroom leaders, teachers of young children need to reconcile their need for authority and autonomy with the children's needs for self-initiation and choice.

As important, teachers need to come to grips with their own attitudes toward play. Burdened by comments from colleagues and friends, teachers need to be emotionally and verbally prepared to handle the quips, "So, all you do is play all day?" Once armed with a value orientation that supports play generally, teachers need to examine their own philosophic play orientation:

- What do I believe is the appropriate balance between cooperation and competition, between aggressive and passive behavior?
- What do I believe is the function of solitary play?
- How much should cultural variations affect play?
- Should my beliefs about play hold constant for all children or should they vary?

Not easy, facilitating children's play feels like rowing a boat upstream with one oar. While the direction may be clear, incipient barriers—in this case attitudinal barriers—make the challenge great.

Structural Barriers

Certainly, mounting attitudinal hurdles is the greatest challenge, but dealing with structural barriers is not an easy feat either. When queried about why play is not prevalent in early childhood settings, teacher trainers, after pointing out the attitudinal constraints, focus on limitations imposed by structured curricula, space, materials, and time. Beyond anecdotal evidence, studies demonstrate that program structure and curriculum significantly influence children's activity. For example, Spivack and Shure's (1974) social-problem-solving curriculum is more likely to encourage children to engage in sociodramatic play than a more rigid "prepared environment" traditionally associated with Montessori is. Studies (Huston-Stein, Friedrich-Cofer, & Sussman, 1977) indicate that the degree to which the program was prepared and directed by adults correlates negatively with pretend play.

There is no question that in many settings space is also a problem. Whereas few attempts have been made to research the measurement of space for young children (Phyfe-Perkins, 1980), licensing codes generally include square feet per child as one requirement. However, because many settings are exempt from licensure and because square footage deals with amount, not quality of space, there are still difficulties. Mostly, teachers complain of not having enough indoor space for adequate play. But, in fact, research is mixed on the relationship between spatial availability and social interaction. On the one hand, Hutt and Vaizey (1966) and Smith and Connolly (1972) report that as space decreases the level of social interaction, including aggression, increases. On the other hand, Hartup (1983) has shown that crowding results in fewer social interactions.

In spite of this uncertainty, we do know that teacher-child ratios and group size are important quality-related variables—that if groups are too large, quality diminishes. Consequently, space needs to be designed so that it encourages small, intimate groups and accommodates the need for solitary play. In some classes, tables and chairs consume the bulk of the space. Such arrangements hamper free movement and small group interactions. Building on Goffman's (1961) claim that various physical settings have associated socially designated behavior patterns, it can be hypothesized that rooms laden with tables or desks and chairs will elicit orderly behavior, whereas rooms resembling playrooms could be expected to foster playful activity. In other classes, space may be ample, but access to play materials is impeded. The case of the "blocked blocks" is a poignant example: although blocks were clearly an important part of the curriculum, indicated by the wall photos of elaborate block constructions, in one classroom they were blocked by the angled book shelf. In another, they were placed adjacent to a frequently used door. While having adequate space is the first step, knowing how to use it to maximize play is the second.

There is no question that materials have an important role in the early childhood classroom. Research demonstrates that the type of materials used fosters certain behaviors in children: conversation, passive cooperation, active cooperation, or longer attention spans (Herron and Sutton-Smith, 1971). For example, Campbell and Frost (1978) found that children playing on a creative playground engage in more imaginative and less functional play than children do playing on a traditional playground. Because materials are so important, teachers often lament their lack. In some cases this concern may be a proxy excuse for other inhibitors. In other cases, the "too-few" materials syndrome can be compensated for by creative inservice training or guidance from an experienced teacher. Too many materials are just as likely to be play inhibitors. Johnson (1935) found that more equipment leads to fewer social games and fewer social conflicts. Further, "ready-made" materials, while not necessarily diminishing the incidence of play, certainly inhibit creativity and resourcefulness. In fact, the National Association for the Education of Young Children (Bredekamp, 1986) takes a stand against using adult-made materials with children under age six.

In spite of these difficulties, the greatest structural inhibitor to creative play in today's early education settings is time. In some settings, programs are indeed short, two and a half hours. Allowing for delayed arrivals, other classroom routines, and meals, a hefty hunk of the day is expended. Adding to the regular schedule, time for special events also precludes long, uninterrupted play periods. Some programs overcome this time bind by lengthening their days or modifying the number of intrusions into the main part of the day.

But time is also a problem because teachers have little of it away from children. There are limited opportunities for adults to share their observations of children with others, to reflect on the meaning or intent of children's play behavior. Teachers have little opportunity to give or gain peer support and little opportunity to grow from one another's experiences. Pedagogical issues faced by individual teachers are harbored, only rarely communicated to a broader audience of teachers. Time prevents teachers from learning how to observe more critically or how to use ministudies as a means of garnering insightful information on children.

Functional Barriers

The lack of time for appropriate inservice training or peer learning leads to the third category of barriers—functional barriers. The number one functional problem is personnel. Functionally, the profession has a 41 percent turnover rate. Simultaneously, programs are expanding and the field is not attracting sufficient personnel to fill the turnover gaps, much less those occasioned by new program slots. People who delightedly entered early education are now flocking to other fields where salaries are higher. Enrollment in teacher preparation programs, particularly at the early childhood level, has decreased dramatically with only a few exceptions. Further, many individuals who join the profession have less than adequate training. No amount of sporadic inservice training is sufficient compensation for solid pedagogical preservice training. Well intentioned, but undertrained and insecure, newer classroom personnel forgo play for "easier" and more controlled activities. Packaged curriculum and table-top games provide the antidote for the natural insecurities associated with the first years of teaching. All totaled, attitudinal, structural, and functional barriers present a nearly unpenetrable panoply of obstacles.

POSSIBLE STRATEGIES

Given the multiple and varied settings in which early education occurs, it is hard to envision a policy that would affect them all. Further, the pedagogical nature of play does not lend itself well to policy construction. Nonetheless, important steps have and need to be taken to foster environments where play can thrive. First, there is a need for a strong professional commitment to play to emerge. Individually, scholars have carried the burden, and they are attracting increasing attention. But a stronger, more collective stance is necessary. Organizations representing young children traditionally have trouble reaching agreement: the play commitment is, however, one that is rather neutral and with advocacy efforts could be a coalescing issue for organizations like NAEYC, Head Start, the Association for Supervision and Curriculum Development (ASCD), the National Association of State Boards of Education (NASBE), the National Black Child Development Institute (NBCDI), and the Chief State School Officers to mention a few. Second, to foster recognition of the importance of play, play advocates should be nurtured and its value should be more widely publicized. A public information effort, possibly enlisting support from the manufacturers or retailers of appropriate toys, should be developed. Third, structural issues need to be addressed. Balanced curricula, days of sufficient length, adequate released time for teachers, and appropriate indoor and outdoor space need to be ensured. Creative teaching institutions, for example, Whittier College in California, offer inservice training options that focus on helping teachers organize time, space, and materials. Such institutes should be expanded and replicated.

Fourth, preservice training needs to be more carefully analyzed so that it truly serves as the bridge between theory and practice. Administrators and practitioners need to acknowledge that teachers face Herculean battles as they attempt to implement play. Consequently, teachers need intense support and high-quality training to ensure that they understand

1. What they can expect from children at different stages as they play in solitary or group settings
2. How they can effectively intervene to enhance children's play (What is the difference between passive and active adult interaction? How can play be facilitated during nonplay periods?)
3. How they can use play to support the development of symbolic skills

4. How they can present the benefits of play most effectively to parents and program leaders—how they can convince parents of the value of "parental play"

Fifth, teachers need to be supported as they institute play. A caring individual, familiar with the challenges of changing institutions, needs to be available to guide the teacher. In some cases, this role is referred to as clinical supervisor and is handled by an "outsider"—a college teacher or a district supervisor. Alternatively, teaching peers may be helpful. To assist teachers in becoming more conscious of their play strategies, they may conduct a "play impact analysis" that focuses on the dimensions of play and its impact on children as individuals and as a group. In most situations, a reorientation to play is a change; changes are best handled incrementally, with support and with specific goals and strategies in hand.

Sixth, those concerned with the role of play in early childhood need to realize that inhibitors to the practice of play will not be rectified by these strategies alone. Play, and the collective resistance to it, are symptoms of greater problems in the early childhood field and of society. Only when early education is accorded higher status and higher salaries will the field become more competitive and standards of early education competence be met. Until teacher supply is more closely aligned with teacher demand, play will remain an elusive dimension, sacrificed to and by professional mediocrity.

Another unresolved dilemma of the profession—the dichotomy between care and education—does little to emphasize the importance of play. National energy is focused on the heated debate regarding who can and who should serve young children. While acrimony mounts, with robust arguments supporting each side, the emphasis is on structure and governance, not on curriculum content. Play and other pedagogical issues, which could be unifying variables, have clearly been sidestepped.

Philosophical issues important to early education have also been sidestepped. Who, in this profession, could deny the inequities that have been ignored for decades? Certainly the two-tier system segregates children into programs by economics, de jure, and by race, de facto. That there are separate programs for very poor and for wealthy youngsters belies this nation's commitment to integration that is the law, if not the spirit, of the land. Some contend that programs for the wealthy are of higher quality—perhaps even characterized by more play than programs for the poor, which have a more didactic orientation. Presently, the question is open for empirical review. That it exists as a question, that it is available for analysis, is itself an indictment and a national embarrassment.

As with these hard and ubiquitous philosophic issues, we have not been able to solve the play issue. With both play and these systematic problems the early childhood field knows what it wants, and knows what should be, but is stymied in its efforts to get it. When the field reconciles practice and theory— what is with what should be—it will have traversed the rainbow. The reward, far more significant than the pot of gold, will be a just and joyous system where all children thrive.

REFERENCES

Athey, I. (1988). The relationship of play to cognitive, language and moral development. In D. Bergen (Ed.), *Play as a medium for learning and development*. Portsmouth, NH: Heinemann.

Berlyne, D. E. (1969). Laughter, humor and play. In G. Lindzey & E. Aronson (Eds.), *The Handbook of Social Psychology* (Vol. 3, 2nd ed., pp. 795–852). Reading, MA: Addison-Wesley.

Bredekamp, S. (1986). *Developmentally appropriate practice in early childhood programs serving children from birth through age eight*. Washington, DC: National Association for the Education of Young Children.

Breger, L. (1974). On the origins of play. In P. K. Smith (Ed.), *Play in animals and humans*. New York: Basil Blackwell.

Bruner, J. (1982). *Under five in Britain* (Vol. II). Oxford Preschool Research Project. Ypsilanti, MI: High/Scope Foundation.

Caldwell, B. M. (1985). Parent-child play: A playful evaluation. In C. C. Brown & A. W. Gottfried (Eds.), *Play interactions: The role of toys and parental involvement in children's development* (pp. 167–178). Skillman, NJ: Johnson & Johnson.

California School Readiness Task Force. (1988). *Here they come: Ready or not!* Sacramento, CA: California State Department of Education.

Campbell, S. D. & Frost, J. L. (1978). *The effects of playground type on the cognitive and social play behaviors of grade two children*. Paper presented at the Seventh World Congress of the International Playground Association, Ottawa, Canada.

Curry, N. E. (1972). *Current issues in play: Theoretical and practical considerations for its use as a curricular tool in the preschool*. Unpublished thesis, University of Pittsburgh.

Elkind, D. (1988). Play. *Young Children, 43*(5), 2.

Erikson, E. H. (1950). *Childhood and society* (2nd ed.). New York: Norton.

Fagan, R. (1984). Play and behavioral flexibility. In P. K. Smith (Ed.), *Play in animals and humans* (pp. 159–173). New York: Basil Blackwell.

Fein, G. G. (1984). The self-building potential of preschool play in "I got a fish all by myself." In T. D. Yawkey & A. D. Pellegrin (Eds.), *Child's play: Developmental and applied* (pp. 125–170). Hillsdale, NJ: Earlbaum.

Goffman, I. (1961). *Encounters*. Indianapolis, IN: Bobbs-Merrill.

Groos, K. (1901). *The play of man*. New York: Appleton.

Guilford, J. P. (1967). *The nature of human intelligence*. New York: McGraw-Hill.

Hall, G. S. (1906). *Youth.* New York: Appleton.

Hartley, R. E., Frank, L., & Goldenson, R. (1952). *Understanding children's play.* New York: Columbia University Press.

Hartup, W. W. (1983). Peer relations. In E. M. Hetherington (Ed.), P. H. Mussen (Series Ed.), *Handbook of child psychology: Vol. 4. Socialization, personality and social development* (pp. 103–196). New York: Wiley.

Herron, R. E., & Sutton-Smith, B. (Eds.). (1971). *Child's play.* New York: Wiley.

Huston-Stein, A., Friedrich-Cofer, L., & Sussman, E. J. (1977). The relation of classroom structure to social behavior, imaginative play, and self-regulation of economically disadvantaged children. *Child Development, 48,* 908–916.

Hutt, C., & Vaizey, M. J. (1966). Differential effects of group density on social behavior. *Nature,* 209, 1371–1372.

Isaacs, S. (1933). *Social development in young children.* New York: Schocken.

Johnson, M. W. (1935). The effect on behavior of variations in the amount of play equipment. *Child Development, 6,* 56–68.

Manosevitz, M., Prentice, N. M., & Wilson, F. (1973). Individual and family correlates of imaginary companions in preschool children. *Developmental Psychology, 8,* 72–79.

Monighan-Nourot, P., Scales, B., Van Horn, J., & Almy, M. (1987). *Looking at children's play: A bridge between theory and practice.* New York: Teachers College Press.

National Association for the Education of Young Children. (1988). *Testing of young children: Concerns and cautions.* Washington, DC: NAEYC.

National Association of Early Childhood Specialists in State Departments of Education. (1987). *Unacceptable trends in kindergarten entry and placement: A position statement.* Chicago: NAECSD.

Neill, S. R. St. J. (1976). Aggressive and non-aggressive fighting in twelve- to thirteen-year-old pre-adolescent boys. *Journal of Child Psychology and Psychiatry, 17,* 213–220.

Partington, J. T., & Grant, C. (1984). Imaginary playmates and other useful fantasies. In P. K. Smith (Ed.), *Play in animals and humans.* New York: Basil Blackwell.

Phyfe-Perkins, E. (1980). Children's behavior in pre-school settings: Review of research concerning the influence of the physical environment. In L. G. Katz (Ed.), *Current topics in early childhood education* (Vol. 3, pp. 91–125). Norwood, NJ: Ablex.

Singer, J. L. (1973). *The child's world of make-believe: Experimental studies of imaginative play.* New York: Academic Press.

Smith, D. (1987). *California kindergarten practices 1986.* Fresno, CA: School of Education and Human Development, California State University.

Smith, P. K., & Connolly, K. J. (1972). Patterns of play and social interaction in preschool children. In N. B. Jones (Ed.), *Ethological studies of child behavior* (pp. 65–69). Cambridge, England: Cambridge University Press.

Smith, P. K., & Simon, T. (1984). Object play, problem solving and creativity in children. In P. K. Smith (Ed.), *Play in animals and humans.* New York: Basil Blackwell.

Spivack, G., & Shure, M. B. (1974). *Social adjustment of young children*. San Francisco, CA: Jossey-Bass.

Wells, G. (1983). Talking with children: The complementary roles of parents and teachers. In M. Donaldson, R. Grieve, & C. Pratt (Eds.), *Early childhood development and education*. London: Guilford Press.

CHAPTER 11

Early Childhood Moves into the Public Schools: Mix or Meld

Edgar Klugman

Social energy can be defined as public concern and pressure "for or against" an issue or issues. Its buildup occurs developmentally. One can almost predict the rhythm it takes. At the early stages of the continuum there is "surface calm." It is at this point that a problem gains recognition and is defined. At the other end of the spectrum, the problem becomes of public concern and receives pressure that may eventually result in legislative action. We are currently witnessing a buildup of social energy in relation to many crucial aspects of early childhood education.

THE BUILDUP OF SOCIAL ENERGY IN SUPPORT OF EARLY CHILDHOOD EDUCATION

Since the 1970s, there has been an exponential buildup of social energy in support of early childhood education. The early years of childhood have now emerged as a public issue of high economical and political priority. This perspective stems from a number of factors, including major changes in the demographic picture that relate to the family, a dramatic shift of work force participation on the part of women who have children under six, and new research findings relative to the efficacy and cost benefits to the community when children benefit from high-quality early childhood education programs.

This social energy has been translated into such tangible evidence as the 1985 report by state governors and state legislatures, through the National Conference of State Legislatures, which cited child care services and early childhood education as the most significant new area of legislative activity in education (Early Childhood Education, 1985). The National Governors' Association subsequently published two additional Task Force reports (National Governors' Association, 1986a, b) focused on education reform, both of which call for investment of state resources in prekindergarten programs. As a result of this concern 28 state prekindergarten early childhood legislative initiatives (Marx & Seligson, 1988) are currently in existence.

The Committee for Economic Development, which is composed of many of the nation's top business leaders and presidents of major universities, added support through their report, which emphasized the importance of directing efforts and resources toward parents and their children from the prenatal stage through age five. These efforts, they state, will have long range benefits for society (Committee for Economic Development, 1987).

Professional organizations such as the National Association for Elementary School Principals and the Association for Supervision and Curriculum Development have published both monographs and articles focused on the needs of the early childhood community. The National Association for the Education of Young Children has produced important position statements relative to early childhood development and education (Bredekamp, 1987). Of equal importance is the fact that in 1989, in the first four months of the 101st Congress, more than 100 bills carried child care provisions (Bureau of National Affairs, 1989). Both the Democratic and Republican platforms of 1988 incorporated as strong planks policy statements that addressed the need for American society to support the years of early childhood. It is expected that positive legislation on behalf of young children and their families will be forthcoming in the near future.

Many state proposals that focus on the child care needs of three-, four-, and five-year-olds now frequently include the public schools either as the primary sponsor or as the conduit for receiving funds to be used in contracting out to a community provider, or a combination of these. It has now become clear that many of the new programs for three-, four-, and five-year-olds will be conducted under the auspices of the public schools.

If public school administrators are, indeed, taking on this additional new role, it is incumbent upon them to work toward understanding how the early childhood profession defines itself and how the professional leadership to which this new responsibility is being assigned views the field of early childhood education.

Early Childhood: Toward a New Definition

Traditionally the field of early childhood education has viewed the ages of three through eight as a developmental and psychological unit. Included in this perception are such programs as day care, nursery schools, kindergarten, and the primary grades. In the 1960s, however, an increased interest in infancy and the toddler years moved toward incorporation of these age groups as integral parts of the growth cycle. The term *early childhood* became expanded to encompass all children under, and including, eight years of age (Weber, 1970). While there has been no formal agreement concerning this definition (Deighton, 1971) among early childhood professionals, the definition as stated delineates the current and generally accepted age parameters covered by early childhood education.

Marilyn Smith, Executive Director of the National Association for the Education of Young Children (NAEYC), has stated that "the Governing Board minutes of the Association are silent as to exactly when the definition of early childhood education changed to include infants and toddlers" (Smith, personal communication, June 1988). It is, however, clear that with the published NAEYC (1986), position statement on care for children from birth to age three which incorporated the ages heretofore left uncovered, the previously somewhat amorphous definition of early childhood education as covering children from birth to age eight had now become adopted by the early childhood field.

The 28 early childhood legislative initiatives (to which previous reference has been made) have frequently referenced their own definitions to coincide with the one that has now been adopted by the field (e.g., Massachusetts Board of Education, 1986), although their mandates do not necessarily always encompass the birth-through-age-three population.

Increasing Role of the Public Schools

What is clear, however, is that approximately half of the states with prekindergarten legislation limit program operation to the public schools; the remaining states may permit the public schools to subcontract with other agencies for services and/or permit private agencies to contract directly with the state (Marx & Seligson, 1988). One can deduce from these initial steps taken by individual states that in the future additional states will also introduce legislative initiatives and that the public schools will have an increasingly major role in administering and/or supervising early childhood education programs. If this will be the case, states will need to study the level of preparedness of the leadership at the local school site for assuming this new or expanded responsibility.

It is well documented in the organizational development literature that the educational leader of a local school sets the climate and tone of that school in relation to such dimensions as collegiality (Goodlad, 1983; Little, 1982; Moos, 1976; Zigarmi, 1981), supervisory support (Fleischer, 1985; Purkey & Smith, 1982), and involvement in the decision-making processes (Fox, 1974;

Whitebook, Howes, Darrah, & Friedman, 1982). How effective early childhood education programs will ultimately become will be determined to a great degree by the extent to which the leadership and organization adapt to new demands, are informed about the parameters of issues, and encourage staff to find creative ways to solve site-specific problems, such as the interfacing of the new early childhood education programs with the programs already extant.

It is highly likely that the principalship of the elementary school will become the prime role to which the responsibility for planning, development, and/or supervision of these new early childhood programs will be assigned. Both in terms of space and cost this is a likely direction in which communities will move. But questions about what previous training and experience best prepare the principal to support high-quality early childhood programs in a given school remain.

In order to ascertain the perceptions about early childhood education held by school principals, and also what they believe to be the important ingredients in teacher education and in early childhood programs for children, I undertook a study of Massachusetts elementary school principals. The following report of the study findings pinpoints some of the opportunities and some of the problems related to the support of high-quality early childhood education programs in terms of the leadership provided by the elementary school principal.

METHODOLOGY

Data Gathering

The study focused on the public elementary school principal in Massachusetts, frequently the person directly responsible for the implementation of early childhood programs within the school. A questionnaire (see the Appendix) was designed for administrators and included in the March 1988 issue of *The Principal View* (the publication of the Massachusetts Elementary School Principals' Association). The Association has approximately 1,400 members. Of these a total of 79 individuals chose to respond to the questionnaire. In addition, 14 follow-up telephone interviews were conducted with respondents who had indicated their willingness to participate in this additional phase of the investigation (43 percent of the respondents—34 of the 79 who returned their questionnaires—had indicated their willingness to be interviewed further). Time limitations did not, however, permit interviews with a larger number. The interviewees were selected to be a representative sample from urban, suburban, and rural areas in Massachusetts.

The Instrument

The printed questionnaire included in *The Principal View* was pretested with eight elementary school principals. The questions were also reviewed by appropriate persons in the Massachusetts Department of Education, Bureau of Early Childhood Programs, and faculty members at Wheelock College, in Boston. Their suggestions and comments were incorporated in the revised form of the questionnaire.

Questions were designed to provide information about the principals' understanding of early childhood education, their capacity to support a developmentally appropriate program, and the extent to which administrators had previous backgrounds in at least some aspect of early childhood education. The construction of the follow-up interview questionnaire took into account the previously elicited written response in order to further validate the data that had been collected and to elicit anecdotal material about the views of early childhood education held by the respondents.

RESULTS

To the question, "What is your title?" the respondents with only four exceptions indicated that they were principals. Three of the four exceptions were early childhood coordinators who carried the responsibility for the early childhood programs for one school or for a school district. The fourth exception was an assistant principal who, in addition to this role, carried the responsibility for the early childhood program of her school.

To the question, "For how many years have you been a principal?" the respondents indicated great variation in their years of experience. The range was from one year of experience (7 individuals) to 36 years (one individual, see Table 11.1). The median range of experience was 13.5 years.

Administrators were asked: "Who holds the administrative responsibility for the early childhood program(s) in your school(s)?" Seventy-five of the respondents (94.9%) reported that they themselves carried the responsibility for the early childhood education programs in their schools. When asked "At what levels have you taught?" only 9 of the 79 (11.3%) reported having had previous kindergarten or preschool experience.

In the follow-up interviews, 6 of 14 principals stressed the importance of administrators' having had previous preschool experience. Three of this group had had prior early childhood experience themselves.

To the question, "Are you the person responsible for the early childhood program(s) in your school(s)?" 94.9% of the principals indicated that they were the persons responsible for the early childhood education programs in

Table 11.1   Distribution of Years of Experience as Principal

Number of Principals	Number of Years as Principal	Percent of Total Number
7	1	8.9
4	2	5.1
6	3	7.6
3	4	3.8
5	5	6.3
4	6	5.1
1	9	1.3
2	10	2.5
4	11	5.1
4	12	5.1
2	13	2.5
2	14	2.5
1	15	1.3
3	16	3.8
4	17	5.1
3	18	3.8
1	19	1.3
4	22	5.1
3	23	3.8
2	24	2.5
1	25	1.3
1	29	1.3
3	30	3.8
1	31	1.3
1	32	1.3
1	34	1.3
1	36	1.3
5	Missing	6.3
79		100.0

their schools. Additional data came to light in the interviews relative to four individual administrators' responsibilities and supervision of the early childhood programs under their jurisdictions. A brief description of each of these four unique local practices seems in order, for they do not appear to form a distinct pattern.

In one setting, the principal was the person in charge of the overall program and activities for her school. She had the support of an early childhood coordinator who was the actual spearhead of both the early childhood effort and the work being done between parents and the school. This early childhood coordinator also acted as an advocate for the teachers, the children, and the parents and generally served as an early childhood education ombudsperson in this setting, though the final authority and responsibility fell to the principal.

In the second setting, the responsibility for the early childhood program was turned over to one of the early childhood teachers who was the team leader. The program in this setting was forged by an outside consultant in conjunction with the principal and the team leader, though the team leader carried this responsibility in addition to her regular classroom assignment.

In the third setting, a similar practice was initiated. The team leader taught for only a half day and worked with teachers and parents on programmatic issues for the remainder of her workday.

In the fourth setting, the elementary principal was also the special education director. This was an eight-hundred-pupil school serving students ranging from three years old to grade six. When the investigator inquired whether the principal was in charge of the whole school, he replied, "Yes, the community is unable to afford more administrative support." The principal mentioned that much of the three- to five-year-old program is delegated directly to the head teacher of this group.

Administrators were asked "Which of the following courses have you taken as part of your educational preparation?" They reported that their training included (in descending order of frequency) the following courses and practica:

> Educational Psychology (100%)
> Elementary Education Theory (96.2%)
> General Psychology (87.3%)
> Child Development (86.6%)
> Human Growth and Development.(83.5%)
> Educational Administration Theory (81.0%)
> Elementary Education Practicum (67.1%)
> Administration Practicum (35.4%)
> Preschool Education Theory (27.8%)
> Secondary Education Theory (26.6%)
> Junior High School Theory (22.8%)
> Play Theory (21.5%)
> Junior High School Practicum (15.2%)
> Secondary Education Practicum (11.4%)
> Preschool Education Practicum (8.9%)

A large majority of respondents had taken courses in Child Development (86.6%) and Human Development (83.5%), prerequisites for persons majoring in early childhood education.

Respondents were asked to indicate both the grade levels and number of years they had taught from preschool through grade twelve. Although not all responded to the question, Table 11.2 indicates the distribution of responses. Only a few of the principals had come to their roles with experience in teach-

Table 11.2   Distribution of Grades Taught by Respondents

Number of Respondents	Percentage of Total(%)	Grades Taught	Total Number Who Responded to Question
9	11.7	Pre-K	77
	23.0	K	
19	31.9	1	77
24	32.9	2	75
32	40.7	3	74
31	40.7	4	74
42	39.5	5	76
48	61.0	6	77
25	32.9	7-12	77

ing preschool education. The majority of the principals who responded had taught in grades three through six.

Questions were designed to elicit administrators' responses as to whether children's play is important for their development. Since play is a focal point in early childhood education curricula, and a growing body of research has emerged affirming that children learn most effectively through a concrete, play-oriented approach (Bredekamp, 1987), principals were asked, "In your opinion, is children's play important for their development?"

Collating the responses on a scale of 1 (not important) to 5 (very important) resulted in 85% of the respondents' scoring play as being very important, and the remaining 15% scored play as quite important (4 on the scale).

Although none of the respondents marked the lower end of the scale, the perception of play as important for children's development *when applied concretely to school programs* drops off dramatically. This is shown in Table 11.3 in response to the question, "Should play be an integral part of the following programs (excluding recess)?" The programs listed were preschool, kindergarten, first grade, second grade, and third grade. The respondents were given the option of selecting always, often, sometimes, seldom, or never. Table 11.3 shows a dramatic drop between each grade and the next (e.g., kindergarten and first grade, first and second grade, and second and third grade).

As Table 11.3 indicates, principals felt that play should be considered an integral part of the early childhood program at the preschool level. The majority of respondents selected "always" and 2.5% of the respondents did not answer this question. However, when the same question was posed relative to kindergarten, 75.9% of the respondents checked "always," 20.3% selected "often," 2.5% selected "sometimes," and 1.3% did not respond. Play takes on less importance to administrators as the curriculum moves from first through third grade. This becomes particularly evident when one looks specifically at

Table 11.3 Distribution of Response to the Questionnaire
            Item: "Should Play be Considered an Integral
            Part of the Following Programs (excluding
            recess)?"

Grades	Always (%)	Often (%)	Some-times (%)	Seldom (%)	Never (%)	Missing Cases (%)
Preschool	88.6	8.9	–	–	–	2.5
Kindergarten	75.9	20.3	2.5	–	–	1.3
First grade	31.6	38.0	27.8	1.3	–	1.3
Second grade	16.5	27.8	48.1	5.1	–	2.5
Third grade	8.9	19.0	51.9	12.7	–	7.6

the "always" category and finds an 85% drop in the importance of play between kindergarten level and grade three.

It would appear that although principals feel play to be important, they seriously question the importance of play within the structure of traditional school work when children get beyond the kindergarten level. This was validated as principals responded to the realities in their schools. They were asked to check those headings listed in the left-hand column of Table 11.4 that are actually included in the early childhood program in their schools.

One can divide Table 11.4 into two parts: (1) curricular components that are generally associated with the "academic areas" (down to and including art) and (2) those components generally associated with early childhood education (up to and including art). This division allows yet another way to view the dichotomy that seems to exist relative to early childhood education in preschool and early childhood education programs within programs that also encompass the first through the third grades. In a high-quality early childhood education program, wherever it is housed, all of the areas listed in Table 11.4 are integrated in some way into the daily (or weekly) activities of the children.

The frequency of the activities listed from art down in Table 11.4, those generally associated with the traditional view of early childhood education, drops dramatically between kindergarten and the early grades. This provides a graphic confirmation of the reality of current curriculum and practice. It also offers a rationale that can explain the commonly held perception on the part of many principals that play in the grades is not an important curricular component (see Table 11.3).

Issues of Academic and Peer Pressure

A great deal has been written about the academic pressures placed on young children in early childhood programs (Elkind, 1986; NASBE, 1988). It

Table 11.4   Percent of Current Status of Curriculum Areas
            by Grade Level

	Pre-K (%)	K (%)	1 (%)	2 (%)	3 (%)
Reading	26.6	84.8	65.8	49.4	48.1
Writing	19.0	72.2	75.9	59.5	54.4
Arithmetic	22.8	82.3	70.9	55.7	53.2
Science	20.3	82.3	65.8	58.2	53.2
Social studies	19.6	77.2	67.1	55.7	50.6
Art	34.2	81.0	55.7	45.6	43.0
Sand play	36.7	72.2	16.5	7.6	3.8
Water play	38.0	68.4	11.4	2.5	13.9
House play	38.0	84.8	16.5	1.3	1.3
Block play	39.2	88.6	27.8	10.1	3.8
Dramatic play	35.4	77.2	36.7	21.5	16.5
Movement education	36.7	70.9	36.7	22.8	17.7
Dancing	22.8	46.8	24.1	16.5	15.2
Cooking	32.9	72.2	27.8	17.7	11.4

is, therefore, no surprise that both the questionnaire results and the follow-up interviews with principals underscore the fact that very young children are experiencing severe and undue academic pressures. These pressures, as we know, have long-term negative results for children and their learning. During the follow-up interviews, concern about the pressure currently being placed on young children was emphasized in two different ways by 4 of the 14 principals. One related to teacher peer pressure and the expectation of high scores on achievement tests. The second reflected the community's expectations of schools.

Peer pressure and testing. Peer pressure seems to stem in part from the way in which schools are organized. Three of the principals interviewed for the study referred to their concern that teachers in the intermediate grades have somewhat unrealistic expectations for both teachers and children at the primary level. These teachers, in turn, have unrealistic expectations of their colleagues and the children at the kindergarten level. Expectations for teachers in programs for three- and four-year olds were not mentioned by the respondents. When asked to be more precise about the types of pressure felt by teachers, the respondents indicated expectations relative to reading, testing, and general preparedness to sit, to listen, and to follow through on directions. As one principal stated:

First grades don't look like early childhood programs. They are primarily academic with a heavy focus on reading and writing. There are desks in each classroom—one for each child and that's where they stay most of the day. The peer pressure comes from the staff [who often push very hard to assure that] students are going to "make it." In first grade, you [the student] have to fit in somehow in order to be successful.

Another principal said:

We have a kindergarten program in our school. The program is heavily geared toward preparing children for an academic program in first grade. At the moment, the early childhood program [meaning the kindergarten program, since the district does not at this time have a program for three- and four-year-olds] collides with the heavy academic emphasis in first grade. . . . The kindergarten program is determined by the first grade.

Another principal attributed the pressure to the achievement tests:

Teachers throughout the school system feel that *they* [are the ones who] are measured [italics added]. We administer the Stanford Achievement tests in kindergarten through grade 12. In first grade, children must read through at least the first primer. I work with those kindergarten parents whose children should spend another year [in kindergarten].

Community pressures on the curriculum.   Another pressure that was reported by administrators in the interviews was the community pressure for academics, coming particularly from parents. This kind of pressure is widely felt both by principals and by their teaching staffs.

Pressures on the schools are expressed in a variety of different ways. A perspective held by many principals that relates to expectations of the first-grade level learning was expressed by one principal as follows:

Since we have a very academic first grade (meaning children really have to read) we have established a K-1 transitional class for the children who would have had to spend another year in kindergarten.

Or, as stated by another interviewee:

I feel a lot of pressure from the parents when their child is about to enter first grade. I feel they really don't understand what is meant by developmentally appropriate activities. They are so concerned that their child might not learn how to read right away.

One principal stated that her community, as a whole, had very serious questions about whether early childhood programs really have a place in elementary schools at all. As she implied in her interview, early childhood programs are usually associated with an academic orientation.

> I have become very sensitive to the fact that a lot of people in the community don't feel that early childhood is within the realm of the public schools. And this includes school committee members, people in the community and teaching staff. Schools are set up for formal instruction and not for play.

It is now quite clear that the pressure for academic learning that parents and communities put on both children and the schools needs to be both recognized and addressed.

Understanding the Definition of Early Childhood

The current definition of early childhood education now includes children from birth through age eight. While this may be the definition agreed upon by the profession, an understanding of this definition has not yet become fully integrated in the minds of people who administer the programs for children of these ages within the public schools. This became particularly evident in the follow-up interviews with principals when they were asked "What early childhood programs are offered in your school?"

The response of 9 of the 14 principals who were interviewed was to cite the three- to five-year-old special education programs in their schools. When asked for descriptions of other early childhood programs, they either did not answer the question (3) or stated that their schools offered a half-day or full-day kindergarten (6).

A group of four respondents included first grade in their response to the question "What early childhood programs are offered in your school?" Only one respondent included the second grade. None included third grade within the definition of early childhood education.

When asked subsequently, "What is your definition of early childhood education?" the principal, in every instance but one, reiterated an understanding of early childhood as defined by the local community. This held true also for principals who had received their professional training and experience as teachers at the preschool and K-2 levels.

IMPLICATIONS OF FINDINGS

The study uncovered three major areas requiring reconsideration:

1. The preparation of the elementary school principal for work with programs for young children

2. The implications of the new definition of early childhood education
3. A reconceptualization of the organizational structure of the elementary school.

The Preparation of Principals

As these study findings indicate, early childhood programs currently fall within the responsibility of the elementary school principal. Two recommendations, therefore, center around the principalship.

1. The person responsible for the early childhood education component in a school should have had at least a minimum level of preparation and experience in the field of early childhood education.

Few principals have had first-hand experience with preschool or early childhood programs. A study undertaken by Ferratier (1985), for the Illinois State Board of Education (1985) relative to attitudes toward, and experience in, early childhood education shows the Massachusetts principals participating in this study have had far more (although still insufficient) preschool experience than their counterparts in Illinois have. (From a total of 3,492 Illinois principals, 3.6% of the group, representing both public and nonpublic schools, had had previous preschool experience, in contrast to 11.3% of their Massachusetts counterparts.)

Concern about the dearth of experience and lack of preparation for carrying out the responsibilities for early childhood education programs was emphasized by the Massachusetts principals who were interviewed, some of whom had had extensive preparation and experience in the early childhood field. This concern is not unique to early childhood education. The teaching profession as a whole values individuals who have had previous experience in the roles that they are to fulfill (Sarason, 1982). The assumption is that trained and experienced administrators will be able to relate more easily to the issues faced by teachers and children, will have more empathy and understanding, and, in general, will be more capable of taking on the role of advocate for the program than persons with little or no related experience will.

2. Those states and communities that require that the elementary principal be the supervisor of early childhood education programs should also, under the requirements for certification, insure appropriate preparation of the principal in this field.

As has been indicated, there was general agreement among the respondents that the administrative leader in charge of early childhood programs should have had background and experience with children between the ages of three and eight years. In spite of the fact that the principal's certificate has been designed to cover nursery school through sixth grade, the Massachusetts administrative certification and training evaluation indicates that very few of the respondents had worked in preschools prior to assuming responsibility for programs serving this age group.

It is our recommendation, therefore, that the person in charge of early childhood programs should have had

1. Prior practical experience at this level
2. A background in child development and developmentally appropriate curriculum including play and its importance
3. Skill in working with professional staff and parents
4. The more commonly accepted requirements for elementary school principals such as administration, supervision, adult development, adult learning theory, and school finance.

Since the implementation of these and other recommendations needs to be thought of as a long-range goal, some interim steps that emerge from the research findings are suggested.

Offering seminars.   As one example of an appropriate interim step, the Massachusetts Department of Education is currently offering a series of in-depth, inservice education seminars for administrators through its Leadership Academy. The seminars begin in the spring with a needs identification, followed by a one-week residential program in the summer. These seminars permit principals and others responsible for the early childhood programs to develop ongoing structures for their settings through the study of such topics as developmental education, the home-school partnership, screening and assessment, and the development of action plans that assist individuals to start programs in their home districts. Support structures are set up so that individuals receive the benefit of consultations during the year and continue to participate in monthly networking support-group meetings.

Appointing early childhood coordinators.   Another pattern that has emerged recently in Massachusetts is the appointment of an early childhood coordinator either for one school or for a school system. This person, who is usually both prepared and knowledgeable about early childhood education, assumes the administration of all aspects of the early childhood education program and reports to the local elementary school principal or to a central office administrator.

Designating head teachers.   Some elementary school principals have delegated the early childhood education program responsibility to individual teachers within their schools. What these selected personnel have in common is that each has had training and extensive experience in the field of early childhood education. The titles held by the persons carrying this responsibility have included lead teacher, team leader, and head teacher (in the instance where a preschool teacher has undertaken this role). The responsibility usually carries with it providing time for supervision, selecting and developing curriculum, meeting with the principal and central office personnel, and serving as an advocate for the program. The teacher carrying this added responsibility is compensated by having a half-day classroom responsibility or an assistant teacher in the classroom. There have been instances, however, where individuals have undertaken this task in addition to their full-day teaching assignments. This is emphatically discouraged because of the many inherent and obvious difficulties associated with work overload.

Implications of the Definition of Early Childhood Education

The agreed-upon definition of early childhood as including children from birth through age eight seems to be a relatively new concept for the practicing professional in the field, for parents, for policy makers, and for the community at large. As the research findings indicate, principals have found that in most instances, the community has defined what early childhood education means. This even held true for those individuals interviewed who had received professional preparation in early childhood education. It would seem that it takes time to shift old perceptions. Changing ideas and definitions is clearly not an easy process.

Implications drawn from the data indicate that the early childhood profession needs to undertake a massive reeducation effort within its own ranks. This effort should include a wide dissemination of the current definition of early childhood, as well as a clear explanation of what makes the birth-through-eight age group such a distinct and unique group when contrasted with the current views and values held for the elementary school years.

Reconceptualizing the Organizational Structure of the Elementary School

Perhaps the most critical issue addressed by the study is the opportunity that must be afforded to school districts to impact and reconceptualize the structure of the elementary school through the establishment of early childhood units. See also the report published by the National Association of State Boards of Education (1988), which comes to a similar conclusion.

Restructuring of the elementary school, particularly as it relates to the early childhood component of a school district, merits consideration from structural, cultural, and programmatic points of view. Many have come to associate the elementary school experience with the beginning of "real" school. As one respondent in the study said, "When children go from our early childhood program [to] downtown, they [the parents and the community] associate the hard playground . . . with hard core academics." Many parents, as well as members of the teaching profession, feel that once you get to elementary school you will *really* learn. What happens before that time is generally associated with early childhood, kindergarten, nursery school, preschool, day care in its various forms, and other modes of child care. These are frequently not perceived as providing recognizable opportunities for "real" learning.

Interestingly, this perception is also held by most of the administrators who were interviewed in the study. It became increasingly apparent as more extensive explorations were made into their definitions of early childhood education. Only 3 of the 14 principals saw early childhood as extending beyond the kindergarten level. As he reflected further, one additional principal decided to include first grade in his definition of early childhood. Three other respondents modified their earlier interview definitions of early childhood to include the kindergarten level within the sphere of early childhood. Two indicated that they would even include first grade, as well.

Reflection upon these responses helps to clarify how for decades educators, parents, and the community have subscribed to the following delineations: *early childhood* has been seen as nursery school through kindergarten; the *primary grades* have been viewed as grades 1–3; the *intermediate grades* have been accepted as grades 4–6; *junior high school* has generally been seen as grades 7–8; and *senior high school* has comprised grades 9–12. Of course, there have been variations of this structure. It seems evident, however, that in the minds of most people, early childhood is something that occurs before the "real" education of children, which is assumed to begin in the first grade.

In response to the new definition of early childhood education, now seen as comprising birth through age eight, public school programs require reconceptualization in order to ensure high-quality programs that maintain children as both their focus and the highest priority of programmatic development. Where shall it begin?

The physical plant that houses an early childhood program has been shown to have a profound effect on that program. The culture of a school exerts many influences on the program, both positive and negative. The undue pressure of first- and second-grade teacher expectations on kindergarten and preschool programs is more difficult to mitigate against in an organization that encompasses K-6, K-4, or Pre-K-6. The mere fact that professional staff will have to share the human, material, physical, and economic resources can put programs into competition with one another.

The parents of the children are another crucial factor. Each setting that reported having developed a separate early childhood center found that the simple physical separation from the elementary school resulted in a more positive mind set and more relaxed interactions between and among teachers and parents. Parents' expectations of their children were also tempered and became more realistic. It became easier for the center to provide such things as exhibits of children's work through which to explain the stages and experiences of young children in child development terms. An exhibit of how a child moves into the symbolic world provides many rich and concrete illustrations of children's growth and development. It can also serve to illustrate how a well-designed environment can reinforce adult learning about a particular span of "age and stage."

In other words, it appears that, whenever possible, the children, their parents, their teachers, and the administrative leadership are all better served by an early childhood component of the school district (through grade three, when feasible) that is housed in its own appropriately designed and supported facility. When this option is not feasible, the early childhood "unit" will benefit by having its own developmentally appropriate environment, which should be self-contained to the extent possible and physically set apart from the setting and activities of the older children.

From a programmatic point of view, a high-quality early childhood program to be housed in a public school includes children from ages three through eight. This structure supports a setting that will serve well those children who fall within the new definition of early childhood and will allow the design of plans for developmental continuity throughout the child's days, weeks, and years in that particular unit. Programs can be coordinated in the best interests of the child and the family. This may mean half-day children's programs, as well as full-day programs. It will also mean offering comprehensive services that address cognitive/academic requirements within the context of a full child development curriculum while simultaneously meeting the child's need for social, emotional, physical, and cognitive experiences to foster well-rounded growth. Such a program also provides needed health, speech, and other services directly or refers children and families to community services as appropriate (Mitchell, 1988).

In early childhood programs, parents are viewed as partners. They are involved in meaningful ways in the program. Whether this involvement is actual participation, communication with staff, or just coming to visit the classroom, parents are welcomed as integral to the overall program.

While these are not new or extraordinary concepts, together they form the core of an early childhood program that may find itself in conflict with some aspects of the present philosophy and practice in the current elementary school structure. It may appear that the most expedient way of solving the influx of early childhood into the public schools is to locate "empty nooks and crannies" in existing facilities. Communities should, however, select their responses within the context of the needs of the young child and the family, which is a very different context from that of the middle years of childhood addressed by the elementary school. As the Plowden Report states so succinctly:

> At the heart of the educational process lies the child. No advances in policy, no acquisitions of new equipment have their desired effect unless they are in harmony with the nature of the child, unless they are fundamentally acceptable to him.
>
> Knowledge of the manner in which children develop, therefore, is of prime importance, both in avoiding educationally harmful practices and in introducing effective ones. (Plowden, 1966)

APPENDIX
The Role of Early Childhood Education in the Elementary School

1. Please check the spaces which are appropriate for you.
   Elementary Principal _____ Number of years_____
   Other title (please state) _____
                                                      Number of years _____
2. Responsibility for: K-8 _____ K-6_____ K-3_____
   Pre-K _____ Other (please indicate) _____
   Number of years _____
3. What is the total length of time you have been in the field of education? _____
4. At what levels have you taught? (Mark all levels that apply. Indicate the number of years at each level.)
   Preschool _____ _____   Grade 4 _____
   Kindergarten _____ _____   Grade 5 _____
   Grade 1 _____ _____   Grade 6 _____
   Grade 2 _____ _____   Grades 7–12 _____
   Grade 3 _____ _____
5. Circle above (question 4 check list) your favorite age group(s) or grade level(s) to teach.
6. What is your highest level of education?
   BS _____ MS(MA) _____ Doctorate _____ Other _____
7. Which of the following courses have you taken as part of your own educational preparation? (Mark all that apply.)
   Child Development   _____
   Educational Psychology   _____
   Human Growth and Development   _____
   General Psychology   _____
   Play Theory   _____

Preschool Education, Theory   ____   Practicum ____
Elementary Education, Theory   ____   Practicum ____
Junior High School, Theory   ____   Practicum ____
Secondary Education, Theory   ____   Practicum ____
Educational Admin., Theory   ____   Practicum ____

8. What college-level courses do you feel are essential in the preparation of early childhood personnel?

9. Who holds the administrative responsibility for the early childhood program(s) in your school(s)?

_____

(Job title; or brief job description)

10a. Are you the person responsible for the early childhood programs(s) in your school(s)? Yes ____ No ____

b. Have you had the opportunity to prepare for this responsibility? Yes ____ No ____

c. To what extent do you feel prepared for this responsibility? Please circle appropriate number.

1	2	3	4	5
Not Well Prepared				Very Well Prepared

d. In your opinion and/or experience, what are the best ways to prepare for the administrative responsibility of early childhood programs?

11. Which of the following are included in your early childhood program?

	by Specialist	by Pre-K	by Kind.	by Gr. 1	by Gr. 2	by Gr. 3
Pre-reading or Reading						
Arithmetic						
Science						
Social Science						
Art						
Sand Play						
Water Play						
House Play						
Block Play						
Dramatic Play						
Movement Educ.						
Dancing						
Cooking						

12. In your opinion, is children's play important for their development? Please circle appropriate number below.

1	2	3	4	5

Not				Very
Important				Important

13a. Should play be an integral part of the following programs (excluding recess)? Please mark all which are applicable.

	Al-ways	Often	Some-times	Seldom	Never
Preschool	____	____	____	____	____
Kindergarten	____	____	____	____	____
First Grade	____	____	____	____	____
Second Grade	____	____	____	____	____
Third Grade	____	____	____	____	____

b. To what extent is play an integral part of the program of your school?

1	2	3	4	5
Not At All			To a Great Extent	

14. Please check all of the definitions of play below which are complementary to your own point of view.
   a. Play is freedom from external rules. ____
   b. Children's play represents individual growth, development and learning about the physical, emotional, social, intellectual, creative and sociocultural facets of their world. ____
   c. Play can be a purposeless activity. ____
   d. Play can be voluntary and intrinsically motivated. ____
   e. Play skills can be learned through teacher direction and intervention. ____
   f. Scheduling playtime for children allows adults time to attend to other important matters. ____
   g. Play must never be interfered with by adults and should be kept as a kind of "sacred ground" for children. ____
   h. In sociodramatic play the child's efforts are aimed at reproducing, as exactly as possible, the world as he observes it, as he understands it, and insofar as he remembers it. ____
   i. Play is child's work. ____

15. Feel free to write your own definition of play.

Please check your age range.
25–29 ____ 30–34 ____ 35–39 ____ 40–44 ____ 45–49 ____
50–54 ____ 55–59 ____ 60–64 ____ 65 or more ____
Gender: M ____ F ____

16. If you have a spouse, does s/he work in the field of early childhood? Yes ____ No ____

17. Are you a parent? Yes ____ No ____
Ages of children _____

18. Are you a grandparent? Yes____ No____
    Ages of grandchildren _____

Other comments (please add an additional page if you wish):

THANK YOU!

I will contact selected respondents for a follow-up interview. If you would be willing to meet with me, would you include your:
Name _____ School Address _____
Home Tel. _____ Work Tel. _____

Your participation is most appreciated!

REFERENCES

Bredekamp, S. (Ed.). (1987). *Developmentally appropriate practice in early childhood programs serving children from birth through age 8.* Washington, DC: National Association for the Education of Young Children.

Bureau of National Affairs. (1989, May). *Child day care in the 101st Congress: Early initiatives.* BNA special report series on work and family. Special Report No. 17, Washington, DC: Author.

Committee for Economic Development. (1987). *Children in need: Investment strategies for the educationally disadvantaged.* New York: Author.

Deighton, L. C. (1971). *The encyclopedia of education* (Vol. 3). New York: Macmillan and The Free Press.

Bridgman, A. (1985, October 16). Early childhood education: States already on the move. *Education Week, 1,* 14–15

Educational Policies Commission. (1966). Universal opportunity for early childhood education, p. 1. Washington, DC: National Education Association

Elkind, D. (1986, May). Formal education and early childhood education: An essential difference. *Phi Delta Kappan,* pp. 631–636.

Ferratier, L. (1985). *Attitudes, experience and education of Illinois elementary principals concerning early childhood education.* EDRS 264 036.

Fleischer, B. (1985). Identification of strategies to reduce turnover among child care workers. *Child Care Quarterly, 14,* 130–139.

Fox, R. (1974). *School climate improvement: A challenge to the school administrator.* Bloomington, IN: Phi Delta Kappa.

Goodlad, J. I. (1983). The school as a workplace. In G. A. Griffin (Ed.), *Staff development: The eighty-second yearbook of the National Society for the Study of Education* (pp. 36–61) Chicago: The University of Chicago Press.

Little, J. W. (1982). Norms of collegiality and experimentation: Workplace conditions of school success. *American Educational Research Journal, 19* (3), 325–340.

Lundgren, E. C. (1976). Perspectives on curriculum development 1776–1976. Washington, DC: Association for Supervision and Curriculum Development.

Marx, F., & Seligson, M. (1988). *The public school early childhood study: The state survey.* New York: Bank Street College of Education.

Massachusetts Board of Education. (1986, January). *Policy statement on early childhood education.* Quincy, MA: Author.

Mitchell, A. (1988). *The public school early childhood study: The district survey.* New York: Bank Street College of Education.

Moos, R. H. (1976). *The human context.* New York: Wiley.

National Association of State Boards of Education. (1988). *Right from the start.* Alexandria, VA: NASBE.

NAEYC. (1986). *NAEYC position statement on developmentally appropriate practice in programs for 4- or 5-year-olds.* Washington, DC: National Association for the Education of Young Children.

National Governors' Association. (1986a). *Focus on the first sixty months: Proceedings of the National Early Childhood Conference* (No. 3058). Washington, DC: Author.

National Governors' Association. (1986b). *Report on the Task Force on Readiness. Time for results: The Governors' 1991 report on education* (No. 3049). Washington, DC: Author.

Plowden, B. (1966). *Children and their primary schools: A report of the central Advisory Council for Education: Vol. 1. The report.* London: Her Majesty's Stationery Office.

Purkey, S. C., & Smith, M. (1982). Too soon to cheer? Synthesis of research on effective schools. *Educational Leadership, 40* (3), 64–69.

Sarason, S. B. (1982). *The culture of the school and the problem of change* (2nd ed.). Boston: Allyn & Bacon, Inc.

Weber, E. (1970). *Early childhood education: Perspective on change.* Belmont, CA: Wadsworth Publishing Company, Inc.

Whitebook, M., Howes, C., Darrah, R., & Friedman, J. (1982). Caring for the caregivers: Staff burnout in child care. In L. Katz (Ed.), *Current topics in early childhood education* (Vol. 4). Norwood, NJ: Ablex.

Zigarmi, D. (1981). Leadership and school climate: Data base approach to administrative training. *Journal of Staff Development, 2* (1).

Part VI
PLAY AND THE
RESEARCH PERSPECTIVE

Johnson and Fromberg provide a rich overview of play research findings related to a wide range of developmental factors in young children. These chapters are a powerful resource for the continuing work of both researchers and practitioners in the field of early childhood education. The two authors point toward an agenda for research and teaching.

Johnson highlights selected major research findings and discusses the developmental significance of play. He meticulously reviews the play research literature, discusses the role of play in the overall cognitive development of young children, and offers a summary and explanation of major findings in the current literature. Johnson hypothesizes that it is possible that the two components of play training have an impact on different areas of development: adult instruction primarily affects cognition and play itself primarily affects social competence. Direction and recommendations are suggested for future research and for using the implications of both past and future research findings in the development of early childhood education curriculum.

Fromberg focuses on the need for a proactive research paradigm. She cites research literature that points to the need for more reciprocity between "the researched" and "the researcher." This reciprocity may lead to the transformation of both theory and practice. She feels this reciprocity to be particularly relevant for early childhood education at this time in history when distance among practice, beliefs, and theories has increased. Fromberg comments on the existing research into play and differentiates the experimental from the ethnographic paradigms. She reviews ethnographic studies of play and describes the issues. She emphasizes the need for increased understanding and documentation of children's play and thematic content. She concludes by raising important questions about play relative to instruction, gender, development, dynamics, and the need for the researcher to separate and exit in a formal way from a given research activity.

CHAPTER 12

The Role of Play
in Cognitive Development

James E. Johnson

Positive attitudes toward the play of the preschool or kindergarten child can be traced to the longstanding belief that play behaviors assist in the development of prosocial aptitudes and in the formation of moral character (see Bloch, 1988, for a historical review), while at the same time nourishing the intellectual and language development of the child (Isaacs, 1933). The basic difference separating past convictions from present-day sentiments is that after the last 20 years of unabated scientific research (spurred in no small way by the publication of Sara Smilansky's book, *The Effects of Sociodramatic Play on Disadvantaged Preschool Children,* 1968) early childhood educators have an even stronger empirical base with which to better understand and communicate to others the nature of play and its developmental underpinnings. There is also, in general, a greater grasp of how situational or ecological arrangements impact the play activities and behavior of the young child for better or for worse. Accordingly, it is currently possible for researchers to inform practitioners and for practitioners to inform the uninitiated (which includes researchers in certain ways) about the landscape of this island of study and inquiry called children's play.

The terrain mapped out for our present excursion concerns the role of play in cognitive development. Here one finds a voluminous literature. I first summarize it by highlighting selected major findings with respect to epistemic or ludic play (defined in the next paragraph) and convergent or integrative, as well as divergent, processing, identifying as I go along the major research perspectives and methodologies which have been used by investigators thus far, as well as the conceptual and methodological problems they have encountered. Secondly, I recommend directions that future research should take to explore virgin territories and to probe further the cultivated ones. Third, I make some practical recommendations with respect to research and curriculum development in early childhood education.

The hypothesis that play serves more than expressive or compensatory functions in child development is being increasingly discussed (Athey, 1988; Pepler, 1987). Although not without qualifiers and some disclaimers (see Smith, 1988), there is growing consensus based on empirical research that play has a constructive part or serves a generative role in cognitive development. Play behavior, then, not only reflects or is a window on child development but also contributes to it both by consolidating or reinforcing recent learnings and conceptual acquisitions and by providing opportunities for new masteries and novel insights. *General* and *specific* functions of play as epistemic behavior and as ludic behavior are now better understood in relation to cognitive development during the preschool years, epistemic behavior being defined as concerned with acquiring and processing knowledge cued from an external source of stimulation, and ludic behavior, as cognitive activity that is more affectively charged or mood dependent and not necessarily cued from external sources. These behaviors are reciprocally related to cognitive development as both a cause and an effect of the child's developmental status.

Cognitive development can be described both in general and in specific terms. According to Athey (1988), the three most important general signs of mental growth during the early years are the ability to discriminate between information that is relevant or irrelevant to a given purpose, increased adeptness in using fewer cues to generate more information, and higher levels of abstraction. Under each of these three general areas are numerous specific cognitive processes, some of which are more discriminatory or integrative, while others are more divergent, as opposed to convergent. All are related to either the child's network of concepts (knowledge base) or the ability to solve problems (operations), or both. How is play, and especially social pretense play (sociodramatic play), implicated in each of these cognitive processes? What does research tell us? What does the practitioner recognize from experience?

BUILDING AND USING REPRESENTATIONAL KNOWLEDGE

Concept development and the development of representational competence entail a number of specific cognitive processes including perceiving or inferring similarities and differences, dichotomous sorting, cross-classifying over a number of dimensions, generalizing, enumerating instances of a category, class inclusion, and other concept acquisitions. Play, and certainly sociodramatic play, often uses or enhances these processes separately or in concert. Building conceptual networks enables the developing child to impose order and establish predictable patterns across diverse arrays of experiences. Integrating reality into structures is the process of assimilation for Piaget, and play is considered to be a predominantly assimilatory activity. Piaget (1962) has theorized that the organizational and adaptational features of intelligence and development depend on the complementary processes of accommodation and assimilation. Play serves an important cognitive consolidating function by assisting in the child's construction of meaning from experience. According to Smilansky (1968), a chief developmental task during the preschool years is to become able to interrelate and thus comprehend events that, to the child, often at first seem to be disconnected. Young children, particularly from homes that are economically impoverished, are very limited in their capacity to read the various scripts of everyday life—the sequence of events involved in going to the drug store or doctor's office, for example. Smilansky proposed that an advanced form of social pretense—sociodramatic play, which is common in middle-class children—is instrumental in helping children get behind the scenes and read what is going on: "By its (sociodramatic play) very nature it demands from the child that he utilize his potential abilities and knowledge, combine his scattered experiences in a flexible way, in an almost lifelike situation" (p. 3). Sociodramatic play, in other words, helps the child integrate experiences that are separate and seem unrelated at first. Through role playing emerges coherence. This is achieved in part by seeing the different characters' points of view on the same event in a particular scene, like a grocery store. Smilansky found that sociodramatic play enhanced children's cognitive and language skills.

Other cognitive theorists or researchers have emphasized how play serves integrative functions through enabling children to replay and record experiences (Singer, 1973). Similar to Piaget's theory, Singer proposed that the internal activity accompanying imaginative play enables preschoolers to practice and consolidate recently acquired skills. Imaginative play enables children to assimilate new information. While such play often reflects children's limited capacity for logical thought, nonetheless, for Singer and others, it is also constructive activity, not compensatory as it is to Piaget. Play represents children's efforts to comprehend and create meaning. Singer and Singer (1988) have further noted that symbolic or imaginative play of preschoolers is an important way children learn to develop new schemas and script structures on which adaptive interaction with the environment depends. The young child possesses "a limited repertory of preestablished schemas or action-oriented scripts" (p. 71). Make-believe processes occur during the child's attempt to assimilate complex stimulation from the physical and social environment. The young child can control novel and strange experiences by creating imaginative microcosms of reality in attempts to assimilate previously imitated actions or overheard conversations, reducing them to mind-size bites or manageable portions.

Saltz and Johnson (1974) and Saltz, Dixon, and Johnson (1977) tested the hypothesis that social pretense can help children connect discrete events. Preschool children who were from economically impoverished backgrounds were randomly assigned, within their regular classroom, either to social pretense or dimensionality training groups (Saltz & Johnson, 1974) or to sociodramatic play or thematic-fantasy play training groups (Saltz et al., 1977). Thematic fantasy training consisted of helping children learn to enact the plot of simple fairy tales. Other control or comparison groups were used that controlled for the effects of adult attention and language use. One important finding to emerge from this research was that training in social pretense (sociodramatic and especially thematic-fantasy play) had a significant and positive effect on children's ability to score high on sequence and comprehension tests that required a reconstruction of the order of pictures representing a story line and an explanation of the relationship between pictures. Evidently, social pretense play fostered this type of integrative skill.

Further empirical support that play promotes categorization skills and better discrimination and attention to relevant cues comes from Rubin and Maioni (1975) and Johnson, Ershler, and Lawton (1982). More mature play in preschoolers is positively correlated with their classification skills.

Play affords opportunities not only to group incoming stimuli in different ways but also to transfer relevant cues to new situations or to generalize (Athey, 1988). During play children deal with external situations in pace with their ability, and matches are made, often leading to feelings of control and emotions of joy (Singer, 1973; Tomkins, 1962–63). Thus, new situations are sufficiently similar to the old ones so that transfer or generalization can take place. Generalizations learned by young children are many and varied (Kamii & DeVries, 1978). A wealth of anecdotal evidence exists to support the view that play provides optimum opportunities for children to draw generalizations. For instance, during sociodramatic play children form many generalizations dealing with both the play content and the play context. For example, adventuresome themes are associated with more fast-paced action than domesticated themes are; children learn that one child has strong preferences for certain roles while another child is more susceptible to group pressure and goes along with the crowd. The child's storehouse of concepts increases geometrically during the early childhood, and sociodramatic play can greatly facilitate this process.

Moreover, immature concepts of space, time, probability, and causality are tested and revised during play and sociodramatic play, and children often also learn to group concepts hierarchically. Topological geometric notions such as near versus far, in versus out, in between, separate, together, etc. are used in play. The more difficult concept of time also comes to have meaning through the medium of play. As Athey (1988) pointed out, when children wait for their turn to use a toy or to perform their part in a script, expressions such as "in a few minutes," "a little while," "tomorrow," and even "next week" come to make more sense. Although time and space are often transformed in social pretense, sequence and structure are usually preserved and become better grasped. Notions of chance, possibility, and certainty in cause-and-effect relations are firmed up as children interact with materials and observe events and relate with peers and adults. Class inclusion or the differentiation into a superordinate and subordinate class system (an ant is also an insect) is concept learning often resistant to direct instruction, but evidence shows it is a significant correlate of high-level play (Johnson, Ershler, & Bell, 1982). By participating in sociodramatic play, preschool and kindergarten children often form and reflect on class hierarchies.

Using representational knowledge to solve problems and mentally operating on symbolic objects to reason, to test hypotheses, or to produce divergent and potentially creative outcomes are all higher order thinking abilities related to play. Bretherton (1984), for instance, provides evidence of the increase in reasoning ability in the symbolic play of preschoolers. During sociodramatic play children often make predictions and verify outcomes, plan, reconstruct, estimate, elaborate, reason about cause and effect, and so forth. Both in the sense of putting various mental operational demands upon themselves and of using their representational competence in general in transforming and transcending the concrete "here and now" ostensive reality, young children, during sociodramatic play, are performing a kind of self-distancing behavior. Distancing behaviors, according to Sigel (1987), are those behaviors that serve to activate and channelize representational thinking in the developing child. According to the distancing view of cognitive socialization, the agents are typically parents and teachers who strategically manipulate the environment verbally and nonverbally to produce outcomes in the young child (Copple, Sigel, & Saunders, 1984). The case can be made for peers and the self to serve as distancing agents. Sociodramatic play situations frequently expose children to other children who are operating at a slightly higher level of cognitive and language functioning; this is optimal for promoting imitation or distancing communications leading to cognitive growth in the lower functioning child. Indeed, research has documented that mixed age groups or integrated or mainstreamed play groups often yield elevated levels of social and cognitive play (Guralnick & Groom, 1987, 1988).

The preschool years correspond to Piaget's preoperational period of intelligence, with the child characterized as egocentric or unable to deploy attention on more than one aspect of a situation at one time. Progressive decentering of the young child's thought is gained through play experiences (Kamii & DeVries, 1980). The role-playing that is part and parcel of sociodramatic play assists in the development of the ability to decenter. Saltz and Brodie (1982), for instance, discuss the role of fantasy play training in developing perspective-taking skills in young children. By engaging in group dramatizations children act out a variety of roles. A child might, on different occasions, take on the role of a baby, parent, grandparent, firefighter, and superhero. To portray such characters accurately, children must be able to mentally put themselves in other people's places and experience the world from others' points of view. This act of consciously transforming their own identities into a variety of make-believe identities may hasten the decentration process, thereby promoting perspective-taking and a number of other social cognitive and cognitive abilities, including conservation ability (Fink, 1976; Golomb & Bonen, 1981; Golomb, Gowing, & Friedman, 1982; Guthrie & Hudson, 1979; Johnson et al., 1982; Johnson & Ershler, 1980; Rubin, Fein, & Vandenburg, 1983).

In recent years research has generally supported the proposed link between sociodramatic play and decentration. Correlational studies (see Table 12.1) have reported positive relationships between levels of group dramatic play and children's perspective-taking abilities (Cole & LaVoie, 1985; Connolly & Doyle, 1984; Rubin & Maioni, 1975). Play-training studies have also shown that training in sociodramatic play results in gains in children's performance on visual and cognitive perspective-taking tasks (Burns & Brainerd, 1979; Rosen, 1974; Smith & Syddall, 1978) and on affective perspective-taking (Burns & Brainerd, 1979; Saltz & Johnson, 1974). Correlational studies suffer from one's being unable to determine from them cause-and-effect relationships among the variables, and the play training studies suffer from a number of other methodological problems, primarily the problem of other variables' confounding the treatment variable, questioning the internal validity of the play-training research.

Research has shown that training in group dramatic play can result in gains in social skills and perspective-taking. There is some controversy over which aspect or component of the play training is primarily responsible for these gains in social development. There are several possibilities:

1. The play itself—object and role transformations that occur in dramatic play may hasten the decentration process.
2. Adult instruction—the adult-child interaction that occurs during the training may directly or indirectly teach the children new skills.
3. Peer interaction—the conflicts among children that occur in sociodramatic play may cause cognitive imbalance or disequilibrium, resulting in new learning.

Peter Smith tested the first two possibilities by carefully monitoring and controlling the adult-child interaction in a large-scale training study (Smith, Dalgleish, & Herzmark, 1981). Results indicated that adult instruction may have been responsible for many of the cognitive gains brought about by the training, including higher scores on measures of intelligence, creativity, and

Table 12.1 Overview of Research on the Role of Play in Cognitive Development

Type of Study	Cognitive Correlates					
	IQ (Memory, Reasoning, Abstraction)	Conservation	Problem-Solving	Divergent Thinking	Language Development	Perspective Taking
Correlational	Johnson (1976) Johnson et al. (1982) Rubin & Maioni (1975)	Johnson et al. (1982)		Johnson (1976) Lieberman (1965)		
Experimental		Golomb & Cornelius (1977) Guthrie & Hudson (1979)	Sylva et al. (1976) Smith & Dutton (1979) Pepler & Ross (1981) Hughes (1987) Vandenberg (1981)	Sutton-Smith (1968) Dansky & Silverman (1973, 1975) Hughes (1987)		
Training	Saltz & Johnson (1974) Saltz et al. (1977) Dansky (1980) Christie (1983)	Fink (1976)	Rosen (1974)	Dansky (1980a) Feitelson & Ross (1973) Christie (1983)	Lovinger (1974) Smilansky (1968) Levy (1988)	Burns & Brainerd (1979) Smith & Syddall (1978) Rosen (1974)
Longitudinal	Johnson & Ershler (1980)	Johnson & Ershler (1980)		Clark, Griffing & Johnson (1988)		

perspective-taking. The play itself appeared, however, to be responsible for the increased positive social interaction resulting from the play training. Thus it is possible that the two components of play training have an impact on different areas of development: adult instruction primarily affects cognition, and play itself primarily affects social competence. This hypothesis is purely speculative and needs to be confirmed by further research.

Observational research by Garvey (1977) and others has revealed that children often engage in conflicts during group dramatic play. They argue over roles, rules, the story line, and the make-believe identities of objects. These conflicts do not occur during the dramatic play itself; rather, they occur during "frame breaks" in which the children temporarily leave their make-believe roles and assume their real-life identities. Once the conflicts are resolved, the children resume their make-believe roles and the play continues.

The peer conflicts that occur during sociodramatic play are undoubtedly responsible for some of play training's impact on perspective-taking and social development. Rubin (1980) explains:

> Rule understanding, the comprehension of obligations and prohibitions, and the ability to consider reciprocal role relations may be less a function of non-literal social play per se and more the outcome of peer interaction and conflict. . . . When children beg to differ concerning issues of importance to them, cognitive disequilibria are likely to ensue. Since such mental states are not pleasurable, conflict resolution is necessary. Often, when disequilibrium is provoked by social conflict, compromise results. Suffice it to say that compromise is accommodative and ·adaptive. In short, given conflict, the child comes to realize that: (1) survival in the social world, as well as (2) popularity among peers are marked by compromises and socialized thoughts. (p. 80).

Because peer interaction and conflict are integral parts of group dramatic play, their effects are difficult if not impossible to separate from those of other aspects of play. It may be best to think of play training as a context in which make-believe role enactment, peer conflicts, and adult instruction all combine to promote children's social-cognitive development. Perhaps some day researchers may be able to untangle the separate contributions of each component of play training, but for now the fact remains that such training appears to be effective in the development of perspective-taking and social competence.

The educational significance of sociodramatic play is not diminished by these methodological and conceptual concerns. These problems will need to be addressed with longitudinal and cross-lagged studies, of which to date there have been few (Clark, Griffing, & Johnson, 1988; Johnson & Ershler, 1980), and other studies that document more thoroughly the nature of the treatment condition (Smith & Syddall, 1978).

Other higher order thinking abilities include hypothesis testing, problem-solving, and divergent thinking. Theoretical presupposition or empirical research shows these abilities to be significant correlates of sociodramatic play. As noted earlier, an important benefit of sociodramatic play is that such play helps children impose meaning onto their experiences. Hypothesis testing, or postulating and testing relationships between events, is possible because there is order and uniformity of events in the universe (Athey, 1988). Being able to reconstruct past events in sociodramatic play relates to the ability to construct fruitful hypotheses in anticipating the future and the immediate present. In other words, the social context of play is fertile ground for playing with ideas and for formulating and testing hypotheses (Isaacs, (1930/1966). Moreover, with language development, which itself is influenced by sociodramatic play (Levy, 1988; Lovinger, 1974; Rogow, 1981; Shores, Hester, & Strain, 1976; Smilansky, 1968), nonverbal expectations about objects, people, and events are more likely to be verbalized and thus become more accessible to processes of logic and reasoning.

Problem-solving can involve either convergent or divergent thinking for successful solutions. The first type of problem-solving has typically been studied in relation to play using the lure-retrieval paradigm (Smith & Dutton, 1979; Sylva, Bruner, & Genova, 1976; Vandenberg, 1981). This type of experimental research methodology has not been used in evaluating the merits of sociodramatic play. However, similar research has examined play as a vehicle for promoting or using problem-solving skills (Hughes, 1987; Rosen, 1974; Pepler, 1979; Pepler & Ross, 1981). For instance, Hughes (1987), who in marked contrast to the Smith and Dutton (1979) experiment, tried to have children feel secure and free in the "play condition" (i.e., they did not have to sit formally at a table as in the procedure used by Smith and Dutton), did find that exploratory behavior facilitated convergent thinking. She found that exploring novel objects in the play setting gave children an advantage when it came time to use materials in a problem-solving task. Pepler (1979; Pepler & Ross, 1981) also found that children who played with convergent materials demonstrated a higher proportion of strategy moves in solving convergent problems when the task closely related to the convergent play experience. Finally, Rosen (1974) conducted a study in which training and practice in sociodramatic play for disadvantaged kindergarten children resulted in significant improvement in posttest group problem-solving skills on the Madsen cooperation board (Madsen, 1967). In this task the objective was to have four children work cooperatively pulling strings to have four pens cross four circles drawn on a large sheet of paper placed on the board. Group effectiveness was significantly higher in the sociodramatic play group than it was in two comparison groups.

Divergent thinking and play have been subjected to a great deal of theoretical and empirical scrutiny using a broad array of research designs (correlational, experimental, training, and longitudinal). Using experimental conditions similar to her convergent problem-solving study, Hughes (1987) performed a second experiment to test the hypothesis that ludic behavior facilitates divergent thinking as exploratory behavior facilitated convergent thinking in her first experiment. She found that children who spontaneously played with familiar objects (e.g., paper towel) for six minutes performed better on a pattern-meaning test and on an alternative-uses task than children did who performed an unrelated task (coloring). These findings are consistent with Sutton-Smith (1968), who found that children gave more divergent responses to those objects with which they preferred to play. Pepler (1979; Pepler & Ross, 1981) reported that puzzle pieces without the form board yielded fantasy play while with it constructive play was seen. Children who played with divergent materials performed better on a divergent problem-solving task. Pepler (1987) noted that the effects of play with convergent materials are very specific (single-solution responses) while divergent play experiences transfer more generally and bring out more flexibility and originality in children. Pepler's (1987) opinion is that the hypothesis concerning the value of play to divergent thinking is more supported by the empirical research literature than the hypothesis concerning the value of play to convergent problem-solving is.

A great deal of research has been conducted examining the relationship between play and divergent thinking or creativity in preschool children. Lieberman (1965) found a relationship between quality of playfulness (i.e., spontaneity, joy, humor) in kindergarten children and certain measures of divergent thinking (e.g., ideational fluency, spontaneous flexibility, and originality). Johnson (1976) reported significant correlations between divergent and convergent thinking task scores and measures of social, but not nonsocial, fantasy play in preschoolers. Further, a "triangular relationship" was found in that high-intelligence children did or did not display imaginative tendencies but that children who were low in intelligence either did not or rarely displayed them. Note, however, that in this study social pretense and divergent thinking were significantly correlated even after the effects of I.Q. were partialled out. Still, it appears that a minimum level of intelligence is a necessary but not sufficient condition for creativity or imaginative behavior. Parenthetically, these findings are not inconsistent with the observations that children below an I.Q. of 90, on the average, usually do not engage in full-fledged sociodramatic play (Smilansky, 1968). These findings are also not inconsistent with the results of Saltz et al. (1977), showing that thematic fantasy training yielded cognitive outcome benefits disproportionately more so for children above the median pretest intelligence score compared with children below the median intelligence pretest level. The early childhood special education literature on the play of cognitively delayed young children supports this generalization as well (Beeghly & Cicchetti, 1987).

Further cross-sectional research points to a linkage between pretense play and divergent thinking or creativity during early childhood (Dansky, 1980a; Dansky & Silverman, 1973, 1975; Feitelson & Ross, 1973; Li 1978; Smith & Whitney, 1987). Dansky and Silverman (1973) experimentally investigated the problem of whether there is a connection between playing with objects and generating alternative uses with play objects. Children who had play experience were superior to an imitation and a control group in terms of giving nonstandard uses for the objects on the divergent thinking task. This finding has been replicated in other research using different objects in play and task situations (Dansky & Silverman, 1975). Evidently, the effects of play generalize to divergent problem solving with unfamiliar objects.

In subsequent research Dansky (1980a) found the significant and positive relationship between play with objects and divergent thinking task performance was restricted to children who typically engaged in make-believe play in school. Furthermore, Li (1978) found that a group directed in make-believe play scored higher than a free-play group in naming diverse uses for a novel object. Other researchers employing the play-training paradigm have demonstrated play effects on divergent thinking or creativity (Christie, 1983; Dansky, 1980b; Feitelson & Ross, 1973). The cognitive underpinnings for the association between pretend play and divergent thinking may be the increasing symbolic capacity of the child and the growing cognitive ability to shift one's thinking from the concrete to the abstract or, in a word, decentration (Johnson, 1976; Johnson & Ershler, 1980; Singer & Rummo, 1973).

Recently, Smith and Whitney (1987) have raised serious methodological questions about this research that suggests that play is related to and perhaps facilitative of divergent thinking ability. Specifically, they note that, in these studies, the same experimenter usually made all the observations and administered all the tests (i.e., failure to control for experimenter effects). Secondly, they complain that this research is not longitudinal, and thus it remains unknown whether the effects of play on divergent thinking are long term or simply transitory.

Longitudinal research on the effects of play on cognitive development is sparse but not nonexistent either with respect to divergent thinking (e.g., Clark, et al., 1988; Hutt & Bhavnani, 1972) or with respect to convergent thinking (e.g., Christie, 1983; Johnson & Ershler, 1980; Smith, et al., 1981). Clark et al. (1988) reported findings concerning concurrent relations of preschool pretend play with creativity as well as the relations of play with creativity scores of children three years later. Play observations were made by members of the research team who were not involved in the creativity testing and who were "blind" to the research hypothesis. Using a symbolic play aggregate score, the study showed that make-believe play was significantly and positively correlated with alternative-uses fluency scores and total fluency scores on the Torrance Thinking Creatively with Action and Movement Test (Torrance, 1981) during the preschool years. Preschool symbolic play predicted creativity scores three years later for males but not for females, and with creativity indexed, not by fluency scores, but by originality and flexibility scores. These relations held up even after the effects of intelligence were partialled out. Interestingly, the gender differences found accord with earlier work done by Hutt and her colleagues (Hutt & Bhavnani, 1972).

Johnson & Ershler (1980) conducted a longitudinal study in which various measures of play and cognitive functioning were compared concomitantly and from one year to the next. A group of 24 middle-class preschool children were studied. The average age of these children during the first year was 43 months. Children were tested each year on the Peabody Picture Vocabulary Test and Raven Progressive Matrices tests of intelligence, and on a battery of classification tasks (dichotomous sort, cross-classification, and class inclusion) and conservation tasks (liquid substance, number, length, area, and weight). Preschoolers were observed for 20 one-minute play observations, with play coded by use of categories for both social level (solitary, onlooker, parallel, and interactive) and cognitive level (functional, constructive, and imaginative). Imaginative play was further scored for number and type of transformations (person, object, situations) and for thematic content (sociodramatic or fantasy).

Pairing of play and cognitive test change scores from year one to year two revealed that, generally, more children increased in cognitive ability without increasing in imaginative play than increased in dramatic play without increasing in cognitive ability. This suggests that directional influence between these two variables moves from cognitive ability to imaginative play and not vice versa. Two statistically significant results were obtained by use of McNemar tests for evaluating proportions in change cells. From year one to year two significantly more children ($n = 11$) increased in conservation ability without increasing in thematic-fantasy play or in increasing situational transformations during pretend play than the number of children ($n = 2$) who increased on these measures of imaginative play while not increasing in conservation ability (see Table 12.2). In other words, these results suggest that cognitive ability may perhaps better be described as an antecedent condition for imaginative play as opposed to play as an antecedent for cognitive development. These findings are not inconsistent with data reported by Emmerich, Cocking, and Sigel (1979), which suggested that cognitive processes facilitate social adaptation but that social adaptation does not influence cognitive growth. Their short-term longitudinal study involved slightly older middle-class preschoolers (mean age at year one beginning of data collection was 48.9 months). In both studies, cognitive measures were restricted to language, intelligence, and conservation, with a form transformation task included in the Emmerich et al. study. Whether this pattern of cognitive prerequisite for play would hold for social cognitive and divergent thinking abilities is an unanswered empirical question at this time.

Table 12.2 Change in Cognitive Ability and Imaginative Play from Year One to Year Two (N=24)

PLAY MEASURES

COGNITIVE MEASURES		Dramatic		Transformations		Socio-Dramatic		Thematic-Fantasy		Situational Transformation	
		+	0	+	0	+	0	+	0	+	0
PPVT IQ	+/0	7/5	6/6	11/5	2/6	8/3	5/8	2/6	11/5	5/3	8/8
RAVEN IQ	+/0	5/7	6/6	8/8	3/5	3/8	8/5	5/3	6/10	5/3	6/10
CONSERVATION ABILITY	+/0	7/5	10/2	11/5	6/2	8/3	9/4	6/2	11/5	6/2	11/5
CLASSIFICA-TION ABILITY	+/0	5/7	7/5	8/8	4/4	6/5	6/7	6/2	6/10	3/5	9/7

Note. Figures refer to number of children showing change pattern.

RESEARCH RECOMMENDATIONS

Certainly more short-term and long-term longitudinal studies are required to test directional hypotheses concerning play and cognitive development, using a broader array of tasks and range of young children (e.g., age, social class, ethnicity). Divergent, convergent, and social cognitive assessments would be useful concomitants to profiling patterns of change in the play behavior of young children during the preschool years. Not only would such longitudinal research increase our understanding of the role of play in cognitive development, but it could also serve to build a case for supplementing or complementing formal tools of screening and assessment with informal play-based observational tools (Miller, 1987). Results of such basic research could have the practical fallout of bringing about more flexibility in the use of developmentally appropriate instruments of evaluation of young children in early childhood education and early childhood special education. However, empirically pinpointing linkages among play measures, cognitive measures, and psychometric measures of developmental functioning would be required before anyone would take seriously the argument for the interchangeability among the three sets of measures, least of all those currently entrenched within the educational establishment wanting business as usual.

The use of longitudinal field-based research methodologies entailing concurrent play and cognitive assessments is recommended as an alternative to the play-training paradigm for evaluating the significance of play in development. However, play-training studies are recommended provided research methods and procedures are tightened. As Brainerd (1982) laments, there has been a lack of consistency across studies, not only in terms of research findings reported but also in terms of length of training, the nature of the treatment conditions, and those of the control or the comparison groups and in terms of the extent and kinds of formative and summative assessments done. In other words, up to now there has not been any systematic program of research among investigators interested in employing the play-training paradigm. Collaboration among researchers is needed to improve this state of affairs.

The extant literature on children's play suggests that higher forms of play participation, such as seen in sociodramatic play, may have a role in facilitating cognitive functioning. However, the opposite hypothesis has not been tested yet; i.e., using cognitive training to determine its effects on sociodramatic play. Now that we have reliable measures of play (Enslein & Fein, 1981), it is possible to treat sociodramatic play not only as an independent variable influencing cognitive development but also as a dependent variable. That is, would training young children in small groups on various cognitive tasks such as perspective-taking tasks improve their performance in sociodramatic play? Not only would such research contribute theoretically and empirically, it would also have some practical import. Brainerd (1982), among others, for instance, has voiced the concern that play-training effects depend on the child's possession of a certain amount of learning or development prior to training. Cognitive training, thus, could be used to prepare young children for sociodramatic play. Since interactive effects of more formal components of an early childhood curriculum on the quality of play have been documented (Johnson, Ershler, Bell, 1980; Tizard, Philps, Plewis, 1977), it is not unreasonable to believe that the more deliberate targeting of certain behaviors and abilities for learning would enhance play competence. Ability to engage in sociodramatic play can thus become a criterion of program effectiveness with respect to the more formal aspects of the preschool or kindergarten curriculum.

Another research recommendation is to perform more fine-grained formative assessments of sociodramatic play. A start has been made in the work by Peter Smith and his colleagues in England (Smith & Syddall, 1978; Smith et al., 1981), who have measured the extent of language behavior and adult contact in play-training treatment conditions. Further progress can be made, for example, by using Sigel's taxonomy of distancing strategies (Copple et al., 1984; Sigel, 1987) to obtain a more detailed description of verbal interactions among children and between children and adults. Delineating the mental operational demand characteristics of the behavior (e.g., reconstructing, inferring, planning, etc.), as well as the level of abstraction and the conceptual difficulty of the play content, would allow for a more molecular appraisal of the processes occurring during play sessions. The notion of the "player-as-a-self-distancing-agent" could become illuminated by such painstaking analyses.

Summative evaluations of play-training conditions would help to clarify the psychological significance of sociodramatic play per se in relation to its cognitive developmental underpinnings by explicating the role of confounding or potentially confounding variables (e.g., adult tuition and warmth, peer interaction, verbal and cognitive stimulation). Although basic descriptive research as suggested above would be useful, factorial studies within the play-training paradigm are also urged for the theoretical and for the applied significance of such research. C. J. Brainerd (personal communication, October 1982) has indicated that one reason for inconsistent results of play training may be differences in personal characteristics of play tutors. Playful adult teachers, for example, may be more effective than less playful ones in conducting sociodramatic play-training sessions. Factorial studies, then, could examine the combined effects of teacher characteristics and play-training conditions. Rather than view adult contact or tuition as a confounding variable, the research purposely and systematically allows the "confounding variable" to remain coupled with the play component. Play is then no longer considered the special ingredient in an idealized, enriched diet decontextualized from the real world. Through such research we can learn what works best, and this has great educational significance. Toys, time, space, and other classroom factors can be systematically included in such factorial research designs to clarify the importance of *play-in-context* for early childhood growth and learning.

EDUCATIONAL RECOMMENDATIONS

The line dividing research and educational concerns is less visible when one focuses on the study of ecological factors and sociodramatic play using factorial or other designs and descriptive procedures to ascertain teacher and child behavior and play within the early childhood curriculum. Researchers need to observe teachers and children more carefully and to report richer descriptive accounts of play interactions. Teachers themselves need to do the same, whether as partners in collaborative research or as independents. Insights culled from such observations can be used to form hypotheses about functional relationships, and, by purposefully inserting gradations or variations in teacher performance with children during interventions, these hypotheses can be put to the test. Practical and reflective interventions with systematic variation form the basis of sound pedagogy and praxis.

Teacher and researcher observations of this nature should make one more cognizant of situational and individual differences in play performances. What may at first appear to be play deficits may turn out to be situational deficits, deficits of opportunity, or children's not feeling at ease in certain situations, for example. Children should be tracked at least informally for their *typical* and *peak* play performances across a variety of classroom play settings and when playing with various materials and playmates. Follow-ups would include teacher intervention to encourage higher play forms in those areas in which performance is low.

A generally as yet untested and underutilized manner in which teachers can intervene to promote high-level imaginative and constructive play in preschool and kindergarten settings is to use to full advantage the new microcomputer technology incorporated within the early childhood educational curriculum. Now, with the production of third- and soon fourth-generation commercial software, we have available many developmentally appropriate selections for use in the classroom (Haugland & Shade, 1988). Many contain attractive graphics and interesting sound effects and other positive features that lend themselves to constructive and dramatic play. COMPUPLAY, a division of the National Lekotek Center, publishes a newsletter that describes creative software ideas for young children. For instance, Jim Gill, Lekotek leader and COMPUPLAY instructor at the National Lekotek Center, uses STICKY BEAR TOWN BUILDER to foster imaginative play ("Creative Software," 1988). After the child builds the town, the teacher or parent can encourage the child to pretend to be a spy who must travel to each site listed; the child is then asked what was found there. When on the road, the child is asked to pretend to eat snack foods or pretend to visit people, improvising and acting out conversations. With the new technology, all children, including those with severe physical involvement, can, with support and encouragement from adults, participate for the first time in sociodramatic play.

Another educational recommendation on a more macrolevel is to better use heterogeneity in the classroom to full-play advantage for all. Admixtures based on age, gender, race, social class, and disability must be reckoned with positively by educators. Multicultural curriculum and instructional strategies for education need to be devised. A very recent study by Urberg (in press) found that without special intervention by the teacher, age-, sex-, and race-homogeneous interactions were not uniformly distributed over social playforms. Interactive play was more common and parallel play less common in homogeneous play groups, with same-age and same-gender, but not same-race, interactions more prevalent overall than would be expected by chance. On the other hand, cognitive playforms (functional vs. constructive vs. dramatic vs. games with rules) did not appear to be influenced by group composition. One wonders, though, whether how the adult's role is defined and implemented in a program might impact the frequency of occurrence of cognitive playforms, which could in turn impact social playforms. Appropriate and carefully planned teacher interventions could possibly lead to more positive and prosocial behavior within mixed or integrated play groups, in line with the tenets of multicultural education.

To come full circle then, the purpose of play in preschool or kindergarten, no matter how important for cognitive development, relates also to the traditional values responsible for why play was put in the kindergarten curriculum in the first place. These long-standing convictions and their rationales must not get lost in the shuffle as we attempt to ground our views on an empirical research base. The original arguments might prove to be effective as well for restoring play in early education.

SUMMARY

This chapter began by noting that research on children's play during the past two decades has proven not to be the fad that some thought it would be. Rather, research has continued and increased in intensity with the prospects for future progress bright. The significance of play was discussed in relation to general and specific cognitive functions. Theoretical and empirical evidence was presented concerning play and growth in the child's knowledge base and problem-solving abilities. The significance of play for integrative functions and concept acquisitions was noted with play seen as a form of distancing behavior.

Empirical research was then reviewed relating play with various convergent, divergent, and social cognitive abilities. Various methodologies, including correlational, experimental, and training procedures, were seen to have been widely employed, although conceptual and methodological limitations in the studies constrain one's being able to draw definitive conclusions at this time. Strongest evidence appears for implicating imaginative play in the development of divergent thinking skill.

Recommendations for research and practice include conducting, in a more programmatic way, research on the effects of and antecedents for sociodramatic play. Longitudinal research involving concurrent assessments of play and cognitive change would explicate the role of play in cognitive development and also have potential practical spinoff in providing an alternative to formal assessment in early childhood education. Within the play-training paradigm three specific research recommendations were made:

1. Tests are needed of the reverse causal hypothesis that training for specific cognitive outcomes would be facilitative of higher level sociodramatic play performance
2. More fine-grained formative assessments of sociodramatic play are needed for a more molecular appraisal of the processes occurring during play sessions
3. Factorial designs can be employed to examine systematically the combined impact of play coupled with other relevant factors such as teacher personal characteristics.

Finally, collaborative research with educational value was urged to help build a theory of practice concerning the teacher's or parent's role in childhood play, with special attention given to situational and individual, as well as developmental, differences in typical and peak play performances. Incorporating microcomputers into the play curriculum in early childhood education was also recommended, as was using heterogenity in the classroom as a challenge to promote education that is multicultural.

REFERENCES

Athey, I. (1988). The relationship of play to cognitive, language, and moral development. In D. Bergen (Ed.), *Play as a medium for learning and development: A handbook of theory and practice* (pp. 81–101). Portsmouth, NH: Heinemann.
Beeghly, M., & Cicchetti, D. (Eds.). (1987, Summer). *Symbolic development in atypi-*

cal children: New directions for child development. No. 36 (whole). San Francisco: Jossey-Bass.

Bloch, M. N. (1988, April). A history of the importance of play in the American kindergarten. Paper presented at the annual meeting of the American Educational Research Association, New Orleans.

Brainerd, C. J. (1982). Effects of group and individualized dramatic play training on cognitive development. In D. J. Pepler and K. H. Rubin (Eds.), The play of children: Current theory and research (pp. 114–129). Basel: Karger.

Bretherton, I. (1984). Symbolic play: The development of social understanding. New York: Academic Press.

Burns, S., & Brainerd, C. (1979). Effects of constructive and dramatic play on perspective-taking in very young children. Developmental Psychology, 15, 512–521.

Christie, J. F. (1983). The effects of play tutoring on young children's cognition performance. Journal of Educational Research, 76, 326–330.

Clark, P., Griffing, P., & Johnson, L. (1988, April). Symbolic play and creativity: Contemporary and longitudinal relationships. Paper presented at the annual meeting of the American Educational Research Association, New Orleans.

Cole, D., & LaVoie, J. (1985). Fantasy play and related cognitive development in 2- to 6-year-olds. Developmental Psychology, 21, 233–240.

Connolly, J. A., & Doyle, A. (1984). Relation of social fantasy play to social competence in preschoolers. Developmental Psychology, 20, 797–806.

Copple, C., Sigel, I., & Saunders, R. (1984). Educating the young thinkers: Classroom strategies for cognitive growth. Hillsdale, NJ: Erlbaum.

Creative software for kids. (1988, Summer). Innotek/Compuplay News, p. 9.

Dansky, J. (1980a). Cognitive consequence of sociodramatic play and exploration training for economically disadvantaged preschoolers. Journal of Child Psychology and Psychiatry, 21, 47–58.

Dansky, J. (1980b). Make-believe: A mediator of the relationship between play and creativity. Child Development, 51, 576–579.

Dansky, J., & Silverman, I. (1973). Effects of play on associative fluency in preschool-aged children. Developmental Psychology, 9, 38–43.

Dansky, J., & Silverman, I. (1975). Play: A general facilitator of associative fluency. Developmental Psychology, 11, 104.

Emmerich, W., Cocking, R., & Sigel, I. (1979). Relationships between cognitive and social functioning in preschool children. Developmental Psychology, 15, 495–504.

Enslein, J. P., & Fein, G. G. (1981). Temporal and cross-situational stability of children's social and play behavior. Developmental Psychology, 17, 760–761.

Feitelson, D., & Ross, G. (1973). The neglected factor—play. Human Development, 16, 202–223.

Fink, R. S. (1976). The role of imaginative play in cognitive development. Psychological Reports, 39, 895–906.

Garvey, C. (1977). Play. Cambridge, MA: Harvard University Press.

Golomb, C., & Bonen, S. (1981). Playing games of make-believe: The effectiveness of symbolic play training with children who failed to benefit from early conservation training. Genetic Psychology Monographs, 104, 137–159.

Golomb, C., & Cornelius, C. (1977). Symbolic play and its cognitive significance. *Developmental Psychology, 13,* 246–252.

Golomb, C., Gowing, E. D., & Friedman, L. (1982). Play and cognition: Studies of pretense play and conservation of quality. *Journal of Experimental Child Psychology, 33,* 257–279.

Guralnick, M. J., & Groom, J. M. (1987). The peer relations of mildly delayed and nonhandicapped preschool children in mainstreamed playgroups. *Child Development, 58,* 1556–1572.

Guralnick, M. J., & Groom, J. M. (1988). Peer interactions in mainstreamed and specialized classrooms: A comparative analysis. *Exceptional Children, 54,* 415–425.

Guthrie, K., & Hudson, L. (1979). Training conservation through symbolic play: A second look. *Child Development, 50,* 1269–1271.

Haugland, S. W., & Shade, D. D. (1988, May). Developmentally appropriate software for young children. *Young Children,* 37–43.

Hughes, M. (1987). The relationship between symbolic and manipulative (object) play. In D. Gorlitz & J. F. Wohlwill (Eds.), *Curiosity, imagination, and play: On the development of spontaneous cognitive and motivational processes* (pp. 248–257). Hillsdale, NJ: Erlbaum.

Hutt, C., & Bhavnani, R. (1972). Predictions from play. *Nature, 23*(7), 171–172.

Isaacs, S. (1933). *Social development in young children.* New York: Schocken.

Isaacs, S. (1966). *Intellectual growth in young children.* New York: Schocken. (Original work published in 1930).

Johnson, J. E. (1976). Relations of divergent thinking and intelligence test scores with social and nonsocial make-believe play of preschool children. *Child Development, 47,* 1200–1203.

Johnson, J. E., & Ershler, J. (1980, September). *Developmental changes in imaginative play and cognitive ability of preschoolers.* Eighty-eighth annual convention of the American Psychological Association, Montreal.

Johnson, J. E., Ershler, J., & Bell, C. (1980). Play behavior in a discovery-based and a formal education preschool program. *Child Development, 51,* 271–274.

Johnson, J. E., Ershler, J., & Lawton, J. (1982). Intellective correlates of preschoolers' spontaneous play. *Journal of General Psychology, 106,* 115–122.

Kamii, C., & DeVries, R. (1978). *Physical knowledge in preschool education.* Englewood Cliffs, NJ: Prentice-Hall.

Kamii, C., & DeVries, R. (1980). *Group games in early education: Implications of Piaget's theory.* Washington, DC: National Association for the Education of Young Children.

Levy, A. (1988, April). *Sociodramatic play as a method for enhancing the language performance of kindergarten age students.* Paper presented at the annual meeting of the American Educational Research Association, New Orleans.

Li, A. K. (1978). Effect of play on novel responses in kindergarten children. *The Alberta Journal of Educational Research, 23,* 31–36.

Lieberman, J. N. (1965). Playfulness and divergent thinking: An investigation of their relationship at the kindergarten level. *The Journal of Genetic Psychology, 107,* 219–224.

Lovinger, S. L. (1974). Socio-dramatic play and language development in preschool disadvantaged children. *Psychology in the Schools, 11*, 313–320.

Madsen, M. C. (1967). Cooperative and competitive motivation of children in three Mexican subcultures. *Psychological Reports, 20*, 1307–1320.

Miller, T. J. (1987). *Exploration and play as assessment components for the identification of preschool handicapped children.* Unpublished doctoral dissertation, The Pennsylvania State University.

Pepler, D. (1979). *Effects of convergent and divergent play experience on preschoolers' problem-solving behaviors.* Unpublished doctoral dissertation, University of Waterloo, Ontario, Canada.

Pepler, D. (1987). Play in schools and schooled in play: A psychological perspective. In J. Black & N. King (Eds.), *School play: A source book* (pp. 75–107). New York: Garland.

Pepler, D., & Ross, H. (1981). Effects of play on convergent and divergent problem solving. *Child Development, 52*, 1202–1210.

Piaget, J. (1962). *Play, dreams, and imitation in childhood.* New York: W. W. Norton.

Rogow, S. M. (1981). Developing play skills and communicative competence in multiple handicapped young people. *Journal of Visual Impairment and Blindness, 75*, 197–202.

Rosen, C. E. (1974). The effects of sociodramatic play on problem-solving behavior among culturally disadvantaged children. *Child Development, 45*, 920–927.

Rubin, K. H. (1980). Fantasy play: Its role in the development of social skills and social cognition. In K. H. Rubin (Ed.), *Children's Play* (pp. 69–84). San Francisco: Jossey-Bass.

Rubin, K. H., Fein, G., & Vandenberg, B. (1983). Play. In E. M. Hetherington (Ed.), & P. H. Mussen (Series Ed.), *Handbook of child psychology: Vol. 4 Socialization, personality, and social development* (pp. 698–774). New York: Wiley.

Rubin, K. H., & Maioni, T. L. (1975). Play preference and its relationship to egocentrism, popularity, and classification skills in preschoolers. *Merrill-Palmer Quarterly, 21*, 171–179.

Saltz, E., & Brodie, J. (1982). Pretend-play: Training in childhood: A review and critique. In D. J. Pepler & K. H. Rubin (Eds.), *The play of children: Current theory and research* (pp. 97–113). Basel, Switzerland: Karger AG.

Saltz, E., Dixon, D., & Johnson, J. E. (1977). Training disadvantaged preschoolers on various fantasy activities: Effects on cognitive functioning and impulse control. *Child Development, 48*, 367–380.

Saltz, E., & Johnson, J. E. (1974). Training for thematic-fantasy play in culturally disadvantaged children: Preliminary results. *Journal of Educational Psychology, 66*, 623–630.

Shores, R., Hester, P., & Strain, P. (1976). Effects of amount and type of teacher-child interaction on child-child interaction during free-play. *Psychology in the Schools, 13*, 171–175.

Sigel, I. E. (1987). Educating the young thinker: A distancing model of preschool education. In J. L. Roopnarine & J. E. Johnson (Eds.), *Approaches to early childhood education* (pp. 237–252). Columbus, OH: Charles E. Merrill.

Singer, D. G., & Rummo, J. (1973). Ideational creativity and behavioral style in kindergarten aged children. *Developmental Psychology, 8*, 154–161.

Singer, J. L. (1973). *The child's world of make-believe: Experimental studies of imaginative play.* New York: Academic Press.

Singer, J. L., & Singer, D. G. (1988). Essay on play: Imaginative play and human development: Schemas, scripts, and possibilities. In D. Bergen (Ed.), *Play as a medium for learning and development: A handbook of theory and practice* (pp. 75–79). Portsmouth, NH: Heinemann.

Smilansky, S. (1968). *The effects of sociodramatic play on disadvantaged preschool children.* New York: Wiley.

Smith, P. K. (1988). Children's play and its role in early development: A re-evaluation of the "Play Ethics." In A. D. Pellegrini (Ed.), *Psychological bases for early education* (pp. 207–226). Chichester, England: Wiley.

Smith, P. K., Dalgleish, L. M., & Herzmark, G. (1981). A comparison of other effects of fantasy play tutoring and skills tutoring in nursery classes. *International Journal of Behavioral Development, 4*, 421–441.

Smith, P. K., & Dutton, S. (1979). Play and training in direct and innovative problem solving. *Child Development, 50*, 830–836.

Smith, P. K., & Syddall, S. (1978). Play and non-play tutoring in preschool children: Is it play or tutoring which matters? *British Journal of Educational Psychology, 48*, 315–325.

Smith, P. K., & Whitney, S. (1987). Play and associative fluency: Experimenter effects may be responsible for previous positive findings. *Developmental Psychology, 23*, 49–53.

Sutton-Smith, B. (1968). Novel responses to toys. *Merrill-Palmer Quarterly, 14*, 151–158.

Sylva, K., Bruner, J., & Genova, P. (1976). The role of play in the problem-solving of children 3–5 years old. In J. Bruner, A. Jolly, & K. Sylva (Eds.), *Play: Its role in development and evaluation* (pp. 244–257). New York: Penguin.

Tizard, B., Philps, J., & Plewis, I. (1977). Play in preschool centers II. Effects on play of the child's social class and the educational orientation of the center. *Journal of Child Psychology and Psychiatry, 17*, 265–274.

Tomkins, S. (1962–63). *Affect, imagery, consciousness* (2 vols.). New York: Springer-Verlag.

Torrance, E. P. (1981). *Thinking creatively in action and movement-manual.* Bensenville, IL: Scholastic Testing Services.

Urberg, K. (in press). An observational study of race-, age-, and sex-heterogeneous interactions in preschoolers. *Journal of Applied Developmental Psychology.*

Vandenberg, B. (1981). The role of play in the development of insightful tool-using strategies. *Merrill-Palmer Quarterly, 27*, 97–109.

CHAPTER 13

An Agenda for Research on Play in Early Childhood Education

Doris Pronin Fromberg

Research needs to proceed from an explicit definition of play and from a clearly stated theoretical base, but neither a single definition of play nor a single theoretical base exists that is acceptable to all. This is apparent in the array of both experimental and ethnographic designs. Definition and research methodology are confounded further by the low status in Western civilization that is accorded to play as contrasted with work. Egan (1988; 1989) further suggests that oral literacy is valued less than written literacy. As a form of oral literacy, therefore, play is again viewed as less significant.

Play is both one integral condition of learning[1] (Fromberg, 1987a) that has lymphatic qualities (Fromberg, 1987b) and a human activity that is worthwhile for its own sake. I have defined the pretend play of young children as behavior that is "Symbolic, . . . Meaningful, . . . Active, . . . Pleasurable, . . . Voluntary and intrinsically motivated, . . . Rule-governed, . . . and Episodic" (1987b, p. 36). The content of play themes is influenced by personal experiences of the child, as well as the context in which play is underway. With this sort of working definition of play, it is apparent that research would need to grapple with the lymphatic aspects of action-in-process.

Sociodramatic play, in particular, is a complex form of pretend play in which children interact with one another and/or adults. Smilansky, in Chapter 2, illuminates a fruitful distinction between sociodramatic and dramatic play as unique forms of pretend play. Bergen (1988) construes sociodramatic play as both cooperative (according to Parten, 1933) and symbolic (within Piaget's 1962 framework) action. Vygotsky credits sociodramatic play as a process that leads development (Reiber & Carton, 1987). Regardless of variations in theo-

I wish to acknowledge the generous encouragement of Carol Seefeldt.

retical perspective, it is apparent that sociodramatic play is a particularly rich form of children's experience of living and being distinctly human. Because of its interactive nature, moreover, sociodramatic play is particularly accessible to study.

There are two major theoretical perspectives from which the various forms of pretend play have been conceptualized and studied. The predominantly psychological perspective or the predominantly cultural/anthropological perspective suggests a respective focus on separate aspects of play that, in reality, are welded within children's experience. A psychocultural perspective may more adequately reflect reality. Earlier chapters and other sources have discussed these issues (Fromberg, 1987b; 1990). This chapter, rather than a re-review of the research literature, focuses on research methodology from a proactive standpoint. I discuss research methodologies that have been emphasized in the study of play, provide a selected look at some alternatives, and consider ways that future research might transform educational practice and theory. That children have opportunities to engage in play and where they play are political issues that require the attention of specific public policy.

A PROACTIVE RESEARCH PARADIGM

Along with other affairs of the heart and head, teaching is often a predictably unpredictable affair. It is unpredictable because of the responsive interactions that take place between children and teachers and among children.

Researchers have traditionally sought to formulate rational questions and to offer predictably rational answers. Teachers and researchers have expected that teachers will take responsibility for using research findings in their teaching. Therefore, the only reasonably predictable outcome of this contrast between unpredictable realities in classrooms and the myths of predictable knowledge about human interaction held by some researchers, teachers, and policy makers is the degree to which slippage of communication occurs. *The ultimate purpose of all this passionate activity is to improve the conditions of children's and teachers' lives in schools, to make a difference in society.*

Typically, even when university-based teachers seek collaboration with classroom-based teachers, they often have been informed by teachers' groups that their job is to do research and the classrooms teacher's job is to implement it. Although there have been recent movements among teachers toward more equitable collaboration (Casanova, 1989), this separation of functions grows out of a tradition of past practices, job descriptions, and incentives. Such compartmentalized arrangements have made little difference in the lives of children in schools.[2] They tend to perpetuate the separation between theory and practice that has been deplored, notably by Dewey (1904). This separation also creates a further schism in the creation of an elitist "producer" researcher class in relation to those who are researched, the intended customers.

In the light of these comments, it is intriguing to consider the work of those who write of the "postpositivist era" (Lather, 1986, p. 259) and of "poststructural investigations" (Cherryholmes, 1988, pp. 186, 187, passim; McDonald, 1988, p. 475). The postpositivist view suggests that there need to be reciprocal, not elitist, relationships between researcher and researched, in order to transform practice, to improve learning and teaching. In a compatible way, the poststructural approach directs our attention to the relationship—the relative balance or imbalance—between what we already may know and what we have yet to discover.

When we consider the nature of research as inclusive of a reciprocity between the participants, theory and practice—rather than separate or sequential—may become illuminated within the same recursive process.[3] This is significant for early childhood education in particular because the gap between practice, beliefs, and theories has been increasing. At the same time that the research literature on the value of play appears to be expanding geometrically, the presence of play in early childhood classrooms has been dwindling impetuously. The tensions between work and play have paralleled increasing academic demands that are defined by narrowly structured standardized tests. In turn, the tests appear increasingly to drive a normatively fueled, linear program.

Vygotsky has made the point that play leads development (Cole, John-Steiner, Scribner, & Souberman, 1978; Reiber & Carton, 1987; Vygotsky, 1976). Without question, there is significant weight in the proliferation of studies of young children's sociodramatic play that supports the notion that play contributes to the development of language, social competence, cognitive skills, and imaginative fluency (creativity). Numerous reviews of relevant literature exist within earlier chapters. (See also Bergen, 1988; Fein & Rivkin, 1986; Fromberg, 1987b; Pellegrini, 1985.) In addition, we are reminded that human beings need to play, that play is a kind of moral imperative (Sutton-Smith, 1989; Morgan, 1982).

COMMENTARY ON EXISTING RESEARCH

Experimental and Ethnographic Paradigms

There is an intermingling of how and where research is done. For example, whereas ethnographic research might be done in a laboratory setting, researchers would be likely to study the effects of the setting on human interaction rather than only on the content of planned interaction. Ethnographic research is more often found in settings where children play in the usual course of living, such as indoors or outdoors at school, in the community, and less often at home.

Experimental research is most often found in laboratory settings in which researchers remove children from their usual physical and human environments. At other times, experimental researchers have altered conditions of ordinary environments and studied children's reactions within them (Singer, 1973). For the most part, these experimental situations are intriguing and ingenious arrangements.

Both ethnographic and experimental methodologies have been used in intervention studies. Ethnographic approaches predominate, however, in naturalistic settings, but experimental approaches predominate in laboratory settings. Thus, there are unique insights available in different situations.

A problem of ethnographic research lies in "catching" children playing. This takes up researcher time in waiting around for things to happen that are relevant to the questions under consideration. If one is to claim to study play, there also is a need to be sure that children are playing. "Play is exceedingly difficult to define adequately and almost by definition is a phenomenon which is easily distorted or suppressed by attempts to manipulate or control it" (Dansky, 1985, p. 279). For example, Dansky (1985), while admiring the rigor of their techniques, criticizes the work of Simon and Smith (1985), claiming that they need to establish that play has occurred. In turn, they criticize him for lack of adequate control procedures (Simon & Smith, 1985).

It may be true that when children are in a controlled laboratory environment, individually or in small groups with familiar or unfamiliar other children, researchers, or parents, the researcher can use time efficiently. The children's experiencing of a change from their natural context may, however, limit the validity of data collected in an artificial environment. For example, the competence of children in the presence of a parent as contrasted with a strange adult, or in interaction with other children in private, may be more or less visible. There are reports of more competent and creative play in familiar and private settings (Dansky, 1985; Fein, 1987; Kelly-Byrne, 1989; Kreye, 1984; Olszewski, 1987; Schwartzman, 1978).

The distinctions between family cultures and school or laboratory settings need to be considered. They have been differentiated in terms of elements such as the use of space, time, language and other forms of communication, classification systems, and aspirations (Janiv, 1976; Silvern, 1988). Mindful of such discontinuity, Bretherton (1984), preliminary to using a laboratory setting with toddlers, arranged home visits in an attempt to familiarize children with the experimenter.

The power of the peer relationship to elicit competent behavior, whether imaginative, social, or cognitive, has been documented by still other researchers (Bruner, 1980, 1986; Dyson, 1987; Johnson, Johnson, Holubec, & Roy, 1984; Piaget et al., 1965). Thus, competence needs to be defined in relation to a situational context rather than as a universal state (Bretherton, 1984; Corrigan, 1987). In effect, play may be depressed or facilitated by contextual variations. The issue of competence in relation to context is particularly significant in light of the "new three Rs"—readiness testing, "redshirting,"[4] and retention (Fromberg, 1989).

Validity and Researchers

There has been an intermingling of who engages in research and the way in which validity is defined. Nevertheless, a hierarchical view would contend that positivist, experimental research, with an idealized neutral experimenter role, is more valid than postpositivist, ethnographic research or collaborative research, with an idealized participant-observer role. Validity is, however, defined from different perspectives within each research paradigm.

The positivist view, positing neutrality of measures, declares that validity has been achieved when measures indeed measure what they were set out to measure, when findings may be confirmed to predict future behavior, and when the purposes of a test collection procedure are supported. The postpositivist view would not exclude such validity but would expect that valid data and findings would result in transformed purposes and practices.

Data, moreover, would need to be analyzed in ways that include a sampling of multiple sources of perceptions from respondents/participants and other data. In particular, the study of play as action-in-process means that observers also need to attend to their own idiosyncratic biases and to make explicit their own priorities and values.

This inclusion of multiple sources is a form of triangulation that may be viewed as additional to, and different from, the positivist use of more than a single quantitative[5] measure in the pursuit of more accurate information. In this way, the positivist notion of validity may be subsumed under the postpositivist notion of validity, but the process is not necessarily reversible.

Research Settings

The predominant experimental paradigm of play research in early childhood involves the use of small populations, the removal of children to laboratory situations by relatively unknown adults, and the relatively brief duration of experiments. In contrast, ethnographic models are represented in a small body of studies that deal with the play of young children in their natural environments.

In one of the most extensive ethnographic studies in which play was part of what was documented, Heath (1983) collected data within families, schools, and communities over a ten-year period. This study continues at the present time (Shirley Brice Heath, personal communication, 1989). Eiferman (1971) amassed data over a period ranging from 14 to 18 months in which 150 observers recorded spontaneous outdoor play activities of 14,000 elementary-school-age children. Inasmuch as each observer focused on five play groups, some shifting in constituent child populations would be expected.

In a school setting, Isaacs (1933/1972; 1930/1960) reports the participation of two to five teachers over a period of three years in the collection of observational material concerning 10 to 20 children. Within other classrooms, there have been studies that ranged from a teacher participant/observer over the course of a year (Paley, 1984) or less (Monighan-Nourot, Scales, Van Hoorn, with Almy, 1987) to outside observers in a descriptive study of 38 children over a period of 20 hours (Giffin, 1984). Studies in which many teachers collaborated in data collection have been reported (Bruner, 1980), as well as those in which one teacher served as a participant-observer (Paley, 1984). There has been periodic collection of case data at school (Shotwell, Wolf, & Gardner, 1979), as well as a periodic collection of data at home over a period of years (Wolf, Rygh, & Altschuler, 1984).

Kelly-Byrne (1989) engaged in an ethnographic study as a participant-observer during 14 sessions of two to three hours, up to five hours' duration, across a one-year period. Taking place in the child's home, this study uniquely focused on an adult and child playing together. Building on a trend in feminist anthropological studies, she studied the possible impact of a researcher's presence, influence, and subjectivity within the research context. Although Levenstein (1976; 1985) collected data at home, it was in the context of a quasi-experimental intervention format.

A much-cited study within ongoing classrooms involved as many as 600 young children in planned teacher curriculum interventions and 600 children in control groups over the period of a nine-week intervention (Smilansky, 1968). Outside observers collected data, while teachers and parents were interviewed, and home visits documented. A notable one-year study that involved a context-based intervention, in which teachers collaborated in data collection, involved one nursery school class (Scales, 1987).

ISSUES FOR FUTURE STUDY

These selected studies highlighted some types of data that have been collected. In addition, there is a need for increased understanding and documentation of how children play and of what their thematic content consists. Surveys and observations in natural settings, using the triangulation of various participants, would provide information concerning the nature of stimulation and opportunities that young children are encountering.

Instructional Questions

There is need for data concerning the play of children within primary and kindergarten classes, as well as in preschools and child care settings. For example, within different curriculum models and organizational and scheduling patterns, what and how do children play? What provisions are teachers making? In what ways are teachers intervening in children's play?

Where does play fit into instructional time? For example, playful time off task has been found to be more fruitful than time on task in learning to write (Dyson, 1987). How time is used, rather than the duration of time in school, has been seen to be significant (Karweit, 1988). With what models of instruction is play compatible? For example, role playing has been found to enhance story recall (Pellegrini & Galda, 1982). While role playing is not typically sociodramatic play, it is also not typically direct instruction. In what ways, for example, does a cooperative learning model (Johnson et al., 1984; Slavin & Madden, 1989) interface with sociodramatic play?

How are teachers using children's play as an indication of their development? For example, teacher observations, which are valid predictors of children's behavior, along with product samples, need to receive greater attention (Gullo, 1988; Seefeldt & Barbour, 1987; Shepard & Smith, 1988; Teale, 1988). If one purpose of research and assessment is to improve conditions for children and teachers, and teacher observations are important in assessing children's development, then we need to provide systematic and political facilitation of the use of such valid observations in making decisions about children.

What research data do administrators and policy makers need in order to understand the importance of play in early childhood? Perhaps it would be useful to reframe the question to include what might be some ways of involving policy makers, as well as practitioners, in the collaborative definition of questions to study.

Gender Questions

The influence of gender on play has been studied from several points of view. Serbin (1978) reported observing classroom differences in access to construction materials and subsequent development of visual-spatial skills. Fagot (1988) noted that boys received more attention for assertive, negative behavior and girls for more compliant, positive behavior.

The issue of competition and cooperation has been discussed in various settings, both in feminist literature (Gilligan, 1982) and in cross-cultural studies. In a New Guinean culture, the goal of games was an equitable outcome for all participants (Burridge, 1976). (Indeed, skill in missing, in order to get even, was greater than striking sticks with tops.) Reviews of rough-and-tumble play suggest that children's subjective experience may be collaborative, although women teachers, among others, may interpret such play as confrontational (Blurton-Jones, 1976; Pellegrini, 1987). A study of the culture of families that tolerate different types and degrees of play would also help to illuminate how cooperation and competition develop.

Kelly-Byrne (1989) suggests that there is a need for research that describes how girls and boys learn about intimacy and bonding with their peers, in contexts in which play relationships are studied. In this regard, it would be useful to reflect on the findings of cross-cultural studies in which girls were kept closer to home and played less than boys did, subsequently becoming more nurturant than boys (Whiting & Edwards et al., 1988). At the same time, although expressed differently, nurturant behavior was equally present across all cultures until school age. It might be fruitful to engage in particular study of those cultures in which deviations from the usual observations appeared.

Developmental Questions

In general, it makes sense to support longitudinal research of sociodramatic play experiences in both cross-cultural study and United States settings. The developmental significance of sociodramatic play needs additional support through longitudinal studies in natural contexts.

There has been some documentation of a decline in play activities around six years of age (Voss, 1987). The problem of washout effects of early childhood programs gains is significant. Although there is the notion that some early childhood program gains are not sustained, one might well ask what is happening during the primary years to depress these gains. Collaborative research that is tied to reflective teaching is a particularly relevant format for documenting such events. Findings of such studies have a potential impact on public policy.

While contextual factors have an influence on the degree and extent of play, thematic contents, and personal relationships, there is a need to study children's subjective feelings as well. In the study of both contextual and personal forces, triangulation procedures within a longitudinal span appear to be reasonable policies to pursue. The development of indicators of "flow"[6] experiences could also be a productive area of study. Children's sociodramatic play, moreover, is particularly accessible to observation and revelatory of children's subjective experiences.

Play Dynamics

The purpose of research that helps adults better understand children's development of play and how they experience their lives is not in the service of tampering with this lymphatic system. The content of sociodramatic play themes can help to illuminate individual children's development and how they experience contexts and relationships.

As a type of syntax that generates changes over time, play has a surface structure and a deep structure. The surface structure consists of what appear to be topics and themes, such as superhero or family play. The deep structure touches on subjective experiences and relationships.

It makes sense to study the transformational aspects of themes and their development. Through such study, it may be possible to identify the deep structure of isomorphic imagery and patterns in children's natural play and its individual variations.

The study of play dynamics can grow out of an emerging theoretical confluence of isomorphic notions such as *personal* affective symbolic templates (Fein, 1987), *interpersonal* script theory as figurative representations (Bretherton, 1984), and *interdisciplinary* perceptual models as the images underlying early experience (Fromberg, 1987a, 1987b). Thus, if the predominantly psychological and predominantly cultural theories of young children's play are wedded into a psychocultural conception, they spawn particular conceptions of content. The lymphatic nature of play suggests that such content is distinctly interdisciplinary and constructed by children. Additional study of these confluent dynamics has the potential to provide insights that are relevant to the improvement of educational practice. At an ethical level, the issue of the moral imperative of play in early childhood education merits integration within this theoretical confluence.

For educational and policy purposes, there is abundant evidence that sociodramatic play is a spontaneous activity of childhood that integrates the many dimensions of development and learning that educators have identified. To eliminate, limit unduly, or warp the generative energy and transformational power of children's sociodramatic play is, in my opinion, an attenuation of childhood, a restraint upon rich learning experiences, and a potential form of child abuse.

Research is needed, therefore, that provides additional information about how environmental contexts and provisions influence the presence and substance of sociodramatic play. Longitudinal, as well as cross-sectional, studies are valuable formats that could extend the knowledge base concerning contextual influences on sociodramatic and other pretend play.

Closedown

Early childhood professionals are usually sensitive to children's weanings and separations. There has been less attention, however, to closedown and separation from research interventions, particularly the temporary routines and presence of researchers in children's lives. Kelly-Byrne (1989), in particular, and others from different points of view (Barnes, Booth, Driscoll, Fromberg, et al., 1979; Goldstein, 1984; Lynn & Garske, 1985[7]), highlight the need for researchers to be sensitive to human beings' needs and feelings about interruptions and separations from a research project.

It makes sense to plan exit activities with care and sensitivity. For example, it might be useful to plan a gradual reduction of duration of contacts along with increased intervals between contacts, coupled with increased focus for children and teachers in other activities. Exit interviews or carefully planned sessions might also take place in conjunction with natural calendar breaks.

Engaging in early childhood research is a courageous act that touches the core of one's ethical stance. The study of play means the integration of content and relationships. In any research on play, the need for contextual sensitivity is particularly significant. With any kind of intervention, moreover, the withdrawal of ethical capital risks escalation. It is essential, therefore, that responsible participants honestly share their perceptions, purposes, and values.

NOTES

1. The other conditions of learning include inductive experiences, cognitive dissonance, social interaction, physical experiences, and competence.

2. There is a difference of opinion concerning the degree to which practice is transformed when teachers have information about research findings. Joyce and Showers (1982) report small impact from information and significant impact from coaching. Peterson, Fennema, and Carpenter (1988/1989) report significant influences on teacher behavior based on information about how children learn. The literature on teacher collaboration in research and reflective practice point toward a clear connection with change in practice (Lieberman, 1987, Spring; Showers, 1985; Stenhouse, 1980).

3. Hofstadter (1980), in particular, illuminates the isomorphic nature of recursive imagery in the context of mathematics, art, and music.

4. "Redshirting" is the practice of postponing entry into a program (Frick, 1986).

5. There have been serious questions raised about the "predictive correlations" of

quantitative tests that are widely used in placing young children (Shepard & Smith, 1988).

6. "Flow" has been identified as the personal "optimal" satisfaction experienced during activities such as play (Csikszentmihayli, 1979; 1988).

7. I appreciate the contribution of the last two sources by Roberta Wiener.

REFERENCES

Barnes, D., Booth, D., Driscoll, M., Fromberg, D., Rothstein, E., Robinsky, R., & To-lan, M. (1979). Getting on with getting out: Reflections on a Teacher Corps project closeout. Hempstead, NY: Unpublished report.

Bergen, D. (Ed.). (1988). *Play: A medium for learning and development.* Portsmouth, NH: Heinemann.

Blurton-Jones, N. (1976). Rough and tumble play among nursery school children. In J. S. Bruner, A. Jolly, & K. Sylva (Eds.), *Play: Its role in development and evolution* (pp. 352–363). New York: Basic Books.

Bretherton, I. (1984). *Symbolic play: The development of social understanding.* New York: Academic Press.

Bruner, J. S. (1980). *Under five in Britain.* Ypsilanti, MI: High/Scope.

Bruner, J. S. (1986). Play, thought and language. *Prospects, 16,* 77–83.

Burridge, K. O. L. (1976). A Tengu game. In J. S. Bruner, A. Jolly, & K. Sylva (Eds.), *Play: Its role in development and evolution* (pp. 364–366). New York: Basic Books.

Casanova, U. (1989, January). Research and practice: We can integrate them. *National Education Association, 7,* 44–49.

Cherryholmes, C. H. (1988). *Power and criticism: Poststructural investigations in education.* New York: Teachers College Press.

Cole, M., John-Steiner, V., Scribner, S., & Souberman, E. (Eds.) (1978). *Mind in Society: L. S. Vygotsky.* Cambridge, MA: Harvard University Press.

Corrigan, R. (1987). A developmental sequence of actor-object pretend play in young children. *Merrill-Palmer Quarterly, 31,* 279–284.

Csikszentmihayli, M. (1979). The concept of flow. In B. Sutton-Smith (Ed.), *Play and learning* (pp. 257–274). New York: Gardner Press.

Csikszentmihayli, M. (1988). Introduction; The flow of experience and its significance for human psychology; The future of flow. In M. Csikszentmihayli & I. S. Csikszentmihayli (Eds.), *Optimal experience: Psychological studies in flow consciousness* (pp. 3–14; 15–35; 364–383). New York: Cambridge University Press.

Dansky, J. L. (1985, July). Questioning "A Paradigm Questioned". A commentary on Simon and Smith. *Merrill-Palmer Quarterly, 31,* 279–284.

Dewey, J. (1904). The relation of theory to practice in education. In C. A. Murry (Ed.), *Third yearbook of the National Society for the Scientific Study of Education* (pp. 9–30). Chicago: University of Chicago Press.

Dyson, A. H. (1987). The value of "time off task:" Young children's spontaneous talk and deliberate text. *Harvard Educational Review, 57,* 396–420.

Egan, K. (1988). The origins of imagination and the curriculum. In K. Egan & D. Nadaner (Eds.), *Imagination and education* (pp. 91–127). New York: Teachers College Press.

Egan, K. (1989). Education and the mental life of young children. In L. R. Williams & D. P. Fromberg (Eds.), *Defining the field of early childhood education: Proceedings of an invitational symposium* (pp. 41–76). Charlottesville, VA: W. Alton Jones Foundation.

Eiferman, R. K. (1971). Social play in childhood. In R. E. Herron & B. Sutton-Smith (Eds.), *Child's play* (pp. 270–297). New York: Wiley.

Fagot, B. I. (1988). Toddlers' play and sex stereotyping. In D. Bergen (Ed.), *Play: A medium for learning and development* (pp. 133–135). Portsmouth, NH: Heinemann.

Fein, G. G. (1987). Pretend play: Creativity and consciousness. In D. Gorlitz & J. F. Wohlwill (Eds.), *Curiosity, imagination, and play* (pp. 281–304). Hillsdale, NJ: Erlbaum.

Fein, G. G., & Rivkin, M. (Eds.). (1986). *The young child at play*. Washington, DC: National Association for the Education of Young Children.

Frich, R. (1986). In support of academic redshirting. *Young Children, 41*(2), 9–10.

Fromberg, D. P. (1987a). *The full-day kindergarten.* New York: Teachers College Press.

Fromberg, D. P. (1987b). Play. In C. Seefeldt (Ed.), *The early childhood curriculum: A review of current research* (pp. 35–74). New York: Teachers College Press.

Fromberg, D. P. (1989, Spring). Kindergarten: Current circumstances affecting curriculum. *Teachers College Record, 90*, 392–403.

Fromberg, D. P. (1990). Play issues in early childhood education. In C. Seefeldt (Eds.), *Continuing issues in early childhood education* (pp. 223–224). Columbus, OH: Merrill.

Giffin, H. (1984). The coordination of meaning in the creation of a shared make-believe reality. In I. Bretherton (Ed.), *Symbolic play: The development of social understanding* (pp. 73–100). New York: Academic Press.

Gilligan, C. (1982). *In a different voice: Psychological theory and women's development.* Cambridge, MA: Harvard University Press.

Goldstein, E. G. (1984). Ego building and termination. In E. L. Baker (Ed.), *Ego psychology and social work practice* (pp. 19–67). New York: Free Press.

Gullo, D. F. (1988). Perspectives on controversial issues related to implementing the all day kindergarten: Assessment and evaluation. Presented at the annual conference of the National Association for the Education of Young Children, Anaheim, CA.

Heath, S. B. (1983). *Ways with words: Language, life, and work in communities and classrooms.* New York: Cambridge University Press.

Hofstadter, D. R. (1980). *Gödel, Escher, Bach: An eternal golden braid.* New York: Schocken.

Isaacs, S. (1960). *Intellectual development in young children.* London: Routledge and Kegan Paul. (Original work published in 1930).

Isaacs, S. (1972). *Social development in young children.* New York: Schocken. (Original work published in 1933).

Janiv, N. N. (1976). Kedmah. Presented at the Bicentennial Conference on Early Childhood Education, Coral Gables, FL.

Johnson, D. W., Johnson, R. T., Holubec, E. J., & Roy, P. (1984). *Circles of learning: Cooperation in the classroom.* Alexandria, VA: Association for Supervision and Curriculum Development.

Joyce, B. R., & Showers, B. (1982, October). The coaching of teaching. *Educational Leadership, 40,* 4–10.

Karweit, N. (1988, November). Quality and quantity of learning time in preprimary programs. *Elementary School Journal, 89,* 119–133.

Kelly-Byrne, D. (1989). *A child's play life: An ethnographic study.* New York: Teachers College Press.

Kreye, M. (1984). Conceptual organization in the play of preschool children: Effects of meaning, context and mother-child interaction. In I. Bretherton (Ed.), *Symbolic play: The development of social understanding* (pp. 299–336). New York: Academic Press.

Lather, P. (1986, August). Research as praxis. *Harvard Educational Review, 56,* 257–277.

Levenstein, P. (1976). Cognitive development through verbalized play: The mother-child home programme. In J. S. Bruner, A. Jolly, & K. Sylva (Eds.), *Play: Its role in development and evolution* (pp. 286–297). New York: Basic Books.

Levenstein, P. (1985). Mothers' interactive play behavior in play sessions and children's educational achievements. In C. C. Brown & A. W. Gottfried (Eds.), *Play interactions* (pp. 160–167). Skillman, NJ: Johnson & Johnson.

Lieberman, A. (1987, Spring). Teacher leadership. *Teachers College Record, 88,* 400–405.

Lynn, S. J., & Garske, J. P. (1985). *Contemporary psychology: Models and methods.* Columbus, OH: Charles E. Merrill.

McDonald, J. P. (1988, Summer). The emergence of the teacher's voice: Implications for the new reform. *Teachers College Record, 89,* 471–486.

Monighan-Nourot, P., Scales, B., Van Hoorn, J., with Almy, M. (1987). *Looking at children's play: A bridge between theory and practice.* New York: Teachers College Press.

Morgan, R. (1982). *The anatomy of freedom: Physics and global politics.* Garden City, NJ: Anchor.

Olszewski, P. (1987). Individual differences in preschool children's production of verbal fantasy play. *Merrill-Palmer Quarterly, 33,* 69–86.

Paley, V. G. (1984). *Boys and girls: Superheroes in the doll corner.* Chicago: University of Chicago Press.

Parten, M. (1933). Social play among pre-school children. *Journal of Abnormal and Social Psychology, 28,* 13–47.

Pellegrini, A. D. (1985). The relations between symbolic play and literate behavior: A review and critique of the empirical literature. *Review of Educational Research, 55,* 107–121.

Pellegrini, A. D. (1987). Rough-and-tumble play: Developmental and educational significance. *Educational Psychologist, 22,* 23–43.

Pellegrini, A. D., & Galda, L. (1982). The effects of thematic-fantasy play training on the development of children's story comprehension. *American Educational Research Journal, 19,* 443–452.

Peterson, P. L., Fennema, E., & Carpenter, T. (1988, December/1989, January). Using knowledge of how students think about mathematics. *Educational Leadership, 46,* 42–46.

Piaget, J. (1962). *Play, dreams, and imitation in childhood* (C. Gattegno & M. F. Hodgson, Trans.). New York: W. W. Norton.

Piaget, J., with the assistance of seven collaborators. (1965). *The moral judgment of the child* (M. Gabain, trans.). New York: The Free Press.

Reiber, R. W., & Carton, A. S. (Eds.). (1987). *The collected works of L. S. Vygotsky: Vol. 1. Problems of General Psychology* (N. Minick, Trans.). New York: Plenum.

Scales, B. (1987). Play: The child's unseen curriculum. In P. Monighan-Nourot, B. Scales, J. Van Hoorn, with M. Almy. *Looking at children's play: A bridge between theory and practice* (pp. 89–115). New York: Teachers College Press.

Schwartzman, H. B. (1978). *Transformations: The anthropology of children's play.* New York: Plenum.

Seefeldt, C., & Barbour, N. (1987, Spring). Functional play: A tool for toddler learning. *Day Care and Early Education, 59,* 6–9.

Serbin, L. A. (1978). Teachers, peers, and play preferences: An environmental approach to sex typing in the preschool. In B. Sprung (Ed.), *Perspectives on nonsexist early childhood education* (pp. 79–93). New York: Teachers College Press.

Shepard, L. A., & Smith, M. L. (1988, November). Escalating academic demand in kindergarten: Counterproductive policies. *Elementary School Journal, 89,* 135–145.

Shotwell, J. M., Wolf, D., & Gardner, H. (1979). Exploring symbolization: Styles of achievement. In B. Sutton-Smith (Ed.), *Play and learning* (pp. 127–156). New York: Gardner.

Showers, B. (1985, April). Teachers coaching teachers. *Educational Leadership, 42,* 43–53.

Silvern, S. B. (1988, November). Continuity/discontinuity between home and early childhood education environments. *Elementary School Journal, 89,* 147–159.

Simon, T., & Smith, P. K. (1985, July). Play and problem solving: A paradigm questioned. *Merrill-Palmer Quarterly, 31,* 265–277.

Singer, J. L. (1973). *The child's world of make-believe: Experimental studies of imaginative play.* New York: Academic Press.

Slavin, R. E., & Madden, N. A. (1989, February). What works for students at risk: A research synthesis. *Educational Leadership, 46,* 4–13.

Smilansky, S. (1968). *The effects of sociodramatic play on disadvantaged preschool children.* New York: Wiley.

Stenhouse, L. (Ed.). (1980). *Curriculum research and development in action.* Portsmouth, NH: Heinemann.

Sutton-Smith, B. (1989). Radicalizing childhood: The multivocal mind. In L. R. Williams & D. P. Fromberg (Eds.), *Defining the field of early childhood education: Proceedings of an invitational symposium* (pp. 77–151). Charlottesville, VA: W. Alton Jones Foundation.

Teale, W. H. (1988, November). Developmentally appropriate assessment of reading and writing in the early childhood classroom. *Elementary School Journal, 89,* 173–183.

Voss, H. G. (1987). An empirical study of exploration-play sequences in early childhood. In D. Gorlitz & J. F. Wohlwill (Eds.), *Curiosity, imagination, and play* (pp. 152–179). Hillsdale, NJ: Erlbaum.

Vygotsky, L. S. (1976). Play and its role in the mental development of the child. In J. S. Bruner, A. Jolly, & K. Sylva (Eds.), *Play: Its role in development and evolution* (pp. 537–554). New York: Basic Books.

Whiting, B. B., & Edwards, C. P., in collaboration with Ember, C. R., Erchar, G. M., Harkness, S., Munroe, R. L., Munroe, R. H., Nerlove, S. B., Seymour, S., Super, C. M., Weisner, T. S., & Wenger, M. (1988). *Children of different worlds: The formation of social behavior.* Cambridge, MA: Harvard University Press.

Wolf, D. H., Rygh, J., & Altshuler, J. (1984). Agency and experience: Actions and states in play narrative. In I. Bretherton (Ed.), *Symbolic play: The development of social understanding* (pp. 195–217). New York: Academic Press.

Where Do We Go From Here?

Edgar Klugman and Sara Smilansky

The breadth of perspectives on play that are brought together in this volume is impressive. Each contributor has developed and expanded the view of play until the fully orchestrated theme emerges. There is overwhelming agreement among the contributors about the crucial importance of play in the wide variety of early childhood education programs presented. Several of the contributors reinforce the position taken by the National Association for the Education of Young Children (Bredekamp, 1986) that play must become fully accepted as part of the core curriculum in early childhood education programs. The foundation of this position is empirical research evidence that shows that play is an important medium through which children's socioemotional, language, and cognitive development is enhanced. Studies (Johnson, 1976; Lewis, 1972; Marshall, 1961; Rubin & Maioni, 1975; Smilansky & Feldman, 1980; Taler, 1976; Tower, Singer, Singer, & Biggs, 1979) also show that without adult facilitation of play, the natural impetus of children toward this activity does not fully develop. There have been only a few attempts, however, to look for ways to constructively intervene in play. Eisner (in Chapter 3) states that play, like art, requires reflection, profits from skill, seeks to generate new forms of experience, leads to invention, and is marginalized in the priorities of both American and Israeli education.

Parents, administrators and teachers, local communities, states, and nations want assurance of the academic success of their children. Academic success is equated with being a "successful individual" and, in turn, becoming successful in the market place. Simultaneously, a strong assumption is made that the earlier children can be introduced to the realm of academics the better it will be, both for the individual and for the community. Although, as Elkind points out (Chapter 1), children have difficulty with this pressure, it is too frequently found in school curricula as children are introduced to workbooks, work sheets, and direct, formalized teaching in their preschool and primary years.

WHAT ARE THE PROBLEMS?

With research pointing toward children's play as a unique way of enhancing social, creative, and cognitive development, why is it so difficult to include play as an integral and valued part of the early childhood curriculum? One can point to several "missing links" in the chain of events. One is the wide division between research findings and actual classroom practice. How can this separation be bridged? One barrier is the historical view of the sanctity of play as a personal and unique expression to be protected from adult interference. The erroneous and widely held belief that young children's play and their cognitive development are unrelated, distinct, and separate from each other is another barrier to progress in this area. Should these historical views be changed? Can ways be developed by which to shift these perceptions?

There is growing awareness of the critical connection between children's play and their future levels of academic achievement. The connection between teacher education in the area of play development and the potential changes in expectations, teaching skills, and supports for play include positive attitudes toward children's play, sufficient and appropriate time and space, a balanced curriculum, and appropriately prepared professional personnel. Also missing has been a cohesive body of suggested steps to take toward ameliorating the dearth of opportunities and support for children's play, once the inadequacy has been recognized.

The Division Between Research and Practice

The separation between research results and actual practice is a good place to begin this aspect of the discussion. Fromberg (Chapter 13) points to the fact that both teachers and researchers have expected that teachers will automatically be able to take on the responsibility for appropriate use of research findings in their daily teaching. Major slippage occurs, however, in communication between the domain of research and the domain of practice. Paul Mort, who taught administration and finance at Teachers College, Columbia University, as long as twenty years ago discussed the 50-year lag between the current levels of theoretical knowledge and actual educational practice (Mort & Vincent, 1946). Today this division may not be quite as great, but it nevertheless adds emphasis to the fact that the transfer of information from research results into practical applications requires a substantial process of rethinking.

A potentially fruitful avenue of approach to this process may be discovered through the observation of other fields such as the rapidly escalating introduction of computers into industry, school, and home or the broad range of methods used in the dissemination of new knowledge about medicine. There is a need for the field of early childhood education to find ways of disseminating information and to recognize the amount of time necessary between the dissemination of research results and their practical application.

As the analysis of play proceeds, it becomes evident that in the field of early childhood education the basic supports for play within the curriculum are frequently unavailable. Some of the critically important tools currently lacking are in-depth training materials for use in teacher education programs that include videotaped analyses of children's dramatic and sociodramatic play and assessment instruments for use by teachers in evaluating children's play. Without the ability to assess a child's current play ability the teacher lacks the basis for planning the types of interventions that are appropriate for facilitating the development of play skills. These materials cannot be developed in isolation but should include "the teacher as researcher" in order to find answers to such questions as what works in this arena with individual children, with small groups, and with large groups.

Effective answers are needed to questions relating to those present policies and procedures that may require adjustment or reconceptualization within a local setting. In this process, not only the psychological needs of children but also the teacher's ability to implement the given tasks or activities should be considered.

Collaborative Efforts: Researcher–Teacher–Policy Maker

Three domains with major foci on early childhood education are research, teaching, and policy/administration. Efforts must be made to assist these groups to work collaboratively in the process of designing and testing research on play and evaluating and generalizing the findings. Only as these groups, with their strong stakes in the process, work together can there be authentic improvement in the schools. The foundation for this proposed collaboration is that all three domains have in common their desire for high-quality teaching and learning settings for both teachers and children. One difficulty that must be worked through is the variety and sometimes disparity among the definitions of "high-quality teaching and learning settings." This may, however, be a very productive place in which to begin a collaborative effort. The "feedback loop," which includes the researcher, the teacher, and the administrator/policy maker permits everyone with a stake in the undertaking to share reactions and suggest changes that will benefit the end product. Through this forum the richness of varied perceptual fields becomes available to the process as a whole.

It will be useful to pilot-test models of cooperative planning and implementation in various settings in order to determine what can work well in most educational environments. In this process, it may indeed be found that the development of a new role is required, that of "researcher-educator-ombudsperson" to help policy makers, administrators, and teachers develop understandings that will allow research results to be used in classroom settings. The person in this new role would function in ways to enhance communication among the three domains and disseminate relevant data and information to constituent groups. This person would have understanding of the needs, interests, and concerns of the various constituents. This person would, for example, understand both the research findings in terms of classroom settings and the new demands that the data may generate in the realm of policy implementation. This person would have skills in imaging and transmitting new knowledge in ways that would allow various constituencies to readily consider, evaluate, and accept appropriate data for use in their ongoing endeavors.

Directors, principals, and other policy makers, like others in the education profession, have been socialized in the belief that academic achievement and play have little, if anything, in common. Therefore, teachers who see play as a very powerful and important medium for learning do not easily find support for their point of view from their respective administrators or communities. It is difficult, under these circumstances, to implement a classroom curriculum that includes play as an important and valued component.

ADDRESSING THE PROBLEMS

Whereas each contributor to this volume has recommended further research in the area(s) in which the discussion has focused, we further recommend that additional research needs to be done in the areas of classroom synthesis of play (working play into the curriculum as is done with language arts and mathematics) and the curricular integration of current knowledge about play (melding theoretical knowledge with actual practice). Special emphasis also needs to be put into researching ways to effect positive attitudinal changes toward play among professionals, policy makers, and parents.

There is a great need for more conscious advocacy work in support of play. If play is to take its rightful place in the curriculum, professional organizations concerned with any part of the early childhood education continuum must become forums in which play is discussed, researched, written about, and through which information is disseminated to members through journals and conferences. Industries with a focus on any aspect of the early years of childhood should be sought as allies in furthering the development of the field and addressing attitudinal issues. The media, a natural and most effective vehicle for demonstrating the uses of play in the education of young children, are a logical instrument for influencing attitudes toward change. It would be very helpful to have articles appear in popular magazines and influential newspapers that could serve to dispel the widely held myths concerning children's play and early learning.

The contributors to this volume are from two countries that use very different forms of policy implementation. In the United States most educational policy is implemented on a decentralized basis, while in Israel the Ministry of Education practices a centralized form of policy making. Yet, no apparent differences exist between the two countries relative to the lack of inclusion of play for young children as an integral part of the curricula in the schools. The same phenomenon holds true for the field of early childhood teacher preparation. In both countries, it has been difficult to find teacher preparation programs that include specific courses focused on play.

Support networks, both formal and informal, are necessary to the processes of both curricular integration and classroom synthesis of play. Those networks already in existence should be made more widely known, and others created as local needs are identified. This process can assist individuals and groups interested in play to share their work, whether in the area of research, classroom practice, or policy development and implementation.

Proceed with Caution

As teachers and administrators become increasingly able to recognize play for what it is, a powerful medium through which the social, emotional, and academic development of young children occurs, one might anticipate that parents may be expected to work toward the development of play ability in their young children. It is conceivable, and of concern, taking into account the school's historical tendency to put blame on the parents for children's areas of weakness, that the child newly arriving at school will be expected to already be a "good player." Parents may be held responsible for the achievement of this goal. In actual fact, although many parents may be well prepared to undertake some of this responsibility, Anna Freud (1952) has shown through research and observation that it is very difficult to function effectively both as parent and as teacher to one's own child.

Another important area of exploration is how parents might, indeed, support the development of their children's play skills. Of course, for some this experience can be relaxed, fun, and rewarding. But the personality structure of other parents may not allow them to undertake such a task constructively. Still others may have home and/or work responsibilities that do not allow them either the time or the energy to engage in such an undertaking.

A number of future research questions are now unfolding, such as, who are the parents who play well with their children? What components make for a successful play experience with a child, and which components mitigate against a successful play experience? Do even those children whose parent is able to offer constructive help in the development of play abilities need systematic teacher intervention and opportunities for sociodramatic play experiences with other children? Can the parents who cannot function as partners in their child's play be assured that their child's ability to play can be developed by teachers from a very early age?

In thinking about these kinds of questions, it must be borne in mind that although the issues are complex, the goal is to foster children's cognitive and socioemotional development through play in joyful, natural, and growth-enhancing ways. When young children play, the alert observer and skilled intervener has astounding opportunities to enhance children's development and skill levels. When one understands the long-term implications of developing good play skills for such milestones as future school achievement or hospital adjustment (Smilansky, Chapter 2), the responsibility becomes clear that those in power must include play as an integral part of early childhood curricula. The development of teacher education programs that include play as an important aspect of early childhood teacher education is an essential corollary. In many crucial ways, play, an old friend, awakens the potential within each child. Play needs to be viewed from fresh perspectives in order to unleash its long-term power. Who can now say where the limits to that power may be?

REFERENCES

Bredekamp, S. (1986). *Developmentally appropriate practice in early childhood programs serving children from birth through age 8.* Washington, DC: National Association for the Education of Young Children.

Freud, A. (1952). Answering teacher's questions. *The writings of Anna Freud: Vol. IV 1945–1956* (pp. 560–568). New York: International Universities Press.

Johnson, J. E. (1976). Relations of divergent thinking and intelligence test scores with social and non-social make-believe play of preschool children. *Child Development, 47,* 1200–1203.

Lewis, H. P. (1972). *The relationship of sociodramatic play to various cognitive abilities in kindergarten children.* Unpublished doctoral dissertation, Ohio State University.

Marshall, H. R. (1961). Relation between home experiences and children's use of language in play interaction with peers. *Psychological Monographs, 75*(5), 509.

Mort, P., & Vincent, W. (1946). *A look at our schools.* New York: Cattell.

Rubin, K. H., & Maioni, T. L. (1975). Play preference and its relation to egocentrism popularity and classification skills in preschool. *Merrill-Palmer Quarterly, 21,* 171–179.

Smilansky, S., & Feldman, N. (1980). *Relationship between sociodramatic play in kindergarten and scholastic achievement in second grade.* Department of Psychology, Tel-Aviv University.

Taler, E. (1976). *Social status of kindergarten children and their level of sociodramatic play.* Unpublished master's thesis, Tel-Aviv University, Department of Psychology.

Tower, R. B., Singer, D. G., Singer, J. L., & Biggs, A. (1979). Development of play. *American Journal of Orthopsychiatry, 49,* 265–281.

About the Editors and the Contributors

Edgar Klugman is Professor of Early Childhood Education at Wheelock College. He has been active in the early childhood field on the local, state, and national levels. He is currently serving on the Massachusetts Early Childhood Advisory Council to the Board of Education. He is on the Board of the New England Association for the Education of Young Children. He received the award of a Mid-Career Fellowship to the Yale Bush Center for Child Development and Social Policy. He has published widely. He co-edited, with Sharon L. Kagan and Ed Zigler, *Children, Families and Government: Perspectives on American Social Policy.*

    Sara Smilansky, a professor in the Department of Psychology at Tel Aviv University, received her graduate degree from Ohio State University. Her books include *Play as a Medium for Cognitive Development of Young Children* (in Hebrew) and *The Effects of Sociodramatic Play on Disadvantaged Preschool Children* (in English).

    Barbara Bowman is Director of Graduate Studies at Erikson Institute of Loyola University in Chicago. She has worked in the field of early childhood education and family development, both in the United States and abroad. She currently directs several projects in the Chicago Public Schools. She is the recipient of the Doctorate of Human Letters from Bank Street College of Education and has served as president of the National Association for the Education of Young Children. She has written and published extensively. Her most recent contribution, *Self-Reflection as an Element of Professionalism*, appeared in the Teachers College Record (1989).

    Elliot W. Eisner is Professor of Education and Art at Stanford University. His major interests are in the use of aesthetic modes of inquiry as a way of studying education practice and in the contributions of the arts to education. He has lectured on these topics around the world. He is the recipient of a number of special awards, including three honorary doctorates. His major publications include *The Educational Imagination, The Art of Educational Evaluation, Cognition and Curriculum,* and forthcoming *The Enlightened Eye: On Doing Qualitative Inquiry.*

David Elkind is Professor of Child Study and Senior Resident Scholar at the Lincoln Filene Center at Tufts University. He formerly was a postdoctoral fellow at Piaget's Institut d'Epistemologie Genetique in Geneva. Professor Elkind's research in the areas of perceptual, cognitive, and social development has developed, in part, out of Piaget's research and theoretical work. He has recently served as the President of the National Association for the Education of Young Children. Professor Elkind's articles have appeared widely in both the academic and popular press, including *The New York Times Magazine, Good Housekeeping,* and *Psychology Today,* and his stories for children have been published in *Jack and Jill.* He is a contributing author of *Parent's Magazine.* His books include *The Hurried Child: Growing Up Too Fast, Too Soon,* and most recently, *Miseducation: Preschoolers at Risk.*

Doris Pronin Fromberg is Professor of Education and Director of Early Childhood Teacher Education at Hofstra University in Hempstead, New York. After having been a teacher and administrator in public and private schools, she received an Ed.D. from Teachers College, Columbia University. She is a member of the National Council of the Association of Teacher Educators Board of Examiners. She has published books, monographs, and articles on the subject of play. Among her publications are *The Full-Day Kindergarten* and *The Successful Classroom: Management Strategies for Regular Elementary and Special Education Teachers* with Maryann Driscoll. She is currently engaged in co-editing, with Dr. Leslie Williams, *The Encyclopedia of Early Childhood Education.*

Rivka Glaubman received her Ph.D. in 1987 from Israel's Bar Ilan University. She is currently associated with Bar Ilan University as Head of the Curriculum Studies and Foundation of Education Program and is a lecturer in Early Childhood Education, Curriculum Studies, and Foundations of Education. She is Director of the Bar Ilan inservice courses for school-based improvement. Dr. Glaubman serves as Advisor to the Israeli Ministry of Education in its Department of Curriculum and Teaching Methods Implementation. Her research interests include analyzing preschool children's play and play negotiations and young children's self-directed learning processes. Among her publications (in Hebrew) are *Children's Questioning: Stages in the Inquiry Process;* with R. Laor, *Learning to Read as an Experience;* and with J. Harrison *Active Learning—Theory and Application.*

James Ewald Johnson is Associate Professor of Education, Curriculum, and Instruction at the Pennsylvania State University. He has undertaken research and published extensively in the area of play. In addition to his numerous articles on play and play theory in preschool age children, Professor Johnson is co-author of *Play and Early Childhood Development, Approaches to Early Childhood Education,* and *Integrative Processes and Socialization: Early to Middle Childhood.*

Sharon L. Kagan is Associate Director of the Yale Bush Center in Child Development and Social Policy and Coordinator of the Bush Network. She is also a research associate at the Child Study Center and is a member of the psychology department at Yale University. She was the Director of Policy Analysis and Evaluation for the Mayor's Office of Early Childhood Education in New York City. Dr. Kagan has directed many early schooling programs of national significance, including Project Developmental Continuity and New York City's Giant Step program. She has lectured and written extensively on early childhood education and child care, parent involvement and also child, family, and educational policy. Some of the publications (which she has co-edited) include *Early Schooling: The National Debate, America's Family Support Programs: Perspectives and Prospects,* and *Children, Families, and Government: Perspectives on American Social Policy.*

Elizabeth Kampe is Program Director at The Center School of the Merrimack Special Education Collaborative, where she manages an educational program for children with severe, special educational, and health care needs. Her interests include play and children with special needs and ethical issues in child life practice. She has served as an Instructor and Program Coordinator of the Child Life Program at the Wheelock College Graduate School. She also was a Supervisor of Therapeutic Recreation and Child Life at the Kennedy Memorial Hospital for Children. Ms. Kampe is a former National Board Member of The Association for the Care of Children's Health and the Child Life Council.

Rina Michalovitz is the Director of Early Childhood Education for the Ministry of Education in Israel. Under her jurisdiction are clustered all of the kindergartens and nursery schools in Israel. She was appointed to her current post after having worked as a supervisor on the regional level. She is a graduate of Bar Ilan University. Her doctoral thesis focused on the development and promotion of imagery and logical operations in young children. She also serves on the faculty of Haifa University, where she teaches developmental and educational psychology.

Patricia Monighan-Nourot is an Assistant Professor at Sonoma State University. She has been a program evaluator, research consultant, and administrator, as well as a teacher of young children. She has produced videos in early childhood education. She is also the author of several articles on play and language development and co-author of the book *Looking at Child's Play: A Bridge Between Theory and Practice.*

Leah Shefatya is senior researcher at the Henrietta Szold National Institute for Research in Jerusalem. She was educated at Hebrew University and at the University of Chicago. Her research interests are broad, including child development, preschool education, education of the hearing impaired, and cultural differences. She has been published extensively in articles, books, and research reports in both Hebrew and English. Some of her publications include *Parents as Partners in the Scholastic Advancement of Their Young Children, Alternative Teaching Methods: Toward Changes in the School Systems, A Formative Evaluation of the Parents Project—A Home-Based Early Intervention Program Based on Portage Materials.*

Index

Ability
   group conception of, 7–8, 16
   individual conception of, 7–15
Academic achievement
   in early childhood education system of Israel, 86–93
   and early childhood programs in public schools, 196–197
   relationship between sociodramatic play and, 29–30
Administrators
   head teachers designated by, 201–202
   on implementation of early childhood education in public schools, 191–208
   need for collaboration between teachers, researchers, and, 252
   preparation of, 200–202
   seminars for, 201
Albino, J. E., 162
Alcott, Bronson, 63
Almy, Millie, 59, 64, 72, 79–81, 103, 108, 180, 240
Altshuler, J., 240
American Educational Research Journal, 102
Anderson, J., 74
Anderson, L. F., 61–62
Angoff, K., 161
Antler, J., 68–69, 75
Argyris, C., 126
Arnheim, Rudolf, 48, 50
Arts
   cognitive benefits of representation in, 53–55
   in cognitive development, 43–55
   reasons for teaching of, 51–53
   relationship between cognition and, 47–51
Ashton, P., 126

Association for Childhood Education International (ACEI), 81, 99, 103
Association for Supervision and Curriculum Development (ASCD), 183, 189
Association for the Care of Children's Health (ACCH), 158
Athey, I., 175, 214, 216–217, 221

Babad, E., 126
Bandura, A., 165
Banet, B., 97, 104
Barbour, N., 241
Barnes, D., 244
Barnett, W. S., xiii
Bates, T. A., 163
Beeghly, M., 222
Behavior
   effect of intervention in children's play on, 31–36
   relationship between sociodramatic play and, 25–26, 31–36
Bell, C., 217, 227
Bell, M., 105
Benham, N., 107
Bereiter, C., 78, 104
Bergen, D., 235, 237
Berger, L., 176
Berlyne, D. E., 175
Berrueta-Clement, J. R., xiii
Bessman, C. A., 161
Betz, C. J., 157
Bhavnani, R., 223–224
Bibace, R., 157
Biber, Barbara, 69, 74, 77, 97, 103
Biggs, A., 27, 29, 250
Bloch, M. N., 213
Bloom, B., 50, 76

261